LEARNING TO LABOUR

To Val

Learning to labour

How working class kids get working class jobs

PAUL E. WILLIS

SAXON HOUSE

Published by
SAXON HOUSE, Teakfield Limited,
Westmead, Farnborough, Hants., England

Reprinted 1978 (twice), 1979 (twice)

ISBN 0 566 00150 0 Cased edition
ISBN 0 566 00227 2 Limp edition

British Library Cataloguing in Publication Data

Willis, Paul E
    Learning to labour.
    1. High school graduates–Employment–Great Britain
    2. Labor and laboring classes–Great Britain
    I. Title
    301.5'5   HD 627.G7   76–58617

    ISBN 0-566-00150-0

Library of Congress Catalog Card Number 76-58617
Printed in Great Britain by Biddles Ltd, Guildford, Surrey

Contents

v

Preface

This book arises out of a project financed by the Social Science Research Council from 1972 to 1975 on the transition from school to work of non-academic working class boys. The methods used were case study work, interviewing, group discussions and participant observation with groups of working class boys as they proceeded through their last two years at school and into the early months of work. Part I presents the empirical data and main findings of this study. It is basically an ethnography of the school, and particularly of oppositional working class cultural forms within it, and a practical contribution to the literature on the transition from school to work. Part II is more theoretical. It analyses the inner meaning, rationality and dynamic of the cultural processes recorded earlier, and the ways in which they contribute, on the one hand, to working class culture in general, and on the other, more unexpectedly, to the maintenance and reproduction of the social order.

A general objective of the book is to make its arguments accessible to audiences of social scientists, practitioners and general readers. The more specialist arguments and references have therefore been removed to end-notes. Practitioners may be most interested in Part I and the Conclusion; social theorists in Part II.

As the book goes to press the SSRC have agreed to fund a continuation of the research described here to focus on 'the young worker and shop floor culture'. It is intended that this research will be written up as a sequel to the present volume.

Acknowledgements

Thanks to the help, advice, encouragement and example of Stuart Hall and Richard Hoggart. Thanks to the people also who have read and substantially commented on drafts of this book: Tony Jefferson, Dan Finn, Michael Green, Allan O'Shea and members of the CCCS Education Group. Thanks to the typists as well: Deirdre Barker, Aleene Hall and Pearl New.

More generally I should like to thank the Centre for Contemporary Cultural Studies and all its members, the schools and all their members and particularly 'the lads' of Hammertown Boys. They made the research possible.

Key to transcripts

[   ]   Background information

. . .   Pause

(. . .)   Material edited out

–   Unidentified speaker

———   Transcription from different discussion follows

*   From field notes, not transcription

Individuals cannot gain mastery over their own social interconnections before they have created them. But it is an insipid notion to conceive of this merely *objective bond* as a spontaneous, natural attribute inherent in individuals and inseparable from their nature (in antithesis to their conscious knowing and willing). This bond is their product. It is a historic product. It belongs to a specific phase of their development. The alien and independent character in which it presently exists *vis à vis* individuals proves only that the latter are still engaged in the creation of the conditions of their social life, and that they have not yet begun, on the basis of these conditions, to live it .... Universally developed individuals . . . are no product of nature, but of history.

Karl Marx, Grundrisse, 1857. [Penguin pp. 161-2]

1 Introduction

The difficult thing to explain about how middle class kids get middle class jobs is why others let them. The difficult thing to explain about how working class kids get working class jobs is why they let themselves.

It is much too facile simply to say that they have no choice. The way in which manual labour is applied to production can range in different societies from the coercion of machine guns, bullets and trucks to the mass ideological conviction of the voluntary industrial army. Our own liberal democratic society is somewhere in between. There is no obvious physical coercion and a degree of self direction. This is despite the inferior rewards for, undesirable social definition, and increasing intrinsic meaninglessness, of manual work: in a word its location at the bottom of a class society.[1] The primary aim of this book is to cast some light on this surprising process.

Too often occupational and educational talents are thought of as on a shallowing line of shrinking capacity with working class people at its lower reaches unquestionningly taking on the worst jobs thinking somehow, 'I accept that I'm so stupid that it's fair and proper that I should spend the rest of my life screwing nuts onto wheels in a car factory'. This gradient model must, of course, assume a zero or near zero reading at its base. The real individuals at the bottom end would scarcely rate a score for being alive, never mind for being human. Since these individuals are currently far from walking corpses but are actually bringing the whole system into crisis this model is clearly in need of revision. The market economy of jobs in a capitalist society emphatically does not extend to a market economy of satisfactions.

I want to suggest that 'failed' working class kids do not simply take up the falling curve of work where the least successful middle class, or the most successful working class kids, leave off. Instead of assuming a continuous shallowing line of ability in the occupational/class structure we must conceive of radical breaks represented by the interface of cultural forms. We shall be looking at the way in which the working class cultural pattern of 'failure' is quite different and discontinuous from the other patterns. Though in a determined context it has its own processes, its own definitions, its own account of those other groups conventionally registered as more successful. And this class culture is not a neutral pattern, a *mental* category, a set of variables impinging on the school from the outside. It comprises experiences, relationships, and ensembles of systematic types of relationship which not only set particular 'choices' and 'decisions' at particular times, but also structure, really and experientially, how these 'choices' come about and are defined in the first place.

A linked and subsidiary aim of the book is to examine important and central aspects of working class culture through the concrete study of one of its most revealing manifestations. My original research interest was, indeed, in working class culture in general and I was led to look at young non-academic disaffected males and their adaption to work as a crucial and privileged moment in the continuous regeneration of working class cultural forms in relation to the most essential structure of society – its working relations.

Both sets of concerns in fact turn on the important concept of labour power and how it is prepared in our society for application to manual work. Labour power is the human capacity to work on nature with the use of tools to produce things for the satisfaction of needs and the reproduction of life. Labouring is not a universal transhistorical changeless human activity. It takes on specific forms and meanings in different kinds of societies. The processes through which labour power comes to be subjectively understood and objectively applied and their interrelationships is of profound significance for the type of society which is produced and the particular nature and formation of its classes. These processes help to construct both the identities of particular subjects and also distinctive class forms at the cultural and symbolic level as well as at the economic and structural level.

Class identity is not truly reproduced until it has properly passed through the individual and the group, until it has been recreated in the context of what appears to be personal and collective volition. The point at which people live, not borrow, their class destiny is when what is given is re-formed, strengthened and applied to new purposes. Labour power is an important pivot of all this because it is the main mode of *active* connection with the world: the way *par excellence* of articulating the innermost self with external reality. It is in fact the dialectic of the self to the self through the concrete world. Once this basic compact with the future has been made everything else can pass for common sense.

The specific milieu, I argue, in which a certain subjective sense of manual labour power, and an objective decision to apply it to manual work, is produced is the working class counter-school culture. It is here where working class themes are mediated to individuals and groups in their own determinate context and where working class kids creatively develop, transform and finally reproduce aspects of the larger culture in their own praxis in such a way as to finally direct them to certain kinds of work. Part I of the book presents an ethnography of the male white working class counter-school culture. For the sake of clarity and incision, and in no way implying their lack of importance, other ethnic and gender variants are not examined.

We may just note here that the existence of this culture has been picked up conventionally and especially by the media in its sensational mode as violence and indiscipline in the class room.[2] The Raising of the School Leaving Age (RSLA) in England in September 1972 seems to have highlighted and further exposed the most aggressive aspects of the culture.[3] Both the major teachers' unions have commissioned special reports[4] and have formalised arrangements for union support in excluding 'trouble-makers' from class. Over half the local authorities in

England and Wales have set up special classes in school, and even quite separate 'sanctuaries' in the case of Inner London for such kids. The Secretary of State for Education has ordered a national investigation into this whole area.[5] Disruption and truancy in schools is high on the agenda of the 'great debate' which Mr Callaghan, the current Prime Minister, called for on education.[6]

In the sense, therefore, that I argue that it is their own culture which most effectively prepares some working class lads for the manual giving of their labour power we may say that there is an element of self-damnation in the taking on of subordinate roles in Western capitalism. However, this damnation is experienced, paradoxically, as true learning, affirmation, appropriation, and as a form of resistance. Furthermore, it will be argued in Part II where I analyse the ethnography presented in Part I that there is an objective basis for these subjective feelings and cultural processes. They involve a partial penetration of the really determining conditions of existence of the working class which are definitely superior to those official versions of their reality which are proffered through the school and various state agencies. It is only on the basis of such a real cultural articulation with their conditions that groups of working class lads come to take a hand in their own damnation. The tragedy and the contradiction is that these forms of 'penetration' are limited, distorted and turned back on themselves, often unintentionally, by complex processes ranging from both general ideological processes and those within the school and guidance agencies to the widespread influence of a form of patriarchal male domination and sexism within working class culture itself.

I shall argue finally in Part II that the processes of self-induction into the labour process constitute an aspect of the regeneration of working class culture in general, and an important example of how this culture is related in complex ways to regulative state institutions. They have an important function in the overall reproduction of the social totality and especially in relation to reproducing the social conditions for a certain kind of production.

This is the spine of the book. In pursuit of these aims the book makes a contribution in a number of other areas. It explores the educational paradigm at the heart of the teaching relationship in our schools, makes a critique of vocational guidance and suggests some explanations for the persistent failure of state education to radically improve the chances in life of working class kids.[7] There is also in Part II an intervention into the discussion of sexual stereotyping in relation to patriarchy and capitalism, and some notes towards an argument within theory about the respective status, and form of relationship between culture and ideology.

The qualitative methods, and Participant Observation used in the research, and the ethnographic format of the presentation were dictated by the nature of my interest in 'the cultural'. These techniques are suited to record this level and have a sensitivity to meanings and values as well as an ability to represent and interpret symbolic articulations, practices and forms of cultural production. In particular the ethnographic account, without always knowing how, can allow a degree of the activity, creativity and human agency within the object of study to come through into the analysis and the reader's experience. This is vital to my purposes where

I view the cultural, not simply as a set of transferred internal structures (as in the usual notions of socialisation) nor as the passive result of the action of dominant ideology downwards (as in certain kinds of marxism), but at least in part as the product of collective human praxis.

The Hammertown case study

One main case study and five comparative studies were made in the research reported in this book. The main study was of a group of twelve non-academic working class lads from a town we shall call Hammertown and attending a school we shall call Hammertown Boys. They were selected on the basis of friendship links and membership of some kind of an oppositional culture in a working class school. The school was built in the inter-war years and lay at the heart of a closely packed inter-war council estate composed of standard, often terraced, reasonably well maintained houses interlinked with a maze of roads, crescents and alleys and served by numerous large pubs and clusters of shops and small supermarkets.

During the period of the research this school was a boys only, non-selective secondary modern school twinned with a girls' school of the same status. After the research finished it was redesignated a single sex comprehensive school as part of the general reorganisation of secondary education in the borough. In view of this expected change and under the pressure of events and in preparation for RSLA the school was expanding in terms of buildings and introducing or experimenting with some new techniques during the period of the research. Streaming was replaced by mixed ability groupings, a resources centre was introduced, experiments were made in team teaching and curriculum development programmes, and a whole range of new 'option' courses were developed for the 'RSLA year'. I made contact with the group at the beginning of the second term of their penultimate year and followed them right through into six months of their working lives (their final year was to be the first year of RSLA). The school population was about 600 and contained substantial West Indian and Asian minorities. Basically this school was selected because it was in the heart of, and drew from, an absolutely characteristic working class inter-war council estate, itself at the heart of Hammertown. The school was exclusively working class in intake, but had the reputation of being a 'good' school. This seemed to mean, in essence, that it had 'reasonable standards' of recognised behaviour and dress enforced by an interested and competent senior staff. I wanted to be as certain as possible that the group selected was typical of the working class in an industrial area, and that the educational provision it enjoyed was as good as, if not slightly better than, any available in similar British contexts. An added advantage of the particular school chosen was that it had a new and well equipped youth wing which was well attended by the pupils and gave the opportunity of a very open and informal initial entry into the school.

Comparative case studies were made over the same period. These were of: a group of conformist lads in the same year of Hammertown Boys; a group of working class conformist lads in a nearby Hammertown mixed secondary modern, informally known as a somewhat 'rougher' school; a group of working class non-conformist lads in the single sex Hammertown grammar school; a similar group in a comprehensive near the middle of the larger conurbation of which Hammertown was part; and a mixed class male non-conformist group in a high status grammar school in the most exclusive residential area of the same larger conurbation. As far as possible, all groups were in the same school year, were friendship groups, and were selected for their likelihood of leaving school at the statutory minimum leaving age of sixteen. In the case of the high status grammar school this latter condition totally determined the membership of the group and its mixed class nature – they were the only boys intending to leave at sixteen in the fourth year (when I first contacted them), and indeed subsequently only two of them actually left at this point. These groups were selected to give a comparative dimension to the study along the parameters of class, ability, school regime, and orientation to the school.

The main group was studied intensively by means of observation and participant observation in class, around the school and during leisure activities; regular recorded group discussions; informal interviews and diaries. I attended all of the different subject classes and options (not as a teacher but as a member of the class) attended by the group at various times, and the complete run of careers classes which were taught by a dedicated and experienced teacher recently returned from secondment to a well-respected careers and counselling course. I also taped long conversations with all the parents of the main group, and with all senior masters of the school, main junior teachers in contact with members of the group, and with the careers officers coming into the school.

I followed all twelve boys from the main group, as well as three selected boys from the comparative groups, into work. Fifteen short periods of participant observation were devoted to actually working alongside each lad in his job, and were concluded with taped interviews with the individual and selected interviews with foremen, managers and shop stewards.

Hammertown is first recorded in the Doomsday Book as a tiny hamlet. It is in the centre of England as part of a much larger conurbation. Like many other small towns around there, its population size and importance exploded during the Industrial Revolution. The coming of canals and the building of a foundry by Boulton and Watt for the construction of metal castings for other manufacturers in the middle of the eighteenth century transformed its nature. It was among the first of the industrial towns, and its population one of the first industrial proletariats. By 1800 it had extensive iron-smelting works and iron foundries as well as soap, lead and glass works. More recently it has become an important centre for bearing engineering, and the production of springs, cycle components, glass, screws, and nuts and bolts. It is indeed a Midlands nuts and bolts town, which was in its time one of the cradles of the Industrial Revolution.

It is now part of a huge industrial conurbation in the Midlands. People still think of it as rough and dirty, even though its civic record in public services and housing

5

provision is better than most in the region. Tumbledown cottages and Victorian slum terraces have now been largely cleared away and replaced by modern council houses and highrise flats. But when boys from Hammertown meet girls away from home they still like to say that they are from the adjacent big city which, conveniently, supplies their postal code.

The population of the town reached its peak in the early 1950s and has been falling since, despite the arrival of substantial numbers of black immigrants. The population is now about 60,000 and, interestingly, has one of the highest 'activity rates'[8] - especially for women - in the country. The age/sex structure of Hammertown is similar to that for the rest of England and Wales, but its class structure is notably different. It is essentially a working class town. Only 8 per cent of its residents are in professional and managerial occupations (half the national rate) and the overwhelming majority of the population are in some form of manual work. There is a startling daily inflow of around 3,000 middle class people from the south and west who will work but not live in Hammertown. The dearth of the middle classes is reflected in the fact that under 2 per cent of adults are in full-time education (again half the national rate).

The structure of employment demonstrates the distinctively industrial nature of the working class community. There is a total labour force of about 36,000 of which fully 79 per cent is involved in manufacturing of some kind compared with 35 per cent nationally and 55 per cent for the conurbation. Metal and metal goods manufacturing accounts for over half of such employment. The other major sources of employment are in food, drinks and tobacco industries, mechanical engineering, vehicles, bricks, pottery and glass, and distribution. Employment prospects are generally good in Hammertown and even during recession its unemployment rate has stayed about 1 per cent under the national average.

Although the town was industrialised over 200 years ago, and has kept many of the same basic industries - especially metal and metal working - it does not have the small firm/family firm infrastructure of many similar towns. In fact its industrial organisational structure is strikingly modern. Much of the employment in Hammertown is in large factories which are often themselves a branch of national or multinational companies. Sixty per cent of the total workforce works in firms employing over 1,000 people. Under 5 per cent of those in manufacturing work in firms employing less than 25 people. Fifty-eight per cent of the total industrial floorspace is concentrated in thirty-eight factories exceeding 100,000 sq. ft. in size. Over 20 per cent of the total area of the town is in industrial use.

Hammertown is altogether something of an archetypal industrial town. It has all the classic industrial hallmarks as well as those of modern monopoly capitalism in conjunction with a proletariat which is just about the oldest in the world.

Notes

[1]   There are masses of statistics demonstrating systematic differences between

the working and middle class in Britain. There is little disagreement about the reliability of these statistics and the latest volume of *Social Trends* (no. 6, 1975, HMSO) brings together most of the official data. Sixty-three per cent of the heads of households are in manual work of some kind. The lower the social class the lower the income, the greater the likelihood of unemployment, the greater the likelihood of poor conditions of work, the greater the likelihood of being off work through sickness. See also for distributions of wealth and income: A. Atkinson, *Unequal Shares*, Penguin, 1974; F. Field, *Unequal Britain*, Arrow, 1974.

[2]   See, for instance, 'Control experiment', *The Guardian*, 18 March 1975; 'They turn our schools into a jungle of violence', *Sunday Express*, 9 June 1974 (by Angus Maude MP); and 'Discipline or terror' and 'In our schools . . . defiance, gang war and mugging', *Sunday People*, 16 June 1974; and the film by Angela Pope on BBC Panorama, 'The Best Years?', broadcast 23 March 1977.

[3]   Even the official government report on the first year of RSLA, mainly notable for its optimism in contrast to all other commentaries, accepted that there was a 'core of dissidents' and recorded 'a strong impression that misbehaviour had increased'. DES Reports on Education, *The First Year After RSLA*, April 1975.

[4]   See National Association of School Masters, 'Discipline in Schools', 1975; NAS, 'The Retreat from Authority', 1976; National Union of Teachers, Executive Report, 'Discipline in Schools', in 1976 Conference Report.

[5]   Reported in *The Guardian*, 27 June 1976. See also J. Mack, 'Disruptive pupils', *New Society*, 5 August 1976.

[6]   In an important speech at Ruskin College, Oxford, in October 1976, Mr Callaghan, the prime minister, called for a 'great debate' on education to examine some of the new teaching techniques, parental 'unease', the possibility of a 'core curriculum' and '(educational) priorities (. . .) to secure high efficiency (. . .) by the skilful use of the £6 billion of existing resources'.

[7]   A. H. Halsley stated recently, even after the help of an OECD seminar on 'Education, Inequality and Life Chance', that 'we are still far from a complete understanding . . . [of why educational] achievement is so stubbornly correlated with social origin' ('Would chance still be a fine thing', *The Guardian*, 11 February 1975).

[8]   The activity rate is the proportion of the population, aged fifteen or over, which is economically active. This and most of the following information is taken from the structure plan of the local borough. Statistics relate usually to 1970.

PART I
ETHNOGRAPHY

2 Elements of a culture

Opposition to authority and rejection of the conformist

The most basic, obvious and explicit dimension of counter-school culture is entrenched general and personalised opposition to 'authority'. This feeling is easily verbalised by 'the lads' (the self-elected title of those in the counter-school culture).

[In a group discussion on teachers]

Joey   (...) they're able to punish us. They're bigger than us, they stand for a bigger establishment than we do, like, we're just little and they stand for bigger things, and you try to get your own back. It's, uh, resenting authority I suppose.

Eddie   The teachers think they're high and mighty 'cos they're teachers, but they're nobody really, they're just ordinary people ain't they?

Bill   Teachers think they're everybody. They are more, they're higher than us, but they think they're a lot higher and they're not.

Spanksy   Wish we could call them first names and that ... think they're God.

Pete   That would be a lot better.

PW   I mean you say they're higher. Do you accept at all that they know better about things?

-

Joey   Yes, but that doesn't rank them above us, just because they are slightly more intelligent.

Bill   They ought to treat us how they'd like us to treat them.

(...)

Joey   (...) the way we're subject to their every whim like. They want something doing and we have to sort of do it, 'cos, er, er, we're just, we're under them like. We were with a woman teacher in here, and 'cos we all wear rings and one or two of them bangles, like he's got one on, and bout of the blue, like, for no special reason, she says, 'take all that off'.

PW   Really?

Joey   Yeah, we says, 'One won't come off', she says, 'Take yours off as well'. I said, 'You'll have to chop my finger off first'.

PW   Why did she want you to take your rings off?

Joey   Just a sort of show like. Teachers do this, like, all of a sudden they'll make you do your ties up and things like this. You're subject to their every whim like. If they want something done, if you don't think it's right, and you object against it, you're down to Simmondsy [the head], or you get the cane, you get some extra work tonight.

PW   You think of most staff as kind of enemies (. . .)?

–   Yeah.

–   Yeah.

–   Most of them.

Joey   It adds a bit of spice to yer life, if you're trying to get him for something he's done to you.

This opposition involves an apparent inversion of the usual values held up by authority. Diligence, deference, respect – these become things which can be read in quite another way.

[In a group discussion]

PW   Evans [the Careers Master] said you were all being very rude (. . .) you didn't have the politeness to listen to the speaker [during a careers session]. He said why didn't you realise that you were just making the world very rude for when you grow up and God help you when you have kids 'cos they're going to be worse. What did you think of that?

Joey   They wouldn't. They'll be outspoken. They wouldn't be submissive fucking twits. They'll be outspoken, upstanding sort of people.

Spanksy If any of my kids are like this, here, I'll be pleased.

This opposition is expressed mainly as a style. It is lived out in countless small ways which are special to the school institution, instantly recognised by the teachers, and an almost ritualistic part of the daily fabric of life for the kids. Teachers are adept conspiracy theorists. They have to be. It partly explains their devotion to finding out 'the truth' from suspected culprits. They live surrounded by conspiracy in its most obvious – though often verbally unexpressed – forms. It can easily become a paranoic conviction of enormous proportions.[1]

As 'the lads' enter the classroom or assembly, there are conspiratorial nods to each other saying, 'Come and sit here with us for a laff', sidelong glances to check where the teacher is and smirking smiles. Frozen for a moment by a direct command or look, seething movement easily resumes with the kids moving about with that 'I'm just passing through, sir' sort of look to get closer to their mates. Stopped again, there is always a ready excuse, 'I've got to take my coat off sir', 'So and So told me to see him sir'. After assembly has started, the kid still marooned from his mates crawls along the backs of the chairs or behind a curtain down the side of the hall, kicking other kids, or trying to dismantle a chair with somebody on it as he passes.

'The lads' specialise in a caged resentment which always stops just short of outright confrontation. Settled in class, as near a group as they can manage, there is a continuous scraping of chairs, a bad tempered 'tut-tutting' at the simplest request, and a continuous fidgeting about which explores every permutation of sitting or lying on a chair. During private study, some openly show disdain by apparently trying to go to sleep with their head sideways down on the desk, some have their backs to the desk gazing out of the window, or even vacantly at the wall. There is an aimless air of insubordination ready with spurious justification and impossible to nail down. If someone is sitting on the radiator it is because his trousers are wet from the rain, if someone is drifting across the classroom he is going to get some paper for written work, or if someone is leaving class he is going to empty the rubbish 'like he usually does'. Comics, newspapers and nudes under half-lifted desks melt into elusive textbooks. A continuous hum of talk flows around injunctions not to, like the inevitable tide over barely dried sand and everywhere there are rolled-back eyeballs and exaggerated mouthings of conspiratorial secrets.

During class teaching a mouthed imaginary dialogue counterpoints the formal instruction: 'No, I don't understand, you cunt'; 'What you on about, twit?'; 'Not fucking likely.; 'Can I go home now please?' At the vaguest sexual double meaning giggles and 'whoas' come from the back accompanied perhaps by someone masturbating a gigantic penis with rounded hands above his head in compressed lipped lechery. If the secret of the conspiracy is challenged, there are V signs behind the teacher's back, the gunfire of cracked knuckles from the side, and evasive innocence at the front. Attention is focused on ties, rings, shoes, fingers, blots on the desk – anything rather than the teacher's eyes.

In the corridors there is a foot-dragging walk, an overfriendly 'hello' or sudden silence as the deputy passes. Derisive or insane laughter erupts which might or might not be about someone who has just passed. It is as demeaning to stop as it is to carry on. There is a way of standing collectively down the sides of the corridor to form an Indian gauntlet run – though this can never be proved: 'We're just waiting for Spanksy, sir'.

Of course individual situations differ, and different kinds of teaching style are more or less able to control or suppress this expressive opposition. But the school conformists – or the 'ear'oles' for the lads – have a visibly different orientation. It is not so much that they support teachers, rather they support *the idea* of teachers. Having invested something of their own identities in the formal aims of education and support of the school institution – in a certain sense having foregone their own right to have a 'laff' – they demand that teachers should at least respect the same authority. There are none like the faithful for reminding the shepherd of his duty.

[In a group discussion with conformists at Hammertown Boys]

Gary   Well, I don't think they'm strict enough now (. . .) I mean like Mr Gracey, and some of the other teachers, I mean with Groucho, even the first years play him up (. . .) they 'the lads' should be punished like, so they grow up not to be cheeky (. . .) Some of the others, you can get on with them all right. I mean from the very beginning with Mr Peters everybody was quiet and if you ain't done the work, you had to come back and do it. I mean some of the other teachers, say from the first years, they give you homework, say you didn't do it, they never asked for it, they didn't bother.

It is essentially what appears to be their enthusiasm for, and complicity with, immediate authority which makes the school conformists - or 'ear'oles' or 'lobes' - the second great target for 'the lads'. The term 'ear'ole' itself connotes the passivity and absurdity of the school conformists for 'the lads'. It seems that they are always listening, never *doing*: never animated with their own internal life, but formless in rigid reception. The ear is one of the least expressive organs of the human body: it responds to the expressivity of others. It is pasty and easy to render obscene. That is how 'the lads' liked to picture those who conformed to the official idea of schooling.

Crucially, 'the lads' not only reject but feel *superior* to the 'ear'oles'. The obvious medium for the enactment of this superiority is that which the 'ear'oles' apparently yield - fun, independence and excitement: having a 'laff'.

[In a group discussion]

PW   (. . .) why not be like the ear'oles, why not try and get CSEs?

-                      They don't get any fun, do they?

Derek   Cos they'm prats like, one kid he's got on his report now, he's got five As and one B.

-                      - Who's that?

Derek   Birchall.

Spanksy   I mean, what will they remember of their school life? What will they have to look back on? Sitting in a classroom, sweating their bollocks off, you know, while we've been . . . I mean look at the things we can look back on, fighting on the Pakis, fighting on the JAs [i.e. Jamaicans]. Some of the things we've done on teachers, it'll be a laff when we look back on it.

(. . .)

Perce   Like you know, he don't get much fun, well say Spanksy plays about all day, he gets fun. Bannister's there sweating, sweating his bollocks off all day while Spanksy's doing fuck all, and he's enjoying it.

Spanksy   In the first and second years I used to be brilliant really. I was in 2A, 3A you know and when I used to get home, I used to lie in bed thinking, 'Ah, school tomorrow', you know, I hadn't done that homework, you know . . . 'Got to do it'.

-                      Yeah, that's right, that is.

Spanksy   But now when I go home, it's quiet, I ain't got nothing to think

	about, I say, 'Oh great, school tomorrow, it'll be a laff', you know.
Will	You still never fucking come!
Spanksy	Who?
Will	You.
[Laughter]	
(...)	
–	You can't imagine . . .
–	You can't imagine [inaudible] going into the Plough and saying, 'A pint of lager please'.
Fred	You can't imagine Bookley goin' home like with the missus, either, and having a good maul on her.
–	I can, I've seen him!
–	He's got a bird, Bookley!
–	He has.
Fred	I can't see him getting to grips with her, though, like we do you know.

It was in the sexual realm especially that 'the lads' felt their superiority over the 'ear'oles'. 'Coming out of your shell', 'losing your timidness' was part of becoming 'one of the lads', but it was also the way to 'chat up birds' successfully. In an odd way there was a distorted reflection here of the teachers' relationships to the 'ear'-oles'. 'The lads' felt that they occupied a similar structural role of superiority and experience, but in a different and more antisocial mode.

[In an individual interview]

Joey	We've [the lads] all bin with women and all that (...) we counted it up the other day, how many kids had actually been with women like, how many kids we know been and actually had a shag, and I think it only come to, I think we got up to twenty-four (...) in the fifth year out of a hundred kids, that's a quarter.
PW	Would you always know though?
Joey	Yes I would (...) It gets around you know, the group within ourself, the kids who we know who are sort of semi-ear'oles like . . . they're a separate group from us and the ear'oles. Kids like Dover, Simms and Willis, and one or two others like. They all mess about with their own realm, but they're still fucking childish, the way they talk, the way they act like. They can't mek us laff, we can mek them laff, they can fucking get in tears when they watch us sometimes, but it's beyond their powers to mek one of us laff, and then there's us (...) some of them [the semi-ear'oles] have been with women and we know about it like. The ear'oles (...) they've got it all to come. I mean look at Tom Bradley, have you ever noticed him. I've always looked at him

and I've thought, Well ... we've been through all life's pleasures and all its fucking displeasures, we've been drinking, we've been fighting, we've known frustration, sex, fucking hatred, love and all this lark, yet he's known none of it. He's never been with a woman, he's never been in a pub. We don't know it, we assume it - I dare say he'd come and tell us if he had - but he's never been with a woman, he's never been drinking, I've never known him in a fight. He's not known so many of the emotions as we've had to experience, and he's got it all to come yet.

Joey was an acknowledged group leader, and inclined at times to act the old experienced man of the world. As is clear here, and elsewhere, he is also a lad of considerable insight and expressive power. In one way this might seem to disqualify him as typical of school non-conformist working class lads. However, although Joey may not be *typical* of working class lads, he is certainly representative of them. He lives in a working class neighbourhood, is from a large family known as a fighting family whose head is a foundryman. He is to leave school without qualifications and is universally identified by teachers as a troublemaker - the more so that 'he has something about him'. Though perhaps exaggerated, and though powerfully expressed, the experiences he reports can only come from what he has experienced in the counter-culture. The cultural system he reports on is representative and central, even if he is related to it in a special way.

It is worth noting that, in his own terms and through the mediations of the group, Joey assumes both complete mastery and understanding of the school year and its social landscape. He assumes that information will find its way to 'the lads' as the focal point of that landscape. A clear hallmark of 'coming out' is the development of this kind of social perspective and evaluative framework. It should also be noted that the alternative standards constructed by 'the lads' are recognised by the teachers in a shadowy sort of way - at least in private. There were often admiring comments in the staff room about the apparent sexual prowess of particular individuals from younger teachers, 'he's had more than me I can tell you'.

Members of the group more conformist to school values do not have the same kind of social map, and nor do they develop an argot for describing other groups. Their response to 'the lads' is mostly one of occasional fear, uneasy jealousy and general anxiety lest they be caught in the same disciplinarian net, and frustration that 'the lads' prevent the smooth flow of education. Their investment in the formal system and sacrifice of what others enjoy (as well as the degree of fear present) means that the school conformists look to the system's acknowledged leaders, the staff, to deal with transgression rather than attempt to suppress it themselves.

[In a group discussion with conformists at Hammertown Boys]
Barry   ... he [one of the teachers] goes on about 'Everybody...', you know. I don't like things like that, when they say, 'Everybody's ... none of you like this, none of you like this, none of you like

16

	that. You're all in trouble'. They should say, 'A few of yer. . .'. Like Mr Peters, he does that, he don't say, 'Everybody', just the odd few. That's better, cos some of us are interested (. . .)
Nigel	The trouble is when they start getting, you know, playing the teachers up (. . .) it means that you're losing time, valuable time, teaching time, and that, so its spoiling it for your, you know, sometimes, I wish they'd just pack up and leave (. . .)
Barry	It's better the way they've done it now (. . .) they've put them all together [CSE groups were not mixed ability groups]. It don't really matter whether they do any work or not . . . You just get on, get on well now [in the CSE groups], cos if anybody's talking, he tells you to shut up, you know, get on with the work.
PW	(. . .) have you ever felt that you should try and stop them? (. . .)
Barry	I've just never bothered with them (. . .) now, in the fifth, they should . . . you know, you don't just go around shouting at people in the classroom, you know, you just talk sensibly. [The teachers] should be more stricter.

Opposition to staff and exclusive distinction from the 'ear'oles' is continuously expressed amongst 'the lads' in the whole ambience of their behaviour, but it is also made concrete in what we may think of as certain stylistic/symbolic discourses centring on the three great consumer goods supplied by capitalism and seized upon in different ways by the working class for its own purposes: clothes, cigarettes and alcohol. As the most visible, personalised and instantly understood element of resistance to staff and ascendancy over 'ear'oles' clothes have great importance to 'the lads'. The first signs of a lad 'coming out' is a fairly rapid change in his clothes and hairstyle. The particular form of this alternative dress is determined by outside influences, especially fashions current in the wider symbolic system of youth culture. At the moment the 'lads' look' includes longish well-groomed hair, platform-type shoes, wide collared shirt turned over waisted coat or denim jerkin, plus the still obligatory flared trousers. Whatever the particular form of dress, it is most certainly *not* school uniform, rarely includes a tie (the second best for many heads if uniform cannot be enforced), and exploits colours calculated to give the maximum distinction from institutional drabness and conformity. There is a clear stereotypical notion of what constitutes institutional clothes – Spike, for instance, trying to describe the shape of a collar: 'You know, like a teacher's!'

We might note the importance the wider system of commercial youth culture has here in supplying a lexicography of style, with already connoted meanings, which can be adapted by 'the lads' to express their own more located meanings. Though much of this style, and the music associated with it, might be accurately described as arising from purely commercial drives and representing no authentic aspirations of its adherents, it should be recognised that the way in which it is taken up and used by the young can have an authenticity and directness of personal expression missing from its original commercial generation.

It is no accident that much of the conflict between staff and students at the moment should take place over dress. To the outsider it might seem fatuous. Concerned staff and involved kids, however, know that it is one of their elected grounds for the struggle over authority. It is one of the current forms of a fight between cultures. It can be resolved, finally, into a question about the legitimacy of school as an institution.

Closely related with the dress style of 'the lads' is, of course, the whole question of their personal attractiveness. Wearing smart and modern clothes gives them the chance, at the same time as 'putting their finger up' at the school and differentiating themselves from the 'ear'oles', to also make themselves more attractive to the opposite sex. It is a matter of objective fact that 'the lads' do go out with girls much more than do any other groups of the same age and that, as we have seen, a good majority of them are sexually experienced. Sexual attractiveness, its association with maturity, and the prohibition on sexual activity in school is what valorises dress and clothes as something more than an artificial code within which to express an institutional/cultural identity. This double articulation is characteristic of the counter-school culture.

If manner of dress is currently the main apparent cause of argument between staff and kids, smoking follows closely. Again we find another distinguishing characteristic of 'the lads' against the 'ear'oles'. The majority of them smoke and, perhaps more importantly, are *seen* to smoke. The essence of schoolboy smoking is school gate smoking. A great deal of time is typically spent by 'the lads' planning their next smoke and 'hopping off' lessons 'for a quick drag'. And if 'the lads' delight in smoking and flaunting their impertinence, senior staff at least cannot ignore it. There are usually strict and frequently publicised rules about smoking. If, for this reason, 'the lads' are spurred, almost as a matter of honour, to continue public smoking, senior staff are incensed by what they take to be the challenge to their authority. This is especially true when allied to that other great challenge: the lie.

[In a group discussion on recent brushes with staff]

Spike   And we went in, I says 'We warn't smoking', he says (. . .) and he went really mad. I thought he was going to punch me or summat.

Spanksy 'Call me a liar', 'I'm not a liar', 'Get back then', and we admitted it in the end; we was smoking (. . .) He was having a fit, he says 'Callin' me a liar'. We said we warn't smoking, tried to stick to it, but Simmondsy was having a fit.

Spike   He'd actually seen us light up.

Punishment for smoking is automatic as far as senior staff are concerned, and this communicates itself to the kids.

Spanksy Well, he couldn't do a thing [the deputy head], he had to give me three. I like that bloke, I think he does his job well, you know. But I was at the front entrance smoking and Bert comes right

behind me. I turns around, been copped, and I went straight to
him and had the cane. Monday morning, soon as I got in school,
three I had . . . . You know he couldn't let me off.

Given this fact of life, and in the context of the continuous guerrilla warfare
within the school, one of the most telling ways for 'the lads' to spot sympathisers,
more often simply the weak and 'daft', in the enemy camp is to see which teachers,
usually the young ones, take no action after an unequivocal sighting of a lighted
cigarette.

Fuzz   I mean Archy, he sees me nearly every morning smoking, coming
                  up by the Padlock, 'cos I'm waiting for me missus, sees me every
                  morning. He ain't never said anything.
Will   He said to me in registration –
PW (interrupt-
ing)   Who's this, Archer?
Will   Archy, yeah, he says, 'Don't get going up there dinner-time'.
                  'What do you mean like, up there?' He says, 'Up there, up that
                  way, the vicinity like'. I says, 'Oh, the Bush', you know, but he's
                  alright, like, we have a laff.

Again, in a very typical conjunction of school-based and outside meanings
cigarette smoking for 'the lads' is valorised as an act of insurrection before the
school by its association with adult values and practices. The adult world, specifically the adult male working class world, is turned to as a source of material for
resistance and exclusion.

As well as inducing a 'nice' effect, drinking is undertaken openly because it is the
most decisive signal to staff and 'ear'oles' that the individual is separate from the
school and has a presence in an alternative, superior and more mature mode of social
being. Accounts of staff sighting kids in pubs are excitedly recounted with much
more relish than mere smoking incidents, and inaction after being 'clocked boozing'
is even more delicious proof of a traitor/sympathiser/weakling in the school camp
than is the blind eye to a lighted 'fag'. Their perception of this particular matrix of
meanings puts some younger and more progressive members of staff in a severe
dilemma. Some of them come up with bizarre solutions which remain incomprehen-
sible to 'the lads': this incident involves a concerned and progressive young teacher.

[In a group discussion about staff]
Derek   And Alf says, er, 'Alright sir' [on meeting a member of staff in
                  a public house] and he dayn't answer, you know, and he says,
                  'Alright sir?', and he turned around and looked at him like that,
                  see, and er . . . and he dayn't answer and he says, in the next day,
                  and he says, 'I want you Alf', goes to him and he says, 'What
                  was you in there last night for?'. He says, 'I was at a football
                  meeting', he says, 'Well don't you think that was like kicking
                  somebody in the teeth?' 'No', he says. 'What would you feel like

if I kicked you in the teeth?', he says. 'What do you mean?', he says. 'Saying hello like that down there', he says, 'what would you expect me to say?'. He says, 'Well don't speak to me again unless I speak to you first'. He says, 'Right sir, I won't say hello again', he says, 'even if I see you in the drive.'

Certainly 'the lads' self-consciously understand the symbolic importance of drinking as an act of affiliation with adults and opposition to the school. It is most important to them that the last lunchtime of their last term should be spent in a pub, and that the maximum possible alcohol be consumed. This is the moment when they finally break free from school, the moment to be remembered in future years:

[Individual interview at work]

PW	Why was it important to get pissed on the last day?
Spanksy	It's a special thing. It only happens once in your life don't it? I mean, you know, on that day we were at school right, you'm school kids, but the next day I was at work, you know what I mean?
PW	Course, you went to work the very next day.
Spanksy	Yeah, I got drunk, had a sleep, and I went to work (. . .) if we hadn't've done that you know, we wouldn't've remembered it, we'd've stopped at school [i.e. instead of going to the pub], it'd've been just another day. No, when we did that, we've got something to remember the last day by, we've got something to remember school by.

In the pub there is indeed a very special atmosphere amongst the Hammertown 'lads'. Spike is expansively explaining that although he had behaved like a 'right vicious cunt' sometimes, he really likes his mates and will miss them. Eddie is determined to have eight pints and hold the 'record' – and is later 'apprehended drunk', in the words of the head, at the school and ingloriously driven home by him. Fuzz is explaining how he had nearly driven Sampson (a teacher) 'off his rocker' that morning and had been sent to see the head, 'but he wasn't off or anything, he was joking'. Most important, they are accepted by the publican and other adult customers in the pub, who are buying them drinks and asking them about their future work. At closing time they leave, exchanging the adult promises which they have not yet learned to disbelieve, calling to particular people that they will do their plumbing, bricklaying or whatever.

That they have not quite broken loose, and that staff want to underline this, is shown when 'the lads' return to the school late, smelling of alcohol and in some cases quite drunk. In a reminder that the power of the school is backed ultimately by the law and state coercion, the head has called in the police. A policeman is waiting outside the school with the head. This frightens 'the lads' and a bizarre scenario develops as they try to dodge the policeman.

20

[Later in a group discussion]

Will   I was walking up the drive [to the school], I was pulling Spike and Spanksy (. . .) I was trying to get these two alright, you know. Joey saw this copper comin' down the drive (. . .) I went into the bogs [at the bottom of the drive bounded at the back only by a fence]. I seen the copper, 'If he don't see me like, I can jump over the fence and get scot free, like, nobody'll see me, I'll be alright'. Then I thought, 'Look well if he comes in or summat', so I undone my trousers like I was having a piss, as though I was late or summat. Then Bill come running in. I thought, 'Christ', and I climbed over the back fence, went creeping off (. . .) Simmondsy had seen Bill, he said, 'Ah, I want to see you *two*', he says, 'You *two*', and I dayn't think you know, I just went walking down.

Eventually 'the lads' are rounded up and delivered in an excited state to the head's study, where they are told off roughly by the policeman: 'He picked me up and bounced me against the wall' - Spike (I did not see this incident myself). The head subsequently writes to all of their parents threatening to withhold their final testimonials until an apology is received: in the case of Spike he wrote:

... your son had obviously been drinking, and his subsequent behaviour was generally uncooperative, insolent, and almost belligerent. He seemed bent on justifying his behaviour and went as far as describing the school as being like Colditz ... as is my practice, I wish to give the parents of the boys an opportunity to come and see me before I finally decide what action to take.[2]

Even sympathetic young staff find the incident 'surprising', and wondered why 'the lads' had not waited until the evening, and then 'really done it properly'. The point is, of course, that the drinking has to be done at lunchtime, and in defiance of the school. It is not done simply to mark a neutral transition - a mere ritual. It is a decisive rejection and closing off. They have, in some way, finally beaten the school in a way which is beyond the 'ear'oles' and nearly unanswerable by staff. It is the transcendance of what they take to be the mature life, the *real* life, over the oppressive adolescence of the school - represented by the behaviour both of the 'ear'oles' *and* of the teachers.

Some of the parents of 'the lads' share their sons' view of the situation. Certainly none of them take up the head's offer to go and see him.

[In a group discussion]

Will   Our mum's kept all the letters, you know, about like the letters Simmondsy's sent [about the drinking]. I says, 'What you keeping them for?' She says, 'Well, it'll be nice to look back on to, won't it', you know, 'show your kids like you know, what a terror you was'. I'm keeping 'em, I am.

[Individual interview at work]

PW   Did your old man understand about having a drink the last day of term?

Spanksy   Oh ah (...) he laughed, he said, 'Fancy them sending a letter', you know. Joey's father come and had a little laugh about it you know.

No matter what the threats, and the fear of the law, the whole episode is 'worth it' to 'the lads'. It is the most frequently recounted, embellished and exaggerated school episode in the future working situation. It soon becomes part of a personalised folklore. As school uniform and smoking cease to be the most obvious causes of conflict in schools as more liberal regimes develop, we may expect drinking to become the next major area where the battle lines are drawn.

The informal group

On a night we go out on
the street
Troubling other people,
I suppose we're anti-social,
But we enjoy it.

The older generation
They don't like our hair,
Or the clothes we wear
They seem to love running
us down,
I don't know what I would
do if I didn't have the gang.

(Extract from a poem by Derek written in an English class.)

In many respects the opposition we have been looking at can be understood as a classic example of the opposition between the formal and the informal. The school is the zone of the formal. It has a clear structure: the school building, school rules, pedagogic practice, a staff hierarchy with powers ultimately sanctioned – as we have seen in small way – by the state, the pomp and majesty of the law, and the repressive arm of state apparatus, the police. The 'ear'oles' invest in this formal structure, and in exchange for some loss in autonomy expect the official guardians to keep the holy rules – often above and beyond their actual call to duty. What is freely sacrificed by the faithful must be taken from the unfaithful.

Counter-school culture is the zone of the informal. It is where the incursive demands of the formal are denied – even if the price is the expression of opposition in style, micro-interactions and non-public discourses. In working class culture

22

generally opposition is frequently marked by a withdrawal into the informal and expressed in its characteristic modes just beyond the reach of 'the rule'.

Even though there are no public rules, physical structures, recognised hierarchies or institutionalised sanctions in the counter-school culture, it cannot run on air. It must have its own material base, its own infrastructure. This is, of course, the social group. The informal group is the basic unit of this culture, the fundamental and elemental source of its resistance. It locates and makes possible all other elements of the culture, and its presence decisively distinguishes 'the lads' from the 'ear'oles'.

The importance of the group is very clear to members of the counter-school culture.

[In a group discussion]

Will	(. . .) we see each other every day, don't we, at school (. . .)
Joey	That's it, we've developed certain ways of talking, certain ways of acting, and we developed disregards for Pakis, Jamaicans and all different . . . for all the scrubs and the fucking ear'oles and all that (. . .) We're getting to know it now, like we're getting to know all the cracks, like, how to get out of lessons and things, and we know where to have a crafty smoke. You can come over here to the youth wing and do summat, and er'm . . . all your friends are here, you know, it's sort of what's there, what's always going to be there for the next year, like, and you know you have to come to school today, if you're feeling bad, your mate'll soon cheer yer up like, 'cos you couldn't go without ten minutes in this school, without having a laff at something or other.
PW	Are your mates a really big important thing at school now?
-	Yeah.
-	Yeah.
-	Yeah.
Joey	They're about the best thing actually.

The essence of being 'one of the lads' lies within the group. It is impossible to form a distinctive culture by yourself. You cannot generate fun, atmosphere and a social identity by yourself. Joining the counter-school culture means joining a group, and enjoying it means being with the group:

[In a group discussion on being 'one of the lads']

Joey	(. . .) when you'm dossing on your own, it's no good, but when you'm dossing with your mates, then you're all together, you're having a laff and it's a doss.
Bill	If you don't do what the others do, you feel out.
Fred	You feel out, yeah, yeah. They sort of, you feel, like, thinking the others are . . .
Will	In the second years . . .

| Spanksy | I can imagine ... you know, when I have a day off school, when you come back the next day, and something happened like in the day you've been off, you feel, 'Why did I have that day off', you know, 'I could have been enjoying myself'. You know what I mean? You come back and they're saying, 'Oorh, you should have been here yesterday', you know. |
| Will | (...) like in the first and second years, you can say er'm ... you're a bit of an ear'ole right. Then you want to try what it's like to be er'm ... say, one of the boys like, you want to have a taste of that, not an ear'ole, and so you like the taste of that. |

Though informal, such groups nevertheless have rules of a kind which can be described – though they are characteristically framed in contrast to what 'rules' are normally taken to mean.

PW	(...) Are there any rules between you lot?
Pete	We just break the other rules.
Fuzz	We ain't got no rules between us though, have we?

(...)

Pete	Changed 'em round.
Will	We ain't got rules but we do things between us, but we do things that y'know, like er ... say, I wouldn't knock off anybody's missus or Joey's missus, and they wouldn't do it to me, y'know what I mean? Things like that or, er ... yer give 'im a fag, you expect one back, like, or summat like that.
Fred	T'ain't rules, it's just an understanding really.
Will	That's it, yes.
PW	(...) What would these understandings be?
Will	Er ... I think, not to ... meself, I think there ain't many of us that play up the first or second years, it really is that, but y'know, say if Fred had cum to me and sez, 'er ... I just got two bob off that second year over there', I'd think, 'What a cunt', you know.

(...)

| Fred | We're as thick as thieves, that's what they say, stick together. |

There is a universal [3] taboo amongst informal groups on the yielding of incriminating information about others to those with formal power. Informing contravenes the essence of the informal group's nature: the maintenance of oppositional meanings against the penetration of 'the rule'. The Hammertown lads call it 'grassing'. Staff call it telling the truth. 'Truth' is the formal complement of 'grassing'. It is only by getting someone to 'grass' – forcing them to break the solemnest taboo – that the primacy of the formal organisation can be maintained. No wonder then, that a whole school can be shaken with paroxysms over a major incident and the purge which follows it. It is an atavistic struggle about authority and the legitimacy of authority. The school has to win, and someone, finally, has to 'grass': this is one of the ways in which the school itself is reproduced and the faith of the 'ear'-oles' restored. But whoever has done the 'grassing' becomes special, weak and marked. There is a massive retrospective and ongoing re-appraisal amongst 'the lads' of the fatal flaw in his personality which had always been immanent but not fully disclosed till now:

[In a group discussion of the infamous 'fire extinguisher incident' in which 'the lads' took a hydrant out of school and let it off in the local park]

PW	It's been the biggest incident of the year as it's turned out, hasn't it?
Joey	It's been blown up into something fucking terrific. It was just like that [snapping his fingers], a gob in the ocean as far as I'm concerned when we did it, just like smoking round the corner, or going down the shop for some crisps.
PW	What happened (. . .)?
-	Webby [on the fringes of the counter-school culture] grassed.
Joey	Simmondsy had me on me own and he said, 'One of the group owned up and tried to put all the blame on Fuzz'. But he'd only had Webby in there.
Spanksy	We was smoking out here.
Spike	He's like that, you'd got a fag, hadn't you [to Fuzz] .
Spanksy	And Webby asks for a drag, so he give Webby the fag. Rogers [a teacher] walked through the door, and he went like that [demonstrating] and he says, 'It ain't mine sir, I'm just holding it for Fuzz'.
Will	Down the park before, (. . .) this loose thing, me and Eddie pulled it off, didn't we, me and Eddie, and the parky was coming round like, he was running round, wor'he, so me and Eddie we went round the other side, and just sat there, like you know, two monkeys. And Webby was standing there, and the parky come up to him and says, 'Come on, get out. Get out of this park. You'm banned'. And he says, he walks past us, me and Eddie, and he says, 'I know you warn't there, you was sitting here'. And Webby went, 'It warn't me, it was . . .', and he was just about to say summat, warn't he?
Eddie	That's it, and I said, 'Shhh', and he just about remembered not to grass us.

Membership of the informal group sensitises the individual to the unseen informal dimension of life in general. Whole hinterlands open up of what lies behind the official definition of things. A kind of double capacity develops to register public descriptions and objectives on the one hand, and to look behind them, consider their implications, and work out what will actually happen, on the other. This interpretative ability is felt very often as a kind of maturation, a feeling of becoming 'worldliwise', of knowing 'how things really work when it comes to it'. It supplies the real 'insider' knowledge which actually helps you get through the day.

PW   Do you think you've learnt anything at school, has it changed or moulded your values?

Joey   I don't think school does fucking anything to you (. . .) It never has had much effect on anybody I don't think [after] you've learnt the basics. I mean school, it's fucking four hours a day. But it ain't the teachers who mould you, it's the fucking kids you meet. You'm only with the teachers 30 per cent of the time in school, the other fucking two-thirds are just talking, fucking pickin' an argument, messing about.

The group also supplies those contacts which allow the individual to build up alternative maps of social reality, it gives the bits and pieces of information for the individual to work out himself what makes things tick. It is basically only through the group that other groups are met, and through them successions of other groups. School groups coalesce and further link up with neighbourhood groups, forming a network for the passing on of distinctive kinds of knowledge and perspectives that progressively place school at a tangent to the overall experience of being a working class teenager in an industrial city. It is the infrastructure of the informal group which makes at all possible a distinctive kind of *class* contact, or class culture, as distinct from the dominant one.

Counter-school culture already has a developed form of unofficial bartering and exchange based on 'nicking', 'fiddles', and 'the foreigner' – a pattern which, of course, emerges much more fully in the adult working class world:

Fuzz   If, say, somebody was to say something like, 'I'm looking, I want a cassette on the cheap like'. Right, talk about it, one of us hears about a cassette on the cheap, y'know, kind of do the deal for 'em and then say, 'Ah, I'll get you the cassette'.

Cultural values and interpretations circulate 'illicitly' and informally just as do commodities.

Dossing, blagging and wagging

Opposition to the school is principally manifested in the struggle to win symbolic and physical space from the institution and its rules and to defeat its main perceived purpose: to make you 'work'. Both the winning and the prize – a form of self-direction – profoundly develop informal cultural meanings and practices. The dynamic aspects of the staff/pupil relationship will be examined later on. By the time a counter-school culture is fully developed its members have become adept at managing the formal system, and limiting its demands to the absolute minimum. Exploiting the complexity of modern regimes of mixed ability groupings, blocked timetabling and multiple RSLA options, in many cases this minimum is simply the act of registration.[4]

[In a group discussion on the school curriculum]

Joey   (. . .) of a Monday afternoon, we'd have nothing right? Nothing hardly relating to school work, Tuesday afternoon we have swimming and they stick you in a classroom for the rest of the afternoon, Wednesday afternoon you have games and there's only Thursday and Friday afternoon that you work, if you call that work. The last lesson Friday afternoon we used to go and doss, half of us wagged out o' lessons and the other half go into the classroom, sit down and just go to sleep (. . .)

Spanksy   (. . .) Skive this lesson, go up on the bank, have a smoke, and the next lesson go to a teacher who, you know, 'll call the register (. . .)

Bill   It's easy to go home as well, like him [Eddie] . . . last Wednesday afternoon, he got his mark and went home (. . .)

Eddie   I ain't supposed to be in school this afternoon, I'm supposed to be at college [on a link course where students spend one day a week at college for vocational instruction]

PW   What's the last time you've done some writing?

Will   When we done some writing?

Fuzz   Oh are, last time was in careers, 'cos I writ 'yes' on a piece of paper, that broke me heart.

PW   Why did it break your heart?

Fuzz   I mean to write, 'cos I was going to try and go through the term without writing anything. 'Cos since we've cum back, I ain't dun nothing [it was half way through term].

Truancy is only a very imprecise – even meaningless – measure of rejection of school. This is not only because of the practice of stopping in school for registration before 'wagging off' (developed to a fine art amongst 'the lads'), but also because it only measures one aspect of what we might more accurately describe as informal student mobility. Some of 'the lads' develop the ability of moving about the school at their own will to a remarkable degree. They construct virtually their own day from what is offered by the school. Truancy is only one relatively unimportant and crude variant of this principle of self-direction which ranges across vast chunks of the syllabus and covers many diverse activities: being free out of class, being in class and doing no work, being in the wrong class, roaming the corridors looking for excitement, being asleep in private. The core skill which articulates these possibilities is being able to get out of any given class: the preservation of personal mobility.

[In a group discussion]

PW   But doesn't anybody worry about your not being in their class?

Fuzz   I get a note off the cooks saying I'm helping them (. . .)

John   You just go up to him [a teacher] and say, 'Can I go and do a job'. He'll say, 'Certainly, by all means', 'cos they want to get rid of you like.

Fuzz   Specially when I ask 'em.

Pete   You know the holes in the corridor, I didn't want to go to games, he told me to fetch his keys, so I dropped them down the hole in the corridor, and had to go and get a torch and find them.

For the successful, there can be an embarrassment of riches. It can become difficult to choose between self-organised routes through the day.

Will   (. . .) what we been doing, playing cards in this room 'cos we can lock the door.

PW   Which room's this now?

Will   Resources centre, where we're making the frames [a new stage for the deputy head], s'posed to be.

PW   Oh! You're still making the frames!

Will   We should have had it finished, we just lie there on top of the frame, playing cards, or trying to get to sleep (. . .) Well, it gets a bit boring, I'd rather go and sit in the classroom, you know.

PW   What sort of lessons would you think of going into?

Will   Uh, science, I think, 'cos you can have a laff in there sometimes.

This self-direction and thwarting of formal organisational aims is also an assault on official notions of time. The most arduous task of the deputy head is the construction of the timetables. In large schools, with several options open to the fifth year, everything has to be fitted in with the greatest of care. The first weeks of term are spent in continuous revision, as junior members of staff complain, and particular combinations are shown to be unworkable. Time, like money, is valuable and not to be squandered. Everything has to be ordered into a kind of massive critical path of the school's purpose. Subjects become measured blocks of time in careful relation to each other. Quite as much as the school buildings the institution over time *is* the syllabus. The complex charts on the deputy's wall shows how it works. In theory it is possible to check where every individual is at every moment of the day. But for 'the lads' this never seems to work. If one wishes to contact them, it is much more important to know and understand their own rhythms and patterns of movement. These rhythms reject the obvious purposes of the timetable and their implicit notions of time. The common complaint about 'the lads' from staff and the 'ear'-oles' is that they 'waste valuable time'. Time for 'the lads' is not something you carefully husband and thoughtfully spend on the achievement of desired objectives in the future. For 'the lads' time is something they want to claim for themselves now as an aspect of their immediate identity and self-direction. Time is used for the preservation of a state – being with 'the lads' – not for the achievement of a goal – qualifications.

Of course there is a sense of urgency sometimes, and individuals can see the end of term approaching and the need to get a job. But as far as their culture is concerned time is importantly simply the state of being free from institutional time. Its own time all passes as essentially the same thing, in the same units. It is not planned, and is not counted in loss, or expected exchange.

'Having a laff'

'Even communists laff' (Joey)

The space won from the school and its rules by the informal group is used for the shaping and development of particular cultural skills principally devoted to 'having a laff'. The 'laff' is a multi-faceted implement of extraordinary importance in the counter-school culture. As we saw before, the ability to produce it is one of the defining characteristics of being one of 'the lads' – 'We can make them laff, they can't make us laff'. But it is also used in many other contexts: to defeat boredom and fear, to overcome hardship and problems – as a way out of almost anything. In many respects the 'laff' is the privileged instrument of the informal, as the command is of the formal. Certainly 'the lads' understand the special importance of the 'laff':

[In an individual discussion]

Joey   I think fuckin' laffing is the most important thing in fuckin' everything. Nothing ever stops me laffing (. . .) I remember once, there was me, John, and this other kid, right, and these two kids cum up and bashed me for some fuckin' reason or another. John and this other kid were away, off (. . .) I tried to give 'em one, but I kept fuckin' coppin' it . . . so I ran off, and as I ran off, I scooped a handful of fuckin' snow up, and put it right over me face, and I was laffing me bollocks off. They kept saying, 'You can't fuckin' laff'. I should have been scared but I was fuckin' laffing (. . .)

PW   What is it about having a laugh, (. . .) why is it so important?

Joey   (. . .) I don't know why I want to laff, I dunno why it's so fuckin' important. It just is (. . .) I think it's just a good gift, that's all, because you can get out of any situation. If you can laff, if you can make yourself laff, I mean really convincingly, it can get you out of millions of things (. . .) You'd go fuckin' berserk if you didn't have a laff occasionally.

29

The school is generally a fertile ground for the 'laff'. The school importantly develops and shapes the particular ambience of 'the lads' distinctive humour. We will look at particular pedagogic styles as material for comic and cultural development in a later chapter. For the moment, however, we can note the ways in which specific themes of authority are explored, played with and used in their humour. Many of their pranks and jokes would not mean the same thing or even be funny anywhere else. When a teacher comes into a classroom he is told, 'It's alright, sir, the deputy's taking us, you can go. He said you could have the period off'. 'The lads' stop second and third years around the school and say, 'Mr Argyle wants to see you, you'm in trouble I think'. Mr Argyle's room is soon choked with worried kids. A new teacher is stopped and told, 'I'm new in the school, the head says could you show me around please'. The new teacher starts to do just that before the turned away laughs give the game away. As a rumour circulates that the head is checking everyone's handwriting to discover who has defaced plaster in the new block, Fuzz boasts, 'The fucker can't check mine, I ain't done none'. In a humorous exploration of the crucial point where authority connects with the informal code through the sacred taboo on informing, there is a stream of telltale stories half goading the teacher into playing his formal role more effectively: 'Please sir, please sir, Joey's talking/pinching some compasses/picking his nose/killing Percival/ having a wank/let your car tyres down'.

In a more general sense, the 'laff' is part of an irreverent marauding misbehaviour. Like an army of occupation of the unseen, informal dimension 'the lads' pour over the countryside in a search for incidents to amuse, subvert and incite. Even strict and well-patrolled formal areas like assembly yield many possibilities in this other mode. During assembly Spanksy empties the side jacket pocket of someone sitting in front of him, and asks ostentatiously 'Whose these belong to', as Joey is clipping jackets to seats, and the others ruin the collective singing:

Joey   The chief occupation when we'm all in the hall is playing with all the little clips what holds the chairs together. You take them off and you clip someone's coat to his chair and just wait until he gets up . . . and you never really listen . . . you have to be really discreet like, so as the Clark [the deputy head] won't see yer, call you out, the other teachers don't matter.

(. . .)

Joey   Even on the hymn . . . when they mek you sing –

PW   But do they make you sing? I didn't notice many of you singing –

–   I was just standing there, moving my mouth.

–   We've only got one of them books between all our class. We've got one between twenty-five –

–   When we do sing we make a joke of it.

Fuzz   Sing the wrong verses . . . So if you're supposed to be singing verse one, you're singing verse three.

[Laughter]

During films in the hall they tie the projector leads into impossible knots, make animal figures or obscene shapes on the screen with their fingers, and gratuitously dig and jab the backs of 'ear'oles' in front of them.

As they wander through the park next to the school at lunchtime they switch on the dynamo on the park-keeper's bike, 'That'll slow the cunt down a bit'. They push and pull everything loose or transportable, empty litterbins and deface signs. Where it looks defenceless private property is also a target:

[In a group discussion on vandalism]

Pete	Gates!
Joey	Gates are the latest crack. Swopping gates over. Get a gate, lift it off, put it on somebody else's.
Bill	That's what we done. We was going to the ten pin bowling, you know, up by the Brompton Road, there was an 'ouse there for sale. We took the 'For Sale' sign out of the one, put it in the next door, then we took the milk carrier from the one, put it next door (. . .) we took a sort of window box on legs from the porch and stuck that next door. We swapped stacks of things.
Spanksy	And dustbins! [Laughter] . . . every night, go in to one garden, tek a dwarf out, and in the end there was a dwarf, a sundial, a bridge, a dwarf fishing, all in this one garden, and there's a big sundial up the road. He got one end of it, I got the other, and carried it all the way and put it in (. . .)

Outside school visits are a nightmare for staff. For instance, the museum trip. The back seats of the coach are left ominously empty for 'the lads' as they arrive late. There is soon a pall of blue smoke at the back of the coach though no red ends are ever visible. When the coach is returned the manager finds all the back seats disfigured with names and doodlings in indelible ink. The head sends the culprits to the garage the next day to clean the coach 'for the sake of the reputation of the school'.

In the museum 'the lads' are a plague of locusts feeding off and blackening out pomp and dignity. In a mock-up Victorian chemist's shop with the clear and prominent injunction 'Please do not touch', 'the lads' are handling, pushing, pulling, trying, testing and mauling everything in sight. Handfuls of old fashioned cough sweets are removed from the tall jars on the counter, and the high-backed chairs are sat upon and balanced back on their legs 'to see how strong they are'.

A model village is surrounded and obscured by fifteen backs from a now and for once attentive attendant. Spanksy says with mock alarm, 'Oh, look, a tram's crashed' as he gives it a good flick with his finger, and Joey takes one of the carefully prepared and stationed little men, 'I've kidnapped one of the citizens'.

They get out into the street for a smoke once they can dodge the teacher. Joey is dissecting his little man 'to see what's inside' and Spanksy is worrying in case the cough sweets have killed him. They all gather around and point to the sky, 'There it is, just above the building', or stare fixedly at the floor, and crack up into laughter when a little crowd gathers. They stop outside a TV shop, and stare at the woman dressing the window, 'Let's all stare at that lady and embarrass her'. They succeed and leave. Finally those with some money detach themselves from the rest and go into the pub for a drink where they talk in overloud voices about school, and snigger a bit uncertainly when someone looks at them. When they get back on the coach, late again, the back seats still empty, they are half 'grassing each other up' to the young teacher: 'There's something wrong with Spanksy, sir, his breath smells', 'Eddie's mouth's on fire sir, would you put it out'.

Next day, back in school, they are called to the headmaster's study because the coach firm has just rung up, but outside the headmaster's door they cannot decide which offence they are going to 'catch it for this time': 'Perhaps it's the cough sweets', 'Perhaps it's the singing on the coach', 'Perhaps it's the boozing', 'Perhaps it's for setting fire to the grass in the park', 'Perhaps it's for telling the parky to fuck off', 'Perhaps it's what we did to the village'. They were surprised and relieved to find it was the ink on the seats. Whenever one of 'the lads' is called to see the head, his first problem is to mentally list the many things he might be interrogated about, and his second problem to construct a likely tale for all of them. When the formal and the informal intersect the guilt and confusion in his mind is much greater than the sharper sense of culpability in the head's mind. There is often real surprise at the trivial and marginal nature of the misdemeanour that has 'caused all the fuss' – especially in view of the hidden country which could have been uncovered.

Of course 'the lads' do not always look to external stimulants or victims for the 'laff'. Interaction and conversation in the group frequently take the form of 'pisstaking'. They are very physical and rough with each other, with kicks, punches, karate blows, arm-twisting, kicking, pushing and tripping going on for long periods and directed against particular individuals often almost to the point of tears. The ribbing or 'pisstaking' is similarly rough and often directed at the same individuals for the same things. Often this is someone's imagined stupidity. This is ironic in view of 'the lads' general rejection of school work, and shows a ghost of conventional values which they would be quick to deny. Though 'the lads' usually resist conventional ways of showing their abilities, certainly the ablest like to be thought of as 'quick'. Certain cultural values, like fast talking and humour, do anyway register in some academic subjects. Joey, for instance, walks a very careful tightrope in English between 'laffing' with 'the lads' and doing the occasional 'brilliant' essay. In certain respects obvious stupidity is penalised more heavily amongst 'the lads' than by staff, who 'expected nothing better'. Very often the topic for the 'pisstake' is sexual, though it can be anything – the more personal, sharper and apposite the better. The soul of wit for them is disparaging relevance: the persistent searching out of weakness. It takes some skill and cultural know-how to mount such attacks, and more to resist them:

[A group of 'lads' during break-time]

Eddie   X gets his missus to hold his prick, while he has a piss. [Laughter]

Will	Ask him who wipes his arse. [Laughter]
Spike	The dirty bastard ... I bet he changes her fucking rags for her.
Spanksy	With his teeth! [More laughter]

[X arrives]

Spanksy	Did you have a piss dinnertime?
Bill	Or a shit?
Spanksy	You disgusting little boy ... I couldn't do that.
Bill	Hold on a minute, I want you to hold my cock while I have a piss. [Laughter]
X	Why am I ...
Will (inter-rupting)	He don't even know.
Bill	Does your missus hold your cock for you when you go for a piss?
X	Who does? [Laughter and interruptions]
-	You do
X	Who?
-	You
X	When?
Spike	You did, you told Joey, Joey told me. *

Plans are continually made to play jokes on individuals who are not there: 'Let's send him to Coventry when he comes', 'Let's laugh at everything he says', 'Let's pretend we can't understand and say, 'How do you mean' all the time'. Particular individuals can get a reputation and attract constant ribbing for being 'dirty', or 'as thick as two short planks', or even for always wearing the 'same tatty jacket'. The language used in the group, especially in the context of derision and the 'pisstake', is much rougher than that used by the 'ear'oles', full of spat-out swearwords, vigorous use of local dialect and special argot. Talking, at least on their own patch and in their own way, comes very naturally to 'the lads':

[In a group discussion on skiving]

Joey	(...) You'm always looking out on somebody [when skiving] and you've always got something to talk about ... something.
PW	So what stops you being bored?
Joey	Talking, we could talk forever, when we get together, it's talk, talk, talk.

Boredom and excitement

PW	What's the opposite of boredom?
Joey	Excitement.
PW	But what's excitement?
Joey	Defying the law, breaking the law like, drinking like.
Spike	Thieving.

Spanksy	Goin' down the streets.
Joey	Vandalising (. . .) that's the opposite of boredom – excitement, defying the law and when you're down The Plough, and you talk to the gaffer, standing by the gaffer, buying drinks and that, knowing that you're 14 and 15 and you're supposed to be 18.

The 'laff', talking and marauding misbehaviour are fairly effective but not wholly so in defeating boredom – a boredom increased by their very success at 'playing the system'.

The particular excitement and kudos of belonging to 'the lads', comes from more antisocial practices than these. It is these more extreme activities which mark them off most completely, both from the 'ear'oles', and from the school. There is a positive joy in fighting, in causing fights through intimidation, in talking about fighting and about the tactics of the whole fight situation. Many important cultural values are expressed through fighting. Masculine hubris, dramatic display, the solidarity of the group, the importance of quick, clear and not over-moral thought, comes out time and again. Attitudes to 'ear'oles' are also expressed clearly and with a surprising degree of precision through physical aggression. Violence and the judgement of violence is the most basic axis of 'the lads' ascendence over the conformists, almost in the way that knowledge is for teachers.

In violence there is the fullest if unspecified commitment to a blind or distorted form of revolt. It breaks the conventional tyranny of 'the rule'. It opposes it with machismo. It is the ultimate way of breaking a flow of meanings which are unsatisfactory, imposed from above, or limited by circumstances. It is one way to make the mundane suddenly *matter*. The usual assumption of the flow of the self from the past to the future is stopped: the dialectic of time is broken. Fights, as accidents and other crises, strand you painfully in 'the now'. Boredom and petty detail disappear. It really does matter how the next seconds pass. And once experienced, the fear of the fight and the ensuing high as the self safely resumes its journey are addictive. They become permanent possibilities for the alleviation of boredom, and pervasive elements of a masculine style and presence.

Joey	There's no chivalry or nothing, none of this cobblers you know, it's just . . . if you'm gonna fight, it's savage fighting anyway, so you might as well go all the way and win it completely by having someone else help ya or by winning by the dirtiest methods you can think of, like poking his eyes out or biting his ear and things like this.
(. . .)	
PW	What do you think, are there kids in the school here that just wouldn't fight?
Spike	It gets you mad, like, if you hit somebody and they won't hit you back.
PW	Why?

34

Eddie	I hate kids like that.
Spanksy	Yeah, 'I'm not going to hit you, you'm me friend'.
PW	Well, what do you think of that attitude?
Joey	It's all accordin' what you got against him, if it's just a trivial thing, like he give you a kick and he wouldn't fight you when it come to a head, but if he's . . . really something mean towards you, like, whether he fights back or not, you still pail him.
PW	What do you feel when you're fighting?
Joey	(. . .) it's exhilarating, it's like being scared . . . it's the feeling you get afterwards . . . I know what I feel when I'm fighting . . . it's that I've got to kill him, do your utmost best to kill him.
PW	Do you actually feel frightened when you're fighting though?
Joey	Yeah, I shake before I start fighting, I'm really scared, but once you're actually in there, then you start to co-ordinate your thoughts like, it gets better and better and then, if you'm good enough, you beat the geezer. You get him down on the floor and just jump all over his head.

It should be noted that despite its destructiveness, anti-social nature and apparent irrationality violence is not completely random, or in any sense the absolute overthrow of social order. Even when directed at outside groups (and thereby, of course, helping to define an 'in-group') one of the most important aspects of violence is precisely its social meaning within 'the lads'' own culture. It marks the last move in, and final validation of, the informal status system. It regulates a kind of 'honour' - displaced, distorted or whatever. The fight is the moment when you are fully tested in the alternative culture. It is disastrous for your informal standing and masculine reputation if you refuse to fight, or perform very amateurishly. Though one of 'the lads' is not necessarily expected to pick fights - it is the 'hard knock' who does this, a respected though often not much liked figure unlikely to be much of a 'laff' - he is certainly expected to fight when insulted or intimidated: to be able to 'look after himself', to be 'no slouch', to stop people 'pushing him about'.

Amongst the leaders and the most influential - not usually the 'hard knocks' - it is the capacity to fight which settles the final pecking order. It is the not often tested ability to fight which valorises status based usually and interestingly on other grounds: masculine presence, being from a 'famous' family, being funny, being good at 'blagging', extensiveness of informal contacts.

Violence is recognised, however, as a dangerous and unpredictable final adjudication which must not be allowed to get out of hand between peers. Verbal or symbolic violence is to be preferred, and if a real fight becomes unavoidable the normal social controls and settled system of status and reputation is to be restored as soon as possible:

PW	(. . .) When was the last fight you had Joey?
Joey	Two weeks ago . . . about a week ago, on Monday night, this silly

rumour got around. It was daft actually, it shouldn've got around to this geezer that I was going to bash him like and it hadn't come from me, so him not wanting to back down from it, put the word out he was going to have me, we had a fight and we was stopped. I marked him up. He give me a bit of a fat lip, and he dropped the nut on me nose, hurt me nose, hurt me nose here. But I gouged his eye out with my thumb, split his head open, then after they pulled us off, I grabbed him and took him in the corner and I told him there that he knows I wasn't scared of him and that I know I wasn't scared of him, he warn't scared of me, that's an end of it. It was a sort of an ... uh ... he was from a family, a big family like us, they're nutters, they're fighters the Jones', and ... uh ... didn't want to start anything between 'em, so I just grabbed him and told him what the strength is like.

In a more general way the ambience of violence with its connotations of masculinity spread through the whole culture. The physicality of all interactions, the mock pushing and fighting, the showing off in front of girls, the demonstrations of superiority and put-downs of the conformists, all borrow from the grammar of the real fight situation. It is difficult to simulate this style unless one has experienced real violence. The theme of fighting frequently surfaces in official school work – especially now in the era of progressivism and relevance. One of Bill's English essays starts, 'We couldn't go Paki bashing with only four', and goes through, 'I saw his foot sink into his groin' and 'kicking the bloke's head in', to 'it all went dark' (when the author himself 'gets done in'). In the RSLA film option where pupils can make their own short films 'the lads' always make stories about bank robberies, muggings and violent chases. Joey gets more worked up than at any time in class during the whole year when he is directing a fight sequence and Spanksy will not challenge his assailant realistically, 'Call him out properly, call him out properly, you'd say, "I'll have you, you fucking bastard" not "Right, let's fight".' Later on he is disgusted when Eddie dives on top of somebody to finish a fight, 'You wouldn't do that, you'd just kick him, save you getting your clothes dirty'.

The perennial themes of symbolic and physical violence, rough presence, and the pressure of a certain kind of masculinity expand and are more clearly expressed amongst 'the lads' at night on the street, and particularly at the commercial dance. Even though they are relatively expensive and not so very different from what is supplied at a tenth of the cost at the Youth Club, commercial dances are the preferred leisure pursuit of 'the lads'. This is basically because there is an edge of danger and competition in the atmosphere and social relations not present at the Youth Club. Commercial provision can be criticised at many levels, not least because of its expense and instrumentalism towards those it caters for. However, it at least responds to its customers' desires, as they are felt, without putting a moral constraint on the way they are expressed. In a sense 'the lads' do have a kind of freedom at the commercial dance. Its alienated and exploited form at least leaves them free from the claustrophobia and constriction of irrelevant or oppressive moral imperatives in official leisure organisations. It is possible for indigenous cultural forms to surface and interact without direction from above:

Spike	If there's a bar there, at a dance, it's good.
Will	Yeah, I think if there's a bar there you have to be more . . . watch what you're doing, not prat about so much, because some people what's got a bit of ale inside 'em (. . .) they see like a lot of birds there, and they think, 'I'll do a bit of showin' off', and they'll go walkin' round, like hard knocks you know (. . .) They just pick a fight anywhere.
Spike	Billy Everett, kids like 'im, he'll go around somebody'll look at 'im and he'll fucking belt 'im one (. . .)
PW	How do you start a fight, look at somebody?
Spike	No, somebody looks at you.
Will	That's it, just walk around so somebody would look at you.
Spike	Or if you walk past somebody, you deliberately bump into 'em and you swear blind that they nudged you.
PW	So if you're at a dance and you want to avoid a fight, you have to look at your feet all the time do you?
-	No.
-	Not really.
Spike	(. . .) Look at 'em, and fucking back away.
Fuzz	If you know a lot of people there, you're talkin' to them, you feel safer as well, if you know a lot of people.
Will	It's OK if you know a lot of people there.
Spike	If you go to a dance where you don't know anybody it's rough.

(. . .)

Spike	The atmosphere ain't there [in the school youth wing] there ain't a bar for one. You drink fuckin' fizzy pop, and eat Mars bars all night.
Will	I think . . . this club might, if they'd got some new kids we'd never seen before.
Spike	It'd be good then.
Will	It'd be good then, 'cos there'd be some atmosphere and you know, you'd be lookin' at each other, then you'd go back and say, 'I don't like that prat, look at the way he's lookin' at us'. And there might be something goin' on outside after . . . but now you're always gettin' Jules [the youth leader] walkin' out or summat, you know.

Evening and weekend activities hold all the divisions of the school plus others – sometimes more shadowy, especially if they involve class differences – further projected onto clothes, music and physical style. Being a 'lad' in school is also associated with 'being out' at night and developing a social understanding not only of the school but also of the neighbourhood, town and streets:

Will   Classin' it like the modern kids, right, the kids who dress modern, right. There's the hard knocks, then there are those who are quiet (. . .) but can look after theirselves, like, dress modern and hang about with the hard knocks or summat. Then there's the money givers, kids who you can blag money off, who'll buy friendship. Then you get into the class of the poufs, the nancies (. . .)

PW   Pouf doesn't mean queer.

Will   No, it means like ear'oles, do-gooders, hear no evil, see no evil (. . .) I think the hard knocks and that like reggae, d'you know what I mean, reggae and soul, they don't listen to this freaky stuff, then the poufs, the nancies, they like . . . the Osmonds, y'know, Gary Glitter.

PW   (. . .) weirdos, freaks, hippy types (. . .) how do they fit into that, Will?

Will   Yeah, well, I dunno (. . .) you find a lot of these freaks are brainy an'all.

Spike   T'aint our scene like (. . .)

Fuzz   I mean take for instance you go down The Plough when the disco's on (. . .) when there's all the heavy music, and you see the kids with their hair long, scruffy clothes (. . .) jeans and everything, and you go down on a soul night, and you see kids with baggy trousers, you know, spread collar shirts, you can tell the difference.

(. . .)

Will   I think you can feel out of it as well, 'cos I've been up the Junction, up town, it's a heavy place, got all the drugs and everything, and everybody was dressed really weirdo (. . .) and I felt I was out, well, I felt, well, out of it, you know what I mean, I felt smarter than the rest, as though I was going to a wedding, or I was at a wedding, and they was working on a farm.

It is the wider scope, extra freedom, and greater opportunities for excitement which make the evening infinitely preferable to the day (in school). In some respects the school is a blank between opportunities for excitement on the street or at a dance with your mates, or trying to 'make it' with a girl. In the diaries kept by 'the lads', meant to record 'the main things that happen in your day', only 'went to school' (or in Will's case gigantic brackets) record school, whilst half a side details events after school, including the all important 'Got home, got changed, went out'. However, although school may be bracketed out of many of these kids' lives, this 'invisibility' should not lead us to believe that school is unimportant in the form of what they do experience (see next chapter).

The pressure to go out at night, to go to a commercial dance rather than a youth club, to go to pubs rather than stop in, to buy modern clothes, smoke, and take girls out – all these things which were felt to constitute 'what life is really about' – put enormous financial pressure on 'the lads'. Shortage of cash is the single biggest pressure, perhaps at any rate after school, in their life:

[In an individual discussion]

Joey   (. . .) after all, you can't live without bread, let's face it, fucking money is the spice of life, money is life. Without money, you'd fucking die. I mean there's nothing fucking round here to eat, you couldn't fucking eat trees, you couldn't eat bark.

All possible contacts in the family and amongst friends and casual acquaintances are exploited and the neighbourhood scoured for jobs in small businesses, shops, on milk rounds, as cleaners, key cutters, ice-cream salesmen, and as stackers in super-markets. Sometimes more than one job is held. Over ten hours work a week is not uncommon. From the fourth form onwards, Spike thinks his work at a linen wholesaler's is more important than school. He gladly takes days and weeks off school to work. He is proud of the money he earns and spends: he even contributes to his parents' gas bill when they've had 'a bad week'. Joey works with his brother as a painter and decorator during the summer. He regards that as 'real' work, and school as some kind of enforced holiday. There is no doubt that this ability to 'make out' in the 'real world', to handle sometimes quite large cash flows (Spike regularly earns over twenty pounds a week, though the average for the others is something under five pounds) and to deal with adults nearly on their own terms strengthens 'the lads' self-confidence and their feeling, at this point anyway, that they 'know better' than the school.

There is even a felt sense of superiority to the teachers. They do not know 'the way of the world', because they have been in schools or colleges all their lives – 'What do they know, telling us . . .?' As the next chapter will show, there are also many profound similarities between school counter-culture and shopfloor culture. The emerging school culture is both strengthened and directly fed material from what 'the lads' take to be the only truly worldliwise source: the working class world of work.

This contact with the world of work, however, is not made for the purposes of cultural edification. It is made within the specific nexus of the need for cash, and responded to and exploited within that nexus. The very manner of approaching the world of work at this stage reproduces one of its characteristic features – the reign of cash. The near universal practice of 'fiddling' and 'doing foreigners', for instance, comes to 'the lads' not as a neutral heritage but as a felt necessity: they need the cash. As Spanksy says, 'If you go out even with just enough money in your pocket for a pint like, you feel different', and it is only the part-time job, and particularly its 'fiddles', which offers the extra variable capacity in their world to supply this free cash. This particular form of early exposure to work helps to set the parameters for their later understanding of labour and reward, authority and its balances, and for a particular kind of contained resentment towards those who manage and direct them:

[In a group discussion on part-time work]

Spike   (. . .) it was about eight o'clock in the morning, this was, he's [a butcher] got a telephone, he's got a big bag of ten bobs, and he'd left the two strings over the telephone so that if I touched it, the strings'd come, you know. I opened the bag, got a handful of ten bobs out, zipped it up and just left it. He says, 'You've touched this fucking bag, the strings was over the telephone'. Well I couldn't say much (. . .) so he told me to fuck off (. . .)

Will   (. . .) like there was an outside toilet [at a greengrocers where he used to work] but it was all blocked with stinking vegetables and all this, and I used to put 'em [cauliflowers] on top of the cistern, you know (. . .) he says, I seen 'im counting 'em, and he says, 'Uh . . . there's one missing here'. I said 'I dunno' (. . .) He says, 'There's one missing here'. I says, 'There ain't'. He says, 'There is'. I says, 'I must have put it in that one, 'ere' have one of 'em', and he dayn't count them, so I was alright. I thought he was laying a trap for me, like, I think it was a Friday night when that happened. The next day (. . .) I had to have a big fire up the back to burn all the rubbish and that, and I set fire to everything like and all the canal bank. It was like the railway bank like, round the back, it was all dry, bone dry, so I got this cardboard, this piece of cardboard box like that, and I threw it over there and set all the bank on fire to get him back like. And I went walking in, I says, 'Is the bank s'posed to be on fire?' [Laughter] He went mad he did. He says, 'Was it you?' I says, 'No, it must have been the butcher, 'cos they was having a fire.' And the fire engines come and everything.

There is some scope for getting money by saving it from dinner money, as well as some possibility for limited extortion from 'ear'oles' and younger boys – though 'blagging off' first and second formers is not highly regarded. Often the last – and sometimes earlier – resort for getting 'money in your pocket' is stealing. Shortage of cash should not be underestimated as the compelling material base for theft. In a very typical articulation of mixed motives, however, 'thieving' is also a source of excitement rather like fighting. It puts you at risk, and breaks up the parochialism of the self. 'The rule', the daily domination of trivia and the entrapment of the formal are broken for a time. In some way a successful theft challenges and beats authority. A strange sort of freedom – even though it is only a private knowledge – comes from defying the conventions and being rewarded for it. If you are 'copped', particular skills in 'blagging your way out of it' can be brought to bear, and renewed excitement and satisfaction is obtained if you 'get away with it'. Sometimes, of course, you do not 'get away with it'. Two of the Hammertown lads are put on probation for stealing car radios during the research. This is disastrous. Parents are brought into it, official reports written up, and all kinds of unspecified worries about the procedures of the court and the interminable proceedings of bureaucracy turn the original excitement to sickness. This is a moment, again, where the formal wins a decisive and irrevocable victory over the informal. The informal meanings do not survive a direct confrontation. Still, given the near universality of theft amongst 'the lads', there are very few convictions for theft. There are many more close scrapes and the dread of 'being done' adds extra excitement and an enhanced feeling of sharpness and adroitness when you do 'get away with it':

[In a group discussion]

Bill   It's just hopeless round here, there's nothing to do. When you've got money, you know, you can go to a pub and have a drink, but, you know, when you ain't got money, you've either got to stop in or just walk round the streets and none of them are any good really. So you walk around and have a laff.

Joey   It ain't only that it's enjoyable, it's that it's there and you think you can get away with it . . . you never think of the risks. You just do it. If there's an opportunity, if the door's open to the warehouse, you'm in there, seeing what you can thieve and then, when you come out like, if you don't get caught immediately, when you come out you'm really happy like.

Bill   'Cos you've showed the others you can do it, that's one reason.

Joey   'Cos you're defying the law again. The law's a big tough authority like and we're just little individuals yet we're getting away with it like.

(. . .)

Fuzz   (. . .) we all went up the copper station [for stealing from a sportshop], he had all our parents in first. Then he had us lot in with our parents and he says, this copper, we was all standing up straight, you know, looks round, he says, 'You! How much pocket money do you get?' he says, 'would you like someone to pinch that'. He says 'NO'. He says, 'Have any of you got anything to say?' 'Yes, cunt, let me go' [under his breath]. 'You should say, "Sorry" ', he said, 'If anything hadn't've been returned, if a dart had been missing, you'd 'ave 'ad it'. Benny Bones had got two air rifles at his house, Steve had got a catapult and a knife, and I'd got two knives at home, and he said, 'If anything'd been missing!'.

(. . .)

Joey	I'd been doing it all night [stealing from handbags], and I was getting drunk and spending the money, and instead of sitting there, doin' it properly, putting your hand down the back of the seat, I lifted the seat up and was kneeling down underneath, getting it out that way, and this bird comes back and says, 'What are you doing under there?'. I says, 'Oh, I just dropped two bob', and then her went on about it, so I just run off like, over the other side of the dance. Her went and told the coppers, and the police sat outside by the bogs. When I went out they just got me into this little cleaning room, and they got me in there and had all me money out. And she'd had four pound pinched, it was a lie really 'cos I'd only pinched three pound, and I'd spent nearly half of it, had a pound on me. If I'd've had four quid on me like, even if it hadn't been hers, I think they'd've done me. I didn't have enough money on me, so they couldn't do me.

Where the target is the school there is a particular heightening of excitement, of challenge to authority, of verve in taking well-calculated risks – and making money as well. Besides being a direct insult to staff, it also puts you absolutely beyond the 'ear'oles'. They have neither the need for the extra cash, nor the imagination to overcome conventional morality, nor the quickness and smartness to carry through the deed. The school break-in sums up many crucial themes: opposition, excitement, exclusivity, and the drive for cash:

X	I couldn't see how we was going to get copped [when they broke into the school some time previously]. If, you know, I could see how them others [the school had recently been broken into] was going to get copped, he was, just bust a door down and walked in. There was footmarks all over the place, smashed a window and shit all over the place, and pulling books off . . . .
Y	I mean we had gloves on and before we left his house we even emptied our pockets out to make sure there was nothing identifying. I left all my stuff at his house and he did, we just went then and I had a brown polo neck on, me jeans, gloves, you know, and he had all black things on.
X	All black, polish on my face. [Laughter]
Y	No. We was going to. Weren't we? We got the polish at your house, we was going to, but we thought, no.
PW	Were you nervous when you were doing it?
Y	Yeah.
X	Oh ar. Like this you know [trembling]. 'Cos it's . . . uh . . . I've always you know, I've pinched out of people's pockets you know, I've seen two bobs lying about and I've gone, but I've never done anything like that before. I enjoyed it!
Y	And I did, really enjoyed it!

X	And after you know coming down the road we were just in a fit, weren't we? We was that, you know, it was that closely worked out.
Y	And we spent it all up The bleeding Fountain, day'nt we. Getting pissed down The Old Boat.
X	Oh ar . . . I saved ten bob for the ice rink, remember?
-	Yeah.
PW	Why did you want to break into the school rather than anything else?
Y	Got no fucking money (. . .)
X	We knew the school well and if you try and break in anything else like houses and that, you know, you're not sure if there's anybody in, it's a bit risky, you know what I mean, but the school you know there's nobody sleeping here, you know there's almost no way you can get copped.

Sexism

Two other groups against whom 'the lads' exclusivity is defined, and through which their own sense of superiority is enacted, are girls and ethnic minority groups.

Their most nuanced and complex attitudes are reserved for the opposite sex. There is a traditional conflict in their view of women: they are both sexual objects and domestic comforters. In essence this means that whilst women must be sexually attractive, they cannot be sexually experienced.

Certainly desire is clear on the part of 'the lads'. Lascivious tales of conquest or jokes turning on the passivity of women or on the particular sexual nature of men are regular topics of conversation. Always it is their *own* experience, and not that of the girl or of their shared relationship, which is the focus of the stories. The girls are afforded no particular identity save that of their sexual attraction:

X	I was at this party snogging this bird, and I was rubbing her up and suddenly I felt a hand on my prick, racking me off . . . I thought, 'Fucking hell, we're in here', and tried to put my hand down her knickers, but she stopped me . . . I thought, 'That's funny, her's racking me off but won't let me get down her knickers'. Anyway we was walking home and Joe said to me, 'How did you get on with that bird, was she racking you off?'. I said, 'Yeah, how do you know?'. He said, 'It warn't her, it was me behind you, putting my hand up between your legs!' [Laughter]
Y	I can never be bothered [to use contraceptives] , I think I must be infertile, the number of times I've fetched inside. I can't be bothered you know . . . I don't want to pull it out, though sometimes I fetch before. You know, you're struggling with her, fighting, to do it, and you've got her knickers down, and you're

43

just getting it out [giving a demonstration, fumbling at flies with feet apart] and pow! [freezes demonstration] you fetch all over the place, that's terrible that is.*

Although they are its object, frank and explicit sexuality is actually denied to women. There is a complex of emotion here. On the one hand, insofar as she is a sex object, a commodity, she is actually diminished by sex; she is literally worthless; she has been romantically and materially partly consumed. To show relish for this diminution is seen as self-destructive. On the other hand, in a half recognition of the human sexuality they have suppressed, there is a fear that once a girl is sexually experienced and has known joy from sex at all, the floodgates of her desire will be opened and she will be completely promiscuous.

Y   After you've been with one like, after you've done it like, well they're scrubbers afterwards, they'll go with anyone. I think it's that once they've had it, they want it all the time, no matter who it's with.

Certainly reputations for 'easiness' – deserved or not – spread very quickly. 'The lads' are after the 'easy lay' at dances, though they think twice about being seen to 'go out' with them.

The 'girlfriend' is a very different category from an 'easy lay'. She represents the human value that is squandered by promiscuity. She is the loyal domestic partner. She cannot be held to be sexually experienced – or at least not with others. Circulated stories about the sexual adventures of 'the missus' are a first-rate challenge to masculinity and pride. They have to be answered in the masculine mode:

[In an individual discussion]

X   He keeps saying things, he went out with me missus before like, and he keeps saying things what I don't like, and y'know like, it gets around . . . he won't learn his fucking lesson, he does summat, he sez summat, right, I bash him for it, he won't hit me back, he runs off like a little wanker, then he sez something else (. . .) he ain't been to school since Friday (. . .) when I fuckin' cop him I'm gonna kill 'im, if I get 'im on the floor he's fucking dead.

Courtship is a serious affair. The common prolepsis of calling girlfriends 'the missus' is no accident amongst 'the lads'. A whole new range of meanings and connotations come into play during serious courting. Their referent is the home: dependability and domesticity – the opposite of the sexy bird on the scene. If the initial attraction is based on sex, the final settlement is based on a strange denial of sex – a denial principally, of course, of the girl's sexuality for others, but also of sexuality as the dominant feature of their own relationship. Possible promiscuity is held firmly in check by domestic glue:

[In an individual interview]

Spike   (. . .) I've got the right bird, I've been goin' with her for eighteen months now. Her's as good as gold. She wouldn't look at another chap. She's fucking done well, she's clean. She loves doing fucking housework. Trousers I brought yesterday, I took 'em up last night, and her turned 'em up for me (...) She's as good as gold and I wanna get married as soon as I can.

The model for the girlfriend is, of course, the mother and she is fundamentally a model of limitation. Though there is a great deal of affection for 'mum', she is definitely accorded an inferior role: 'She's a bit thick, like, never knows what I'm on about', 'She don't understand this sort of stuff, just me dad'. And within the home there is a clear sense that men have a right to be waited on by the mother:

[In an individual interview]

Spanksy   (...) it shouldn't be done, you shouldn't need to help yer mother in the house. You should put your shoes away tidy and hang your coat up, admittedly, but, you know, you shouldn't vacuum and polish and do the beds for her and (...) her housekeeping and that.

The resolution amongst working class girls of the contradiction between being sexually desirable but not sexually experienced leads to behaviour which strengthens 'the lads' ' sense of superiority. This resolution takes the form of romanticism readily fed by teenage magazines. It turns upon the 'crush', and sublimation of sexual feeling into talk, rumours and message-sending within the protective circle of the informal female group.[5] This is not to say that they never have sex – clearly a good proportion must do – but that the dominant social form of their relationship with boys is to be sexy, but in a girlish, latter day courtly love mould which falls short of actual sexual proposition. The clear sexual stimulus which in the first place attracts the boy can thus be reconverted into the respectable values of the home and monogamous submission. If ever the paranoic thought strikes the boy that, having got the 'come on' himself, why shouldn't others, he can be calmed with the thought, 'she's not like that, she's soft inside'. In this way, still, romanticism brokes the sexual within a patriarchal society. It allows sexual display without sexual promise, being sexy but not sexual.

What 'the lads' see of the romantic behaviour they have partly conditioned in the girls, however, is a simple sheepishness, weakness and a silly indirectness in social relationships: 'saft wenches giggling all the time'. Since the girls have abandoned the assertive and the sexual, they leave that ground open to the boys. It is they who take on the drama and initiative, the machismo, of a sexual drive. They have no reservations about making their intentions clear, or of enjoying a form of their sexuality. However, they take it as an aspect of their inherent superiority that they can be frank and direct and unmystified about their desires. The contortions and strange rituals of the girls are seen as part of their girlishness, of their inherent weakness and confusion. Their romanticism is tolerated with a knowing masculinity, which privately feels it knows much more about the world. This sense of masculine pride spreads over into the expressive confidence of the rest of 'the lads' culture. It adds a zest to their language, physical and boisterous relations with each other, humiliation of 'ear'oles', and even to a particular display style of violence.

The combination of these various factors gives a special tone to interaction between the sexes. 'The lads' usually take the initiative in conversation and are the ones who make suggestive comments. The girls respond with giggles and talk amongst themselves. Where girls do make comments they are of the serious, caring or human kind. It is left to 'the lads' to make the jokes, the hard comments, the abrasive summations and to create a spectacle to be appreciated by the girls. The girls are clearly dominated, but they collude in their own domination:

[A mixed group talking 'by the sheds' at dinner time]

Joan	We'm all gonna start crying this afternoon, it's the last.
Bill	You've only got two weeks left ain't yer, we'm gonna laugh when we leave (. . .)
Joan	I like your jumper.
Bill	You can come inside if yer like!
Will	Ain't it terrible when you see these old women with bandages round their ankles.
Mary	I ain't got 'em, and I ain't fat.
Will	I dayn't say you had, I said it was terrible.
Bill	I'm gonna nick Mary's fags and smoke 'em all. [Giggles]
(. . .)	
Eddie	It's time you lot were back in school, go on. [Giggles and whispering about someone who 'fancies' Eddie]. These wenches don't half talk about you behind your back, me ears are burning. [Loud burp from one of 'the lads']
Maggie	Oh, you pig, shut up.
Bill	[Handing cigarettes around] He'are.
Maggie	No thanks, I'll have a big one.
Bill	She likes big ones! He's got a big one, ask him, he'll let you have a look.
The rest	[Singing] He's got a big one, he's got a big one . . . [Bill takes his coat off]
Eddie	Have it off.
Bill	[To Mary] Have you ever had it off?
Will	I've had it off twice today already [Laughter] Do you like having it off? [To Maggie]
Maggie	You cheeky sod.
Will	I mean your coat. *

Interestingly, this kind of banter can be used towards the mother but never the father. It takes on a more kindly tone, responding to the domestic rather than the sexual range, but the initiative, force and the tone remain the same:

[In a group discussion of family]

Will   (. . .) I just play her up like, I'll be lying there, after I'd just woke up or summat. Her won't be sayin' a thing, and I'll say, 'Shurrup', like, 'Shurrup, stop talking' (. . .) Her says to me once, 'I think you're mad as a coot', and like once I lit the oven, a gas oven we got. Her was in the kitchen, and I pulled down the oven door like you know to make sure the gas wasn't on, her come in and sez, 'What the bloody hell you doin' ', I says, 'I'm lookin' for me fags'. [Laughter] (. . .) well, I'll just be lying there and say, I've got the radio on, when a good record comes on I'll start jumping about and goin' about makin' mad noises.

PW   What does your mum think?

Will   Her just sits there, I wouldn't do it in front of our dad.

PW   Why not?

Will   He'd just, he wouldn't see no . . . really, he'd think there was summat wrong, you know, and uh, when I ain't seen our mum like, I'll go home and say, 'Give me a kiss, give me a kiss!' . . . and her pushes me off, you know, sayin' 'Get off, you daft idiot' (. . .) The thing that gets her really mad, say, you go in to hang your coat up, and I'll push her into the corner like, and she'll be trying to get out, and I'll move there, and she'll go that way, and we'll be like that [dodging sideways] for about two minutes and she'll go bloody mad.

Racism

Three distinct groups – Caucasians, Asians and West Indians – are clearly visible in most school settings. Though individual contacts are made, especially in the youth wing, the ethnic groups are clearly separated by the fourth year. Divisions are, if anything, more obvious in informal settings. For a period the head of upper school allows fifth years to use form rooms for 'friendship groups' during break time. This is yet another, this time defensive and accommodating, variant of the continuous if subtle struggle to contain opposition. Its results, however, demonstrate for us what are the clear informal patterns of racial culture beneath and sometimes obscured by the official structures of the school.

Head of
Upper School   We have got the Martins (Bill), Croft (Joey), Rustin, Roberts (Will), Peterson (Eddie), Jeffs (Fuzz) and Barnes (Spike) in the European room. Bucknor, Grant, Samuels, Spence in the West Indian room and Singh, Rajit and co in the Asiatic room. So much for integration! There are three distinct rooms. You go into the white room and you will probably sit down and have a cup of tea made. You go into the Indian room and they are all

playing cards and they are jabbering to each other, and then you go into the West Indian room and they are all dancing to records. In the West Indian room they are sort of stamping around, twisting.

From the point of view of 'the lads' the separation is certainly experienced as rejection of others. There is frequent verbal, if not actual, violence shown to 'the fuckin' wogs', or the 'bastard pakis'. The mere fact of different colour can be enough to justify an attack or intimidation. A clear demarcation between groups and a derogatory view of other racial types is simply assumed as the basis for this and other action: it is a daily form of knowledge in use.

Spanksy   We had a go at the Jamaicans, 'cos you know, we outnumbered them. We dayn't want to fight them when they was all together. We outnumbered them.
Spike   They was all there though.
Spanksy   They was all there, but half of them walked off dayn't they, there was only a couple left. About four of us got this one.
Joey   Not one of us was marked . . . that was really super.

Racial identity for 'the lads' supplants individual identity so that stories to friends concern not 'this kid', but 'this wog'. At Hammertown Boys there is an increasing and worrying tension between the ethnic groups, particularly the Caucasians and the Asians, which sometimes flares up into violence. The deputy head then gets everyone into the hall and lectures them, but this only suppresses the immediate expression of dislike:

[In a group discussion on recent disturbances at the school]
Joey   He [the deputy in the hall after an incident] even started talking about the Israeli war at one stage, 'This is how war starts. . . . Pack it in'.
PW   (. . .) was he convincing you a bit?
Joey   He was just talking, we were just listening thinking, 'Right you black bastard, next time you start, we'll have you' - which we will.

This curiously self-righteous readiness to express and act on dislike is reinforced by what 'the lads' take to be a basically collusive attitude of staff - no matter what the public statements. This is perhaps even an unconscious effect and certainly where racism exists amongst staff it is much less virulent than that in the counter-school culture. There is, however, by and large much less sympathy and rapport between (a massively white) staff and ethnic minorities than between staff and whites. In an almost automatic cultural reflex minorities are seen as strange and less civilised - not 'tea', but 'jabbering to each other' and 'stamping around'. Certainly it is quite explicit that many senior staff associate the mass immigration of the 1960s with the break up of the 'order and quietness' of the 1950s and of what is seen more and more retrospectively as their peaceful, successful schools. Both 'lads' and staff do share, therefore, a sense in their different ways of resentment for the disconcerting intruder. For racism amongst 'the lads' it provides a double support for hostile attitudes. The informal was, for once, backed up by at least the ghost of the formal.

The racism in the counter-school culture is structured by reified though somewhat differentiated stereotypes. Asians come off worst and are often the target for petty intimidation, small pestering attacks, and the physical and symbolic jabbing at weak or unprotected points in which 'the lads' specialise. Asians are seen both as alien, 'smelly' and probably 'unclean', and as sharing some of the most disliked 'ear'ole' characteristics. They are doubly disliked for the contradictory way in which they seem simultaneously to be both further off, and closer to received English cultural models. They are interlopers who do not know their station and try to take that which is not rightfully theirs but which is anyway disliked and discredited on other grounds.

West Indians come off somewhat better at the hands of 'the lads'. Although they are identifiably 'foreign', sometimes 'smelly' and probably 'dirty' and all 'the rest', they at least fit into the cultural topography a little more consistently. Their lack of conformist achievement is seen as more appropriate to their low status, and aspects of their own oppositional, masculine and aggressive culture chime with that of 'the lads'. There is some limited interaction, between males at any rate, on the grounds of shared cultural interests in 'going out', reputation, dancing, soul, R and B, and reggae. The combination of racial dislike with some shared cultural interests meets, however, with most tension in the area of sexual relations where 'the lads' feel direct sexual rivalry and jealousy as well as a general sense of suspicion of male West Indian sexual intentions and practices – ironic, of course, in the light of their own frankly instrumental and exploitative attitudes. 'The lads' feel, however, barely consciously and in an inarticulate way, that they are bound, at least in the serious stage of 'courting', by some unwritten rules of de-sexualisation and monogamy which are not respected in West Indian culture.

To the elements of an enviable style and dubious treatment of women in the stereotype is added finally a notion of the alleged stupidity of West Indians. 'The lads' have their own notions of what constitutes 'sharpness' and 'nous' and the most common butt outside their own circles of denunciations and jokes turning on its opposite, 'thickness', are the West Indians. For the 'ear'oles' there is at least a degree of ambiguity about such charges, but 'wogs' can be safely and deprecatingly seen as 'stupid', 'thick as pudding', 'bone-headed'. This range of prejudice is real and virulent and potentially explosive in the sexual arena but in some important senses more comfortable for 'the lads' than the register of prejudice felt for Asians.

Notes

[1]   It is now recognised that some teachers retained on school teaching staffs are seriously disturbed and that this is a growing problem. See, for instance, J. Lawrence, 'Control experiment', *The Guardian*, 18 March 1975.

[2]   Spike's letter of apology is carefully pitched to maintain his own dignity as well as to secure his leaving certificate: 'I would like you to accept my sincere apologies .... The school *itself* has nothing to resemble 'Colditz' in any way whatsoever .... I realise what I have done, which might I add I find stupid now, *but at the time not so stupid*, so I am now prepared to face the consequence which you see fit' (my italics).

[3]   A recent piece of research on Dartington, the progressive private school in the West of England, claims that its children did not have a taboo on informing. This is extremely unusual and is explained (in that piece of research) by the way in which informal groups and the anti-school culture are inhibited by the exceptional unity, openness and democratic organisation of the school (reported in *The Guardian*, 1 January 1976).

[4]   It has been widely claimed that streaming, traditional subject-based curriculum planning, exams and general achievement orientation are likely to be conducive to the emergence of anti-school or semi-delinquent groups amongst the lower forms.

In Hammertown Boys it was quite clear that oppositional groups had emerged under streaming by the end of the third year. However, after mixed ability grouping was introduced at the beginning of the fourth year, the counter-school groups developed and hardened in exactly the same fashion as may have been expected under streaming. Furthermore, it was by no means only the least able who were involved in the counter-school group. Some of its really central members were highly articulate, clear-sighted, assertive, and able to across a wide range of activities. They had decided that, for them and at that stage, the life of 'the lads' offered more than the conventional road. Although continued streaming may have had a reinforcing effect on those of low ability in the 'ghetto' form with the orthodox effects we have been led to expect, we should also be aware that de-streaming can lead to a creative social mix which is developmental, not only for the overall social system of the school, but also, and in particular, for its informal, radical and oppositional wing. And those verging towards the anti-school perspective were, if anything, aided by the new forms of mixed ability groupings, topic centred teaching, student centred teaching and the obvious confusion caused by the high number of group changes during the course of the day, compounded in particular by the sheer number of RSLA options open to the pupils – on other counts, of course, a desirable thing. See D. H. Hargreaves, *Social Relations in the Secondary School*, RKP, 1967; M. D. Shipman, *Sociology of the School*, Longman, 1968; and R. King, *School Organisation and Pupil Involvement*, RKP, 1973.

[5]   The field work in the main case study was focused on boys in a single sex school. There was a 'twinned' girls' school next door, however, and 'the lads' often

chatted with groups of girls in the park at lunchtime. Angela Macrobbie first suggested to me the pivotal role of romanticism in the experience of working class girls.

3 Class and institutional form of culture

Class form

The main emphasis so far has been upon the apparently creative and self-made forms of opposition and cultural style in the school. It is now time to contextualise the counter-school culture. Its points of contact with the wider working class culture are not accidental, nor its style quite independent, nor its cultural skills unique or special. Though the achievements of counter-school culture are specific, they must be set against the larger pattern of working class culture in order for us to understand their true nature and significance. This section is based on fieldwork carried out in the factories where 'the lads' get jobs after leaving school, and on interviews with their parents at home.

In particular, counter-school culture has many profound similarities with the culture its members are mostly destined for – shopfloor culture. Though one must always take account of regional and occupational variations, the central thing about the working class culture of the shopfloor is that, despite harsh conditions and external direction, people do look for meaning and impose frameworks. They exercise their abilities and seek enjoyment in activity, even where most controlled by others. Paradoxically, they thread through the dead experience of work a living culture which is far from a simple reflex of defeat. This is the same fundamental taking hold of an alienating situation that one finds in counter-school culture and its attempt to weave a tapestry of interest and diversion through the dry institutional text. These cultures are not simply layers of padding between human beings and unpleasantness. They are appropriations in their own right, exercises of skill, motions, activities applied towards particular ends.

The credentials for entry into shopfloor culture proper, as into the counter-school culture, are far from being merely one of the defeated. They are credentials of skill, dexterity and confidence and, above all, a kind of presence which adds to, more than it subtracts from, a living social force. A force which is *on the move*, not supported, structured and organised by a formal named institution, to which one may apply by written application.

The masculinity and toughness of counter-school culture reflects one of the central locating themes of shopfloor culture – a form of masculine chauvinism. The pin-ups with their enormous soft breasts plastered over hard, oily machinery are examples of a direct sexism but the shopfloor is suffused with masculinity in more generalised and symbolic ways too. Here is a foundryman, Joey's father, talking at home about his work. In an inarticulate way, but perhaps all the more convincingly for that, he attests to that elemental, in our culture essentially masculine, self-esteem of doing a hard job well – and being known for it:

I work in a foundry ... you know, drop forging ... do you know anything about it ... no ... well you have the factory down in Bethnal St with the noise ... you can hear it in the street ... I work there on the big hammer ... it's a six tonner. I've worked there twenty-four years now. It's bloody noisy, but I've got used to it now ... and it's hot ... I don't get bored ... there's always new lines coming and you have to work out the best way of doing it ... You have to keep going ... and it's heavy work, the managers couldn't do it, there's not many strong enough to keep lifting the metal ... I earn eighty, ninety pounds a week, and that's not bad, is it? ... It ain't easy like ... you can definitely say that I earn every penny of it ... you have to keep it up you know. And the managing director, I'd say 'hello' to him you know, and the progress manager ... they'll come around and I'll go ... 'Alright' [thumbs up] ... and they know you, you know ... a group standing there watching you ... working ... I like that ... there's something there ... watching you like ... working ... like that ... you have to keep going to get enough out.*

The distinctive complex of chauvinism, toughness and machismo on the shop-floor is not anachronistic, neither is it bound to die away as the pattern of industrial work changes. Rough, unpleasant, demanding jobs which such attitudes seem most to be associated with still exist in considerable numbers. A whole range of jobs from building work to furnace work to deep sea fishing still involve a primitive confrontation with exacting physical tasks. The basic attitudes and values most associated with such jobs are anyway still widely current in the general working class culture, and particularly in the culture of the shopfloor. The ubiquity and strength of such attitudes is vastly out of proportion to the number of people actually involved in heavy work. Even in so-called light industries, or in highly mechanised factories where the awkwardness of the physical task has long since been reduced, the metaphoric figures of strength, masculinity and reputation still move beneath the more varied and visible forms of workplace culture. Despite the increasing numbers of women employed, the most fundamental ethos of the factory is still profoundly masculine.

Another main theme of shopfloor culture - at least as I observed and recorded it in the manufacturing industries of the Midlands - is the massive attempt to gain informal control of the work process. Limitation of output or 'systematic soldiering' and 'gold bricking' have been observed from the particular perspective of management from Taylor [1] onwards, but there is evidence now of a much more concerted - though still informal - attempt to gain control. It sometimes happens now that the men themselves to all intents and purposes actually control at least manning and the speed of production. Again this is effectively mirrored for us by working class kids' attempts, with the aid of the resources of their culture, to take control of classes, substitute their own unofficial timetables, and control their own routines and life spaces. Of course the limit to this similarity is that where 'the lads' can escape entirely, 'work' is done in the factory - at least to the extent of the production of the cost of subsistence of the worker – and a certain level of activity is seen as necessary and justified. Here is the father of one of 'the lads', a factory hand on a track producing car engines, talking at home:

> Actually the foreman, the gaffer, don't run the place, the men run the place. See, I mean you get one of the chaps says, 'Alright, you'm on so and so today'. You can't argue with him. The gaffer don't give you the job, they swop each other about, tek it in turns. Ah, but I mean the job's done. If the gaffer had gi'd you the job you would . . . They tried to do it one morning, gi'd a chap a job you know, but he'd been on it, you know, I think he'd been on all week, and they just downed tools (. . .) There's four hard jobs on the track and there's dozens that's . . . you know, a child of five could do it, quite honestly, but everybody has their turn. That's organised by the men.

Shopfloor culture also rests on the same fundamental organisational unit as counter-school culture. The informal group locates and makes possible all its other elements. It is the zone where strategies for wresting control of symbolic and real space from official authority are generated and disseminated. It is the massive presence of this informal organisation which most decisively marks off shopfloor culture from middle class cultures of work.

Amongst workers it is also the basis for extensive bartering, arranging 'foreigners' and 'fiddling'. These are expanded forms of the same thing which take place in school amongst 'the lads'.

The informal group on the shopfloor also shows the same attitude to conformists and informers as do 'the lads'. 'Winning' things is as widespread on the shopfloor as theft is amongst the lads, and is similarly endorsed by implicit informal criteria. Ostracism is the punishment for not maintaining the integrity of the world in which this is possible against the persistent intrusions of the formal. Here is the father of another of 'the lads' on factory life:

> A foreman is like, you know what I mean, they're trying to get on, they're trying to get up. They'd cut everybody's throat to get there. You get people like this in the factory. Course these people cop it in the neck off the workers, they do all the tricks under the sun. You know what I mean, they don't like to see anyone crawlin' (. . .) Course instead of taking one pair of glasses [from the stores] Jim had two, you see, and a couple of masks and about six pairs o'gloves. Course this Martin was watching and actually two days after we found out that he'd told the foreman see. Had 'im, Jim, in the office about it, the foreman did, and, (. . .) well I mean, his life hasn't been worth living has it? Eh, nobody speaks to him, they won't give him a light, nobody'll give him a light for his fag or nothin' . . . Well, he won't do it again, he won't do it again. I mean he puts his kettle on, on the stove of a morning, so they knock it off, don't they, you know, tek all his water out, put sand in, all this kind of thing (. . .) if he cum to the gaffer, 'Somebody's knocked me water over',

or, er, 'They put sand in me cup' and all this business, 'Who is it then?'. 'I don't know who it is'. He'll never find out who it is.

The distinctive form of language and highly developed intimidatory humour of the shopfloor is also very reminiscent of counter-school culture. Many verbal exchanges on the shopfloor are not serious or about work activities. They are jokes, or 'pisstakes', or 'kiddings' or 'windups'. There is a real skill in being able to use this language with fluency: to identify the points on which you are being 'kidded' and to have appropriate responses ready in order to avoid further baiting.

This badinage is necessarily difficult to record on tape or re-present, but the highly distinctive ambience it gives to shopfloor exchanges is widely recognised by those involved, and to some extent recreated in their accounts of it. This is another foundry worker, father of one of the Hammertown 'lads', talking at home about the atmosphere on his shopfloor:

> Oh, there's all sorts, millions of them [jokes]. 'Want to hear what he said about you', and he never said a thing, you know. Course you know the language, at the work like. 'What you been saying about me?' 'I said nothing.' 'Oh you're a bloody liar', and all this.

Associated with this concrete and expressive verbal humour is a well-developed physical humour: essentially the practical joke. These jokes are vigorous, sharp, sometimes cruel, and often hinged around prime tenets of the culture such as disruption of production or subversion of the boss's authority and status. Here is the man who works in a car engine factory:

> They play jokes on you, blokes knocking the clamps off the boxes, they put paste on the bottom of his hammer you know, soft little thing, puts his hammer down, picks it up, gets a handful of paste, you know, all this. So he comes up and gets a syringe and throws it in the big bucket of paste, and it's about that deep, and it goes right to the bottom, you have to put your hand in and get it out . . . This is a filthy trick, but they do it (. . .) They asked, the gaffers asked X to make the tea. Well it's fifteen years he's been there and they say 'go and make the tea'. He goes up the toilet, he wets in the tea pot, then makes the tea. I mean, you know, this is the truth this is you know. He says, you know, 'I'll piss in it if I mek it, if they've asked me to mek it' (. . .) so he goes up, wees in the pot, then he puts the tea bag, then he puts the hot water in (. . .) Y was bad the next morning, one of the gaffers, 'My stomach isn't half upset this morning'. He told them after and they called him for everything, 'You ain't makin' our tea no more'. He says, 'I know I ain't not now'.

It is also interesting that, as in the counter-school culture, many of the jokes circle around the concept of authority itself and around its informal complement, 'grassing'. The same man:

He [Johnny] says, 'Get a couple of pieces of bread pudding Tony [a new worker] we'll have them with our tea this afternoon see. The woman gi'd him some in a bag, he says, 'Now put them in your pocket, you won't have to pay for them when you go past, you know, the till' (. . .) Tony put 'em in his pocket didn't he and walked past with his dinner (. . .) When we come back out the canteen Johnny was telling everybody that he'd [i.e. Tony] pinched two pieces of bread pudding (. . .) he told Fred, one of the foremen see, 'cos Fred knows, I mean . . . Johnny says, 'I've got to tell you Fred', he says, 'Tony pinched two pieces of bread pudding', I mean serious, the way they look you know (. . .) he called Johnny for everything, young Tony did, Fred said, 'I want to see you in my office in twenty minutes', straight-faced you know, serious. Oh I mean Johnny, he nearly cried (. . .) We said, 'It's serious like, you're in trouble, you'll get the sack', you know and all this (. . .) they never laugh. He says, 'What do you think's gonna happen?'. 'Well what can happen, you'll probably get your cards' (. . .) 'Oh what am I gonna do, bleeding Smith up there, he's really done me, I'll do him'. I says, 'Blimey, Tony', I says, 'It ain't right, if other people can't get away with it, why should you 'a' to get away with it'. 'Ooh'. Anyway Fred knocked the window, and he says, 'Tell Tony I want him'. He says, 'You've got the sack now Tony', you know. 'Hope I haven't', he says, 'I dunno what I'm gonna do' (. . .) After they cum out, laughing, I said, 'What did he say to you Tony'. He says, 'He asked me if I pinched two pieces of bread pudding', so I couldn't deny it, I said I had. He says, 'All I want to know is why you didn't bring me two pieces an' all'.

The rejection of school work by 'the lads' and the omnipresent feeling that they know better is also paralleled by a massive feeling on the shopfloor, and in the working class generally, that practice is more important than theory. As a big handwritten sign, borrowed from the back of a matchbox and put up by one of the workers, announces on one shopfloor: 'An ounce of keenness is worth a whole library of certificates'. The shopfloor abounds with apocryphal stories about the idiocy of purely theoretical knowledge. Practical ability always comes first and is a *condition* of other kinds of knowledge. Whereas in middle class culture knowledge and qualifications are seen as a way of shifting upwards the whole mode of practical alternatives open to an individual, in working class eyes theory is riveted to particular productive practices. If it cannot earn its keep there, it is to be rejected. This is Spanksy's father talking at home. The fable form underlines the centrality and routinisation of this cultural view of 'theory'.

In Toll End Road there's a garage, and I used to work part-time there and . . . there's an elderly fellow there, been a mechanic all his life, and he must have been seventy years of age then. He was an old Hammertown professional, been a professional boxer once, an elderly chap and he was a practical man, he was practical, right? . . . and he told me this (. . .) I was talking to him, was talking about something like this, he says (. . .) 'This chap was all theory and he sends away for books about everything', and he says, 'Do you know', he says, 'he sent away for a book once and it came in a wooden box, and it's still in that box 'cos he can't open it'. Now that in't true, is it? But the point is true. That in't true, that didn't happen, but his point is right. He can't get at that box 'cos he don't know how to open the box! Now what's the good of that?

This can be seen as a clear and usually unremarked class function of knowledge. The working class view would be the rational one were it not located in class society, i.e. that theory is only useful insofar as it really does help to do things, to accomplish practical tasks and change nature. Theory is asked to be in a close dialectic with the material world. For the middle class, more aware of its position in a class society, however, theory is seen partly in its social guise of qualifications as the power to move up the social scale. In this sense theory is well worth having even if it is never applied to nature. It serves its purpose as the *means* to decide precisely which bit of nature one wants to apply it to, or even to choose not to apply it at all. Paradoxically, the working class distrust and rejection of theory comes partly from a kind of recognition, even in the moment that it oppresses, of the hollowness of theory in its social guise.

Even the non-conformists in the high status grammar school in the most exclusive part of the larger conurbation recognise the *social* essence of theory as it is articulated with practice in our society. For them, qualification is choice and mobility in a class society. It is not simply the ability to do the job better. It is this central realisation, in fact, which characteristically limits their anti-school feeling:

Larry   ... What I want to do, I want to get me 'A' levels [he had only
               just finished his 'O' levels and decided to carry on to 'A' level]
               and then go touring the world, then OK, live it fairly rough for
               a few years, just dossing around, then I'll carry on, but at least
               then I've got the choice of whether I want to carry on, whether
               I want to go back and get a decent job. If you've got qualifica-
               tions, then you can choose what you want to do: if you want to
               drop out, or whether you want to carry on being part of the
               system. But if you haven't got, you know ... if I didn't have the
               qualifications, I don't know what I'd do, this is all according if
               I get them, but if I do get them, at least I'll know I'll have
               a choice of whether I want to get a steady job and you know
               pension scheme, car, two kids and wife and house mortgage and
               everything like, or whether I just want to roam the world.

It is, of course, the larger class dimension which gives the working class counter-school culture its special edge and resonance in terms of style, its particular force of opposition and its importance as an experiential preparation for entry into working class jobs. Although all forms of institution are likely to breed their own informal accretions, and although all schools of whatever class always create oppositional cultures, it is the crucial conjunction of institutional opposition with a working class context and mode which gives the special character and significance to 'the lads' ' culture. Institutional opposition has a different meaning according to its class location and expression. The non-conformists in the high status grammar school, although sharing similar attitudes to school, know that they are different from the Hammertown lads. They cannot through institutional means alone transcend their class location. Ultimately, they have not only a different attitude to qualifications but also an inevitable sense of different social position.

Larry   A lot of kids that you've been talking to [in Hammertown], they'd regard us as poufs, 'cos we go to a grammar school. Not only 'cos we go to a grammar school, but because we're from here in the first place which is regarded as a snob area.

Some of the non-conformist group in the grammar school are, in fact, from working class families. Despite even their origins and anti-school attitude, the lack of a dominant working class ethos within their school culture profoundly separates their experience from 'the lads'. It can also lead to artificial attempts to demonstrate solidarity on the street and with street contacts. That the working class cultural forms of school opposition are creative, specific, borne and reproduced by particular individuals and groups from afresh and in particular contexts - though always within a class mode - is shown by the cultural awkwardness and separation of such lads. The lack of the collective school based and generated form of the class culture, even despite a working class background and an inclination to oppositional values, considerably weakens their working class identity:

John   Kids (. . .) have casually bracketed me as that [a snob] (. . .) I live near a school called The Links, and there's a lot of kids there, 'Oh he goes to grammar school. Oh'. Well, my attitude's been, I never want to be called anything like that, I think it's really horrible, so for a start, I've never tried to improve my language. I have these basic things of doing things daft, doing things daft. It's mainly just to make sure that everybody knows that I'm not a typical Percival Jones (. . .), he's got a really posh accent, 'Old chap', Lady Byron Lane type [indicating a middle class accent] of person, you know, not one of us kind, proud of the school and all that (. . .) I've said to kids who've really been getting on my nerves, you know, 'I know I'm better than you', you know, but these things when I muck about, that's trying to make sure that everybody knows I'm not.

It could be suggested that what non-conformists in middle class schools - no matter what their individual origins - are struggling for is some kind of conversion of their institutional opposition into a more resonant working class form. Insofar as they succeed and become influenced by processes discussed in the rest of the book, so does their future 'suffer'. Insofar as they fail, or insofar as, for instance, conformist working class boys in a working class school are insulated from working class culture, and become free from its processes, so they are likely to 'succeed'. Cultural location, especially in terms of shifts between patterns, is a much better model for explaining social mobility than is the mechanistic undialectical notion of 'intelligence'.

Institutional form

No matter how hard the creation, self-making and winning of counter-school culture, it must, then, be placed within a larger pattern of working class culture. This should not lead us however, to think that this culture is all of a piece, undifferentiated or composed of standard clonal culture modules spontaneously reproducing themselves in an inevitable pattern.

Class cultures are created specifically, concretely in determinate conditions, and in particular oppositions. They arise through definite struggles over time with other groups, institutions and tendencies. Particular manifestations of the culture arise in particular circumstances with their own form of marshalling and developing of familiar themes. The themes are *shared* between particular manifestations because all locations at the same level in a class society share similar basic structural properties, and the working class people there face similar problems and are subject to similar ideological constructions. In addition, the class culture is supported by massive webs of informal groupings and countless overlappings of experience, so that central themes and ideas can develop and be influential in practical situations where their direct logic may not be the most appropriate. A pool of styles, meanings and possibilities are continuously reproduced and always available for those who turn in some way from the formalised and official accounts of their position and look for more realistic interpretations of, or relationship to, their domination. As these themes are taken up and recreated in concrete settings, they are reproduced and strengthened and made further available as resources for others in similar structural situations.

However, these processes of borrowing, regeneration and return in particular social regions are not often recognised by those concerned as class processes. Neither the institutionalised, customary and habitual forms in which domination is mediated from basic structural inequality, nor the regional forms in which they are broken out of, opposed and transformed, are recognised for what they are. This is partly because social regions and their institutional supports and relationships really do have a degree of autonomy and separateness from each other and the rest of the social system. They have their own procedures, rules and characteristic ideological balances. They have their own legitimising beliefs, their own particular circles of inversion and informality.

Despite their similarity, it is a mistake, therefore, to reduce particular social forms and regions too quickly to the obvious central class dynamics of domination and resistance. They have simultaneously both a local, or institutional, logic and a larger class logic. The larger class logic could not develop and be articulated without these regional instances of struggle, nor could, however, these instances be differentiated internally and structured systematically in relation to other instances and the reproduction of the whole without the larger logic.

The state school in advanced capitalism, and the most obvious manifestations of oppositional working class culture within it, provide us with a central case of mediated class conflict and of class reproduction in the capitalist order. It is especially significant in showing us a circle of unintended consequences which act finally to reproduce not only a regional culture but the class culture and also the structure of society itself.

Emergence of opposition

Even if there is some form of social division in the junior school, in the first years of the secondary school everyone, it seems, is an 'ear'ole'. Even the few who come to the school with a developed delinquent eye for the social landscape behave in a conformist way because of the lack of any visible support group:

[In a group discussion]

Spike   In the first year ... I could spot the ear'oles. I knew who the fucking high boys was, just looking at 'em walking around the playground - first day I was there (...) I was just quiet for the first two weeks, I just kept meself to meself like, not knowing anybody, it took me two years to get in with a few mates. But, er ... after that, the third year was a right fucking year, fights, having to go to teachers a lot ...

In the second to fourth years, however, some individuals break from this pattern. From the point of view of the student this break is the outstanding landmark of his school life, and is remembered with clarity and zest. 'Coming out' as a 'lad' is a personal accomplishment:

[In an individual interview]

Joey   And in the second year, I thought, 'This is a fucking dead loss', 'cos I'd got no real mates, I saw all the kids palling up with each other, and I thought, 'It's a fucking dead loss, you've got to have someone to knock about with'. So I cracked eyes on Noah and Benson, two kids who weren't in the group, fucking Benson, summat's happened to Benson, summat terrible, he's really turned fucking ear'ole now, but I still like him, he still makes me laff. He can't say his r's properly (...) but I clocked ... I seen these two, 'cos our mum used to be at work then, and our dad used to go out at night, so I grabbed them and I said, 'Do you want to come down to our fucking house tonight?', and skinheads just starting up then, and I think Benson and them had the first fucking levis and monkey boots. And I started knocking about with them, they came down the first night, and we drank a lot of whisky, and I pretended to be fucking drunk like, which we warn't, and it was from there on. We parted off from the rest (. . .) we always used to sit together, we used to start playing up wild, like, 'cos playing up in them days was fucking hitting each other with rulers, and talking, and it just stemmed from there. And Bill started to come with us, Fred and then Spike . . . And from then on it just escalated, just came more and more separated. We used to go out of nights, and carrying on from hitting each other with rulers we used to fucking chuck bottles at each other, so the major occupation was roaming around the streets, looking for bottles to lam at each other. And from that came a bit of vandalism, here and there like.

[In a group discussion]

Fred It's the second year I went astray. Me and Spike first, I used to come, I come twelfth in the first years or twelfth in the second years and then I met Bill and all them (. . .) we went out with them one night, picked up a big crate of bleeding bottles, Bill and them did. I thought if I don't do it they're goin' to think I'm a right wanker . . . Picked up a crate of bottles, threw them, me and Spike you know, shit ourselves like, we was down the end of the road before they'd even started running, and then Bill threw bricks and all this you know, and scratching cars, fucking hell.

'The lads' themselves very rarely identify any deep causes for the changes they describe so vividly. Apparently for them it really is a question of the need for friendship or even of *accidental* causality – sitting by so and so in class, meeting 'the lads' at night by chance or being 'called for' unexpectedly. Of course these accounts do testify to the importance of the group in the change.

Staff too notice these dramatic changes and are not short of explanations. Kids start 'lording it about' and develop 'wrong attitudes' because they become exposed to 'bad influences'. The 'bad influences' arise from behaviour attributed, in the first place, to individual pathology: 'He's made of rubber, there's nothing to him at all', 'If you want the truth, you just take the opposite of what he says', 'He's a mixed up lad, no idea where he's going', 'He worries me stiff, his personality is deficient'. The counter-school culture arises from permutations of these character deficiencies in relation to 'the impressionable'. We have the classic model of a minority of 'troublemakers' being followed by the misguided majority:

Deputy Joey is the outstanding one as far as follow my leader is con-
head cerned (. . .) Spike being the barrack room lawyer would support him, and those two did the stirring (. . .) and Will is easily led.

It is interesting generally to note just how much teachers personalise, and base observations about kids – themselves lost in social and class processes – on what are taken to be concrete individual characteristics. Verbal comments start with 'I like' or 'I haven't much time for', and accounts are interrupted – in a way which is presented as illuminating – with '... a bloody good lad too', or '... a bad lot altogether, have you seen his dad?' Written school leaving and other reports clearly demonstrate notions of pathology in relation to a basic social model of the leaders and the led:

> [Joey] proved himself to be a young man of intelligence and ability who could have done well at most subjects, but decided that he did not want to work to develop this talent to the full and allowed not only his standard of work to deteriorate, except for English, but also attendance and behaviour (...) too often his qualities of leadership were misplaced and not used on behalf of the school.

> [Spanksy] in the first three years was a most co-operative and active member of school. He took part in the school council, school play and school choir in this period and represented the school at cricket, football and cross-country events.
> Unfortunately, this good start did not last and his whole manner and attitude changed. He did not try to develop his ability in either academic or practical skills (...) his early pleasant and cheerful manner deteriorated and he became a most unco-operative member of the school (...) hindered by negative attitudes.

> [Eddie's] conduct and behaviour was very inconsistent and on occasions totally unacceptable to the school. A lack of self-discipline was apparent and a tendency to be swayed by group behaviour revealed itself.

Explanations involving random causality or pathology may or may not hold elements of truth. Certainly they are necessary explanations-in-use for teachers trying to run a school and make decisions in the contemporary situation; they will not do, however, as proper social explanations for the development of an anti-school culture.

Differentiation and the teaching paradigm

The particular process by which working class culture creatively manifests itself as a concrete form within, and separates itself from even as it is influenced by, the particular institution I shall call *differentiation*. *Differentiation* is the process whereby the typical exchanges expected in the formal institutional paradigm are reinterpreted, separated and discriminated with respect to working class interests, feelings and meanings. Its dynamic is opposition to the institution which is taken up and reverberated and given a form of reference to the larger themes and issues of the class culture. *Integration* is the opposite of *differentiation* and is the process whereby class oppositions and intentions are redefined, truncated and deposited within sets of apparently legitimate institutional relationships and exchanges. Where *differentiation* is the instrusion of the informal into the formal, *integration* is the progressive constitution of the informal into the formal or official paradigm. It may be suggested that all institutions hold a balance between *differentiation* and *integration*, and that *differentiation* is by no means synonymous with breakdown or failure in function. Indeed, as I will go on to argue, it is the aspects of *differentiation* in the make up of an institution, and its effects upon particular social regions, which allow it to play a successful, if mystifying, role in social reproduction. *Differentiation* is experienced by those concerned as, on the one hand, a collective process of learning whereby the self and its future are critically separated from the pre-given institutional definitions and, on the other hand, by institutional agents, as inexplicable breakdown, resistance and opposition. What is produced, on the one side, are working class themes and activities reworked and reproduced into particular institutional forms and, on the other, retrenchment, hardening, or softening – all variants of a response to loss of legitimacy – of the formal institutional paradigm. Within the institution of the school the essential official paradigm concerns a particular view of teaching and its *differentiation* produces forms of the counter-school culture.

There are a number of possible relationships between teacher and taught. Recent years have seen a wide variety of experiments and developments as well as a more recent retrenchment and self-examination in this country under the auspices of Callaghan's 'great debate' on teaching.[2] I want to outline the basic teaching paradigm which I suggest locates all others – even as they attempt to go beyond it – and which, I would argue, remains massively dominant in our schools. Whether modified or not, near to the surface or not, its structure is common to all the varied main forms of classroom teaching.

Teachers know quite well that teaching is essentially a relationship between potential contenders for supremacy. It makes sense to speak of, and it does feel like, 'winning and losing':

Deputy head
: It's a funny thing (. . .) you get a situation where you've got a class or a boy and you think, 'God, he's beaten me', but the dividing line is so close, push a bit harder and you're over, and you're there (. . .) this is surprising about kids who are supposed to be dull. They will find a teacher's weakness as quickly as any lad.

Yet the teacher's actual power of direct coercion in modern society is very limited. The kids heavily outnumber the teachers and sanctions can be run through with frightening rapidity. The young teacher often wants a show of force to back him up; the experienced teacher knows that the big guns can only fire once:

Deputy head	You see we have very few sanctions and punishments we can apply. Very few indeed. So it's a question of spacing them out and according them as much gravity as you can. And we've got a reporting system with the staff now, whereby eventually they get through as far as me, the head's the ultimate, the next ultimate in the range (. . .) You can't go throwing suspensions around all the time. Like the football referees today, I mean they're failing because they're reduced to the ultimate so quickly somehow (. . .) the yellow card comes out first of all, and once they've done that, they've either got to send the player off or ignore everything else he does in the game (. . .)
Head	If enough people set out in defiance of anything . . . if all my boys tomorrow in school decide to do something wrong, what chance have I got?

The teacher's authority must therefore be won and maintained on moral not coercive grounds. There must be consent from the taught. However, the permanent battle to assert and legitimate a personal moral supremacy, especially with limited personal power, is tiring and not really a viable strategy for the long term. Sleight of hand is involved. It is this which marks off the 'experienced' teacher. It is the learning of the relative autonomy of the teaching paradigm: the recognition that the ideal of teaching is related only variably to particular individuals. It is the *idea* of the teacher, not the individual, which is legitimised and commands obedience.

This idea concerns teaching as a fair exchange – most basically of knowledge for respect, of guidance for control. Since knowledge is the rarer commodity this gives the teacher his moral superiority. This is the dominant educational paradigm which stands outside particular teachers but enables them to exert control legitimately upon the children. It is legitimated in general because it provides equivalents which can enter into other successive exchanges which are to the advantage of the individual. The most important chain of exchanges is, of course, that of knowledge for qualifications, qualified activity for high pay, and pay for goods and services. The educational is, therefore, the key to many other exchanges.

All of these exchanges are supported in structures which hold and help to define, as well as being themselves to some extent created and maintained by, the particular transaction. The educational exchange is held in a defining framework which establishes an axis of the superiority of the teacher in a particular way. Whilst the exchange and its 'fairness' is open to view and is the basis for consent, the framework which hold and defines the terms is both less explicit and in some ways more powerful. It must be considered as an integral part of our basic view of the teaching paradigm. The exchange spins, as it were, like a giro in this framework which it thus helps to stabilise and orientate. But the framework must be secured and ensured by other means as well. It must be capable both of enforcing definitions to some degree where the exchange itself cannot generate them (which is, of course, the case for such as 'the lads'), and to reinforce the exchange, where it is successful, by guaranteeing the equivalents, the concrete referents, external signs and visible supports.

This framework or axis is held by the school on the material basis of its buildings, organisation, timetable and hierarchy. It is sanctioned (in normal times) by dominant cultural and social values and backed up in the last analysis by larger state apparatuses. The final if messy breakdown of Tyndale,[4] the public enquiry and suspension of seven teachers, shows us on what ultimate basis our other schools stay open. Within the school 'good teaching' is maintained only by the proper establishment and reproduction of this axis. Usually much short of any direct force the establishment of the often implicit structural axis necessary for the explicit teaching paradigm proceeds through the 'slow drip' and the suppression of other or private meanings which might tilt the axis, devalue the teacher's knowledge, or make responses other than politeness appropriate.

Deputy head	In telling them off, you've got to make them feel ever so small, to think, 'Oh, I'm so sorry, I didn't realise'. If you can get them like that, not where you're making them flinch or necessarily cry, the way you can make them realise that you are very upset, or I am very upset, with what has happened, and give them the very good reasons for being upset, you know, convince them that they are a bloody nuisance, if you like, once you get to that stage, I mean, that's the way to tell them off. If you do call a kid a shit bag, you get nowhere do you, he'll call you one back.

The school is the agency of face to face control *par excellence*. The stern look of the inquiring teacher; the relentless pursuit of 'the truth' set up as a value even above good behaviour; the common weapon of ridicule; the techniques learned over time whereby particular troublemakers can 'always be reduced to tears'; the stereotyped deputy head, body poised, head lowered, finger jabbing the culprit; the head unexpectedly bearing down on a group in the corridor – these are all tactics for exposing and destroying, or freezing, the private. What successful conventional teaching cannot tolerate is private reservation, and in the early forms in virtually any school it is plain to see that most kids yield that capacity willingly. The eager first form hands reaching and snapping to answer first are all seeking approval from an acknowledged superior in a very particular institutional form. And in the *individual* competition for approval the possibility of any private reservations becoming *shared* to form any oppositional definition of the situation is decisively controlled.

The relative independence of the paradigm from particular teachers, and the importance of this separation is demonstrated nicely when teachers specifically reverse the teacher/pupil role. They are exploiting the degree to which the educational paradigm has been internalised by – or at least has a degree of legitimacy for – the student.

Head	To actually have to impose a punishment on a fifth year person ... you try to avoid anything inasmuch as you put them in the position, then you ... I think you can make them see from there. I say to these kids quite often, 'What shall I do about it, you say you're old enough to know, what shall we do about it? You get in my chair, now I'll stand over there, now you tell me what you're going to do about it?'.

Discipline becomes a matter not of punishment for wrongs committed in the old testament sense, but of maintaining the institutional axis, of reproducing the social relationships of the school in general: of inducing respect for elemental frameworks in which other transactions can take place.

Deputy head	If you can catch them you do, and you make hay of it. But only to impress on them, of course, that you can't do as you please in this life, and you can't break rules (. . .) every time you bring home to them something that's gone wrong, then it does some good somewhere.

It should also be noted that the basic framework and the teaching paradigm stretch upwards as well, and that deviation from it amongst staff is regarded in an equally pathological light. The position of all teachers, and of the young teacher especially, both in learning their performance as an embodiment of the abstract educational paradigm, maintaining and reproducing what makes it possible, and in fulfilling an expected relationship with other staff, can be extremely exacting:

Deputy head	You've got to be seen to be a man of great integrity, a man who's honest, a man who's just ... now if you become all these things to a member of staff, you can tear a ruddy great strip off him, and the respect will still be there (. . .) they know damn well that when they've done something wrong, they've done something wrong. They know when they've done it wrong, and if they're told off, they haven't a leg to stand on, so ... Some of them argue, of course, out of sheer defence due to some character deficiency, but the fact remains, they know deep down, you can't cheat in golf and you can't cheat at this game either.

It is the moral intensity of maintaining this axis and attempting to exclude or suppress the contradictory, murky cross-currents of normal life which can give to the school a cloying, claustrophobic feel of arrested adolescence. Everything ultimately turns on the fair exchange and the maintenance of the axis which makes it possible. In this sense the school is a kind of totalitarian regime. There is relatively little direct coercion or oppression, but an enormous constriction of the range of moral possibilities. Everything is neatly tied in, every story has the same ending, every analogy has the same analogue. The word 'co-operation' – the common-sense-in-use term for the exchange of 'equivalents' - creeps in everywhere. It is what has *not* happened when one is punished. It is what *has* happened when one is rewarded, ironically often by early release from the very system one has excelled in.

Perhaps the essence of the fair exchange, the quality of the axis which supports it, and the nature of the attempts to maintain it are best illustrated by programmatic statements made in what is still widely regarded as the ritual keystone of the institution of the school: morning assembly. This is the head talking to the school after his office had been broken into and human faeces deposited under his chair:

> I respect you, I respect your abilities. In some areas your abilities are greater than mine. I accept that (...) Last Friday I was feeling pretty low after I found out about this lot, I thought, there's not much here to respect ... but then I went to football on Saturday, there were several lads and teachers there, playing their hearts out, or giving up their time just for the school, and then I thought, 'Perhaps it's not so bad after all' ... I do respect your talents and abilities ... but I expect you to respect my talents as a teacher, and accept what I say ... It's difficult to distinguish between the real and the plastic today ... What's best to swallow isn't always best to eat. It's not always the most brightly packaged item that's best to eat. Here we're trying to do what's best for you, really help you, not give you the easy way out ...*

It is of the utmost importance to appreciate that the exchange relationship in the educational paradigm is not primarily in terms of its own logic a relationship between social classes or in any sense at all a self-conscious attempt on the part of teachers to dominate or suppress either working class individuals or working class culture as such. The teachers, particularly the senior teachers of the Hammertown school, are dedicated, honest and forthright and by their own lights doing an exacting job with patience and humanity. Certainly it would be quite wrong to attribute to them any kind of sinister motive such as miseducating or oppressing working class kids. The teacher is given formal control of his pupils by the state, but he exerts his social control through an educational, not a class, paradigm.

It is important to realise just how far the teaching paradigm and especially the axis of control and definition which makes it possible are clearly bound up, supported and underwritten in countless small and in certain large, as it were, architectural ways by the material structure, organisation and practices of the school as we know it in our society.

In a simple physical sense school students, and their possible views of the pedagogic situation, are subordinated by the constricted and inferior space they occupy. Sitting in tight ranked desks in front of the larger teacher's desk; deprived of private space themselves but outside nervously knocking the forbidden staff room door or the headmaster's door with its foreign rolling country beyond; surrounded by locked up or out of bounds rooms, gyms and equipment cupboards; cleared out of school at break with no quarter given even in the unprivate toilets; told to walk at least two feet away from staff cars in the drive - all of these things help to determine a certain orientation to the physical environment and behind that to a certain kind of social organisation. They speak to the whole *position* of the student.[5]

The social organisation of the school reinforces this relationship. The careful bell rung timetable; the elaborate rituals of patience and respect outside the staff room door and in the classroom where even cheeky comments are prefaced with 'sir'; compulsory attendance and visible staff hierarchies – all these things assert the superiority of staff and of their world. And, of course, finally it is the staff who are the controllers most basically and despite the advent of 'resources centres' of what is implied to be the scarce and valuable commodity of knowledge. The value of knowledge to be exchanged in the teaching paradigm derives not only from an external definition of its worth or importance for qualifications and mobility but also from its protected institutional role: its disposition is the prerogative of the powerful. Teachers distribute text books as if they owned them and behave like outraged, vandalised householders when they are lost, destroyed or defaced; teachers keep the keys and permissions for the cupboards, libraries and desks; they plan courses and initiate discussions, start and end the classes.

Of course much of this is obvious and apparently dictated by 'necessity'. It is perhaps difficult for us to imagine the school in any manner which is basically different or dictated by other 'necessities'. But our familiarity with the institution of the school in our society should not obscure the way in which its accepted material infrastructure and organisation underwrites specific kinds of pedagogic options and places a firm limit on the range of possible change. What is 'obvious' in one instance cannot be forgotten in another.

It is especially important to bear this material limit in mind when considering the extent to which what I have called the basic teaching paradigm can be and is modified in practice. Certainly many teachers would deny that their teaching relationship was so simple or structured, and there have indeed been many pressures towards change from below and from above. Leaving aside individualistic, stoic or heroic solutions there seem to be two main sets of (linked) variants of the basic paradigm identifiable in school: those from 'below' and those from 'above'. Essentially, I argue, both are responses to *differentiation*, or the fear of *differentiation*, whether or not this occurs in particular cases as a direct response to opposition or as an aspect of overall school policy. Neither modify the material basis and organisation of the school in any significant way. No matter what their internal ideologies or justifications, they are attempts, I argue, to *re-integrate* the same basic paradigm on a somewhat different and wider footing.

Many experienced teachers in working class schools sense a potential weakness in the hold of the basic paradigm on their 'less able', disinterested and disaffected students and seek to modify one of its terms in some way or another. Perhaps the classic move here, and one which is absolutely typical of the old secondary modern school and still widespread in working class comprehensives, is the revision from an objective to a moral basis of what is in the teacher's gift and is to be exchanged by him for obedience, politeness and respect from the students. This is the crucial shift and mystification in many forms of cultural and social exchange between unequal territories in late capitalist, society: that the objective nature of the 'equivalents' are transmuted into the fog of moral commitment, humanism and social responsibility. A real exchange becomes an ideal exchange. The importance of all this is not, of course, that the values and stances involved might be admirable or execrable, correct or incorrect, or whatever. The point is a formal one: the moral term, unlike the objective one, is capable of infinite extension and assimilation because it has no real existence except in itself. The real world cannot act as a court of appeal. Moral definitions make their own momentum. So far as the basic teaching paradigm is concerned what it is worth the student striving for becomes, not knowledge and the promise of qualification, but somehow deference and politeness themselves – those things which are associated certainly with academic and other kinds of success but are only actually their cost and precondition. The shift implies that such qualities are desirable in their own right, detachable from the particular project and negotiable for themselves in the market place of jobs and social esteem.

The pivotal notion of 'attitudes' and particularly of 'right attitudes' makes its entry here. Its presence should always warn us of a mystificatory transmutation of basic exchange relationships into illusory, ideal ones. If one approaches school and its authority, it seems, with the 'right attitude' then employers and work will also be approached with the 'right attitude' in such a way indeed that real social and economic advances can be made – all without the help of academic achievement or success. Of course this crucial move renders the basic paradigm strictly circular and tautological since the same thing is being offered on both sides without any disjunctions or transformations occurring in the circle of the relationship. What the student gets all round is deference and subordination to authority. He could learn this for himself. The objective tautology which turns on that too little examined category, 'the right attitude' does not necessarily damage the basic paradigm so long as its nature remains concealed or mystified. Indeed insofar as it maintains the tempo of apparently fair exchange, reinforces the institutionally defined axis and restrains other tendencies this modification strengthens the basic paradigm. It keeps its giro spinning.

These modifications of the teaching paradigm and associated views on life chances and the nature of reward are usually held quite sincerely by the individual teacher and are in no sense machiavellian. This is a powerful reason, of course, for their effectiveness. Often the whole is integrated by a genuinely and strongly-held conservative ethic concerning the organic, harmonious society.

A senior teacher at the Hammertown school	There must be hewers of wood and drawers of water. This is an inescapable fact and people tend to look down on the lad, 'Well, of course, he's gone on the milk round'. But you think of your own milkman. Is he doing a good job in the community? Is he a pleasant fellow? Does he give you good service? And as the answer to all those is 'yes', what the hell's wrong with him,

why should we look down on him? I think it's dreadful and I'm not a socialist, but I do think it's dreadful. Most of our milkmen are blooming charming blokes. 'Morning Sir', I say that to him, why shouldn't I? Invariably he says the same sort of thing back and this boosts your ego. But the fact remains that you can still say good morning sir to the milkman and why the hell shouldn't you. I mean, you have a respect for him as a human being and the job he's doing, and you hope to God he's got one for you. I know there's no such thing as altruism but there you are (. . .) talking in terms of sheer academic ability (. . .) little Jimmy's as thick as two short planks (but) he'd make a marvellous milkman or breadman. And you know it's considered, 'Well, he'll have to go on the milk won't he', instead of saying, 'Just the job for you, you've got personality, you're honest with money, you like people, ideal', you know, so the kid thinks, 'I'm getting the right job, I'm going places'. Why shouldn't they think that? They are, it isn't a question of earning less money than anybody else these days, 'cos they earn good money.

Another, so to speak, grass roots variant of the basic paradigm is also a product of long experience in the school. It concerns a revision of the other item in the expected exchange – respect, politeness and what is expected from the students. Quite simply not much is expected and there is no particular moral indignation when it does not come. Allied with this is often a non-programmatic interest in providing useful information where possible. Though this represents an unillusioned reduction of the teaching relationship, and provides the elements towards a realistic assessment of what is actually possible with disaffected kids, it still remains within the basic paradigm since institutional control remains the essential stake and no effort is made to change the material arrangements and organisation of the school. The yielding of some ground to the students and to their definitions and interests is made in the interests of ensuring a more basic control. The fundamental axis of the teaching relationship is maintained by accepting with good grace battles which are already lost – and making sure that the really important battles can never be fought. Such educational views are often associated with what might be called a pragmatic, not over-hopeful and poorly integrated solidarity with the working class – an uneasy but fatalistic sense of their basic oppression.

A senior teacher at the Hammer-town school

I've never been one who thinks we are really teaching these lads (. . .) even if they are reacting away from the school, they're still experiencing, still growing up, and our job is to listen to them, be around, be there to be argued with (. . .) and we might get something in on the side, quickly (. . .) With the fifth [year] I reckon it's careful containment, we give them little bits you know, let them think they're big tough men getting their own way, but in all the important things they're doing what you want ... you know, don't confront them, let them think it's going their way.*

The other basic set of variants of the teaching paradigm observable in schools come, so to speak, from 'above'. They enjoy a more public and influential provenance, but turn, I argue, on the same broadening and redefinition of the exchange relationship and acceptance of what is basically the same if somewhat modified material structure and organisation of the school. *In situ*, at least, it concerns *reintegration* of a *differentiated* or threatened teaching paradigm.

'Relevant' education proposes that the teacher of the non-academic working class child should start off from where the child is in terms of his/her own interests, rather than from the distanced interests of an academic subject. The local neighbourhood, work, tax matters and dealing with officials, and civics should be the curricula of the boys; home-making, family life and bringing up children those of the girls; and popular music, art and the mass media are to be studied by both. 'Progressivism' suggests that activities should not be imposed, but encouraged: approaches are 'child centred' rather than 'subject centred'; 'individual programmes' allow children to go at their own speed; and 'team teaching' opens up the widest resources possible to the children. In Britain these techniques have made the greatest inroads in the primary sector of education, and have been steadily spreading upwards. In the case of the non-academic at least, progressivism and relevance are usually taken together to denote the *new* specialised, liberal techniques first germinated in specialist centres, universities and colleges.

These ideas and techniques have had a thorough political and theoretical airing.[6] They have been linked to changes in social democratic thought generally since the war and have been the subject of a massive literature and expenditure in research. These are specific determinants and there has been a strong and clear thread of relatively independent theoretical developments which have produced their own concrete techniques and pedagogic objectives *at that level*. Certainly this whole debate and corpus of intellectual work may well have given a form to, and set limits for, educational reform, but I would argue that they have in no real sense determined downwards a new pedagogic practice. In the actual school the two main approaches anyway have an 'elective affinity' with patterns I previously characterised as from 'below'. Though they are interlinked, relevance is concerned *mainly* with what the teacher offers, and progressivism with how the child is supposed to respond. Teachers select from the repertoire of teaching styles and developments which are currently available to deal with the problems as they know them. These still centre on the maintenance of the basic teaching paradigm – which seems the only possible one and which is anyway minutely supported by material infrastructures which have been only marginally changed. The 'new' techniques may or may not have had a radical genesis (there is certainly a case here to be argued for progressivism) but they have been taken up on very different and more ancient grounds. If the new techniques seemed revolutionary they were profoundly post-revolutionary solutions to pre-revolutionary problems. They have been taken up often, in real situations, for control purposes or for the justification and rationalisation of existing tendencies. For those concerned with the 'permissiveness' and 'breakdown' of schools using the 'new' techniques it may seem strange to argue that they are actually mobilised to *reintegrate* failed or threatened traditional models. The alacrity with which some schools, under the pressure of the great debate, straightened circumstances, and return to a somewhat more authoritarian general climate, are further integrating, or attempting to, the teaching paradigm into something very much like the old model, might reassure them that the fundamental issue has always been the same no matter how it is represented at other levels. It will be much easier than it is commonly supposed to 'modify', 'restrain', 'redirect' the 'new permissiveness'. In its essentials the 'great debate' is a fraud which will not and cannot touch the real questions concerning the teaching paradigm and its material supports.

During *differentiation* the basic paradigm (no matter how modified) is to some extent delegitimised. The teacher's superiority is denied because the axis in which it is held has been partially dislodged. Because what the teacher offers is seen to be less than an equivalent the establishment of the framework which guarantees the teaching exchange is regarded with suspicion and is seen more and more obviously in its repressive mode. For 'the lads' other ways of valuing the self and other kinds of possible exchange present themselves. The teacher's authority becomes increasingly the random one of the prison guard, not the necessary one of the pedagogue. Where 'the private' was penetrated and controlled before it now becomes shared, powerful and oppositional. In a system where exchange of knowledge and the educational paradigm is used as a form of social control, denial of knowledge and refusal of its educational 'equivalent', respect, can be used as a barrier to control. 'The lads' become 'ignorant', 'awkward' and 'disobedient'. It should be noted that measured intelligence and exam results in general are much more likely to be based on the individual's position in this social configuration of knowledge than on his 'innate' abilities. Furthermore, many of an individual's 'personal characteristics' should be understood in this social sense rather than in an individual sense.

At any rate the challenge to the formal paradigm, and re-evaluation of the self and the group, comes from those 'private' areas now *shared* and made visible which were held in check before. These private areas are nothing more nor less, of course, than the class experiences of the working class boy and derive basically from outside the school. Where the basic paradigm excludes class from the educational realm, its *differentiation* invites it in.

It is interesting to trace in the earlier accounts of how individuals joined 'the lads', just how the development, both of the culture, and of the individuals in or moving towards it, starts from the school and steadily moves out to the street and neighbourhood, drawing with it a larger and larger content of working class values, attitudes and practices. It is clearly this expanding area which supplies informal and unofficial materials for the *differentiation* of the educational paradigm in the school. Where the cultural location of the school is not working class, then there is of course a different set-up: there is much less for the educational paradigm to be

72

differentiated with respect to, and therefore a much greater possibility of the paradigm holding in the long run.

In the working class area, though, there is a huge reservoir of class feeling to be drawn upon once trust has been decisively withdrawn from the school. Neighbourhood, street and the larger symbolic articulations of working class youth cultures supply themes for, and are themselves strengthened dialectically by counterschool culture. Of course parents and family are very important and influential bearers of working class culture too. Stories are told in the home about shopfloor culture, the things which happen and the attitudes which prevail there – especially attitudes towards authority. The language in the home reproduces (minus the swearwords) that of work culture. There is also a characteristic division of labour and a form of male supremacy in the home. The man earns the living and does practical work around the house, and the wife works for the 'extras' and services the needs of the family. There is also an interface here with the more extreme aspects of working class culture so that the father may 'tip the wink' occasionally about what to do in a fight ('Get one in, then ask questions') or how to approach theft ('Small fish are sweet, son').

Nevertheless parents should only be considered as one set – though important – of many possible 'bearers' of working class culture. Not all parents act in the same way or share the same values. Parents have their own complex and creative relations to class themes and in no sense press their children into a simple standard working class mould. There is a degree of relative independence between parents and kids. Some very conformist, 'respectable' parents who visit the school and try to back it up in everything have kids who inexplicably, to them, 'go wrong' and join 'the lads'. Other parents who are indifferent or even hostile to the school have 'ear'ole' kids – sometimes to their discomfort and dislike. We should be wary of any mechanistic analysis arising from particular indicators such as 'parental attitude'.

Still, there is an undoubted sense in which working class values and feelings – importantly though not always borne by parents – work against the school and provide concrete materials for *differentiation*. Spanksy's father, for instance, voices a profound working class suspicion of formal institutions and their modes of working. Ultimately he is not willing to legitimise the teacher's authority either. It is seen as basically artificial even though fearsome as it exploits, for instance, his own felt weakness in expression. Here he is talking about the last school open night he had attended:

> The headmaster irritated me, I can't put me finger on it now . . .
> 'cos I could see . . . could see, I was 'im, I was 'im, I was standing
> there, and I was 'im. I thought, 'Aye, aye, he's talking to hisself',
> you know, wa'nt talking to me (. . .) he put my back up (. . .) and
> then there was this person, you know, family, father or some-
> thing, instead of coming out, asking the teacher a question he
> knew what he'd gotta ask, he knew what answer he wanted to
> get, you see, I don't know how to explain it, like. I thought like,

	'Mate you'm only asking that question, just to let people know you'm in the room', know what I mean, 'cos he wasn't listening to the bloke's answer, he'd already accepted whatever the bloke was going to say was right, you know what I mean, how can I explain that. I don't know how to put it . . . See now, I can't get up in a room and talk against teachers, like, I couldn't talk against you, because I'd be flabbergasted, I'd be 'umming' and 'ahhing', and I'd be worried stiff you know (. . .) I dunno how to say it, how to put it, 'cos I'd look around me and I'd think, 'These people don't want to know anyway' (. . .) If I could have been in a room with 'im [the head] you know on his own, without anybody hearing us, I could have said . . .
PW	Could have said what?
Father	You're full of bull.
Mother	They say, 'Children's night', go down, they ain't interested really in what you'm saying, am they? They don't want to know.
PW	What's the whole thing in aid of then?
Mother	I don't know.
Father	I think it's trying to show you what good they'm doing for your kid (. . .) They don't tell what they'm doin' wrong for him, they tell you exactly what they're doing right for 'em, what good they're doing.

The letter of invitation for the open night has a tear-off strip saying that unless it is filled in and returned the head will assume parents are not going. It also says that questions must be submitted in writing beforehand and that only selected questions will be called. Even staff underline and put exclamation marks after the part of the information sheet which reads: 'Walk round the school and see for yourself exactly how the school works day to day'. Add to this the curiously pompous and elliptical style which can be used to parents about their children's misbehaviour (Spanksy's father received a letter beginning, 'I would like to discuss with you your son's *possible* future in the school' – my italics) and it can be seen that this working class mistrust is responding to something real. This is not necessarily a criticism of the school. It is doing its own job well in its own terms. But the axis of moral authority underlying its certainties and its style is quite different from the profane confusions, compromises and underlying spirit of resistance in working class culture. Once the working class boy begins to differentiate himself from school authority there is a powerful cultural charge behind him to complete the process:

[In an individual interview]

| Spanksy | He [father] doesn't want me to cheek the teachers, but he wouldn't want me to be a wanker, sitting there working, you know . . . My old man called me an ear'ole once, in the second years, playing football and comin' to the school. It upset me it did, I was surprised (. . .) I'd like to be like him, you know, he |

74

can't stand no bull, if anybody tries it on him, he hates it. It's the same with me, I think I'm gonna be little and fat like him, I'd love to be. I'd love to be like him, he's a great bloke.

It is not quite that the parents become any more influential during the period of *differentiation*, of return to, and regeneration of, working class themes. In a crucial sense they become less influential as their world becomes more so. The development of the young boy and his growing cultural confidence often put him in a role of competition with his father and a kind of attempted half-domination of his mother. He becomes not so much like his father as of the same world: the working class male world of independence, physicality and symbolic intimidation – and standing up to these things. The boy becomes a force to be reckoned with in this world. Despite filial affection there can be a definite tension in the domestic atmosphere where 'measuring up to dad' can mean being able 'to put one on 'im'. Often parents say, 'He goes his own way, like they do', or 'You can't tell 'im a thing', or there is a fatalistic recognition that certain profound cultural processes are already in train strengthened especially by the need for cash.

Spanksy's father
: This is probably one factor you don't . . . People don't probably think it's important, is money today. There's a group of chaps here, they go out every day (. . .) then there's little [his son], 'cos he goes to school, he has to rely on me to give him a pound. I can't afford to give him any more but how does he feel amongst them others. Education's gone by the board now, they'm out there ain't they. Somewhere to go, a discotheque or something, they go and buy sandwiches, ice cream, cake . . . can't, he ain't got it, he's the same age as them or he might be a few months younger you know (. . .) Education is right at the back of their minds you see. Their pockets you see, that's in their minds.

From the boy's side this fatalism can come across as indifference. This underlines the harsh importance of finding your own way through.

[In an individual interview]
Joey
: I asked the old lady . . . 'Ain't you fucking bothered what I become, don't you worry about it like?' Her never said, 'What do you want to be?' Nor the old man never said anything. But she answered it in a nutshell. She said, 'What difference would it make if I fucking said anything?' Her said, 'You'll still be what you want to be'. So I thought, 'Oh well'.

The middle class pattern is different. Though disillusion with the school and affiliation with some group form can be seen, these things do not occur with reference to a distinctive outside culture. Authority is not properly differentiated with respect to class dynamics. The emergent culture does not benefit from the force of working class themes. Consequently optimal conditions exist for the dominant educational axis to recoup its former position. The second term necessary for institutional differentiation is basically lacking.

When the middle class child is thrown back on to his indigenous culture, instead of finding strengthening and confirming oppositional themes there, he finds the same ones. Centripetal forces act to throw him back to the institution.

His relationship at home is not one of competition but of dependence. The axis at home is similar to that at school. Knowledge and guidance are exchanged for hoped-for respect in a relationship of superior/inferior. This relationship is secured particularly by the parents' likely financial ability to support the child. Thus no matter what the crisis, there is likely to be a parental notion of responsibility to a dependent instead of the working class notion of indifference to an independent. This reproduces to some extent the relationship which obtains at school. In particular, there is likely to be a reinforcement of a certain view of the social importance and value of knowledge, though on somewhat different grounds from the school's more idealistic paradigm. Middle class parents, in fact, are more likely than the teacher to insist on the importance of the school as a source not of theory for application to concrete practice, but of qualifications as a means of mobility in the chain of exchanges which characterise our society.

Although in the fourth year they are designated as the anti-school group by teachers ('All the school's problems are in there'), of the ten members of the group from the high status grammar school who say they are going to leave at the earliest opportunity, only two actually do so the end of the fifth year – one of these to be an assistant golf professional taking 'A' levels through a correspondence course.[7] They finally realise the strategic importance of qualifications, and are therefore more open to the rational dimension of careers advice, and can be brought back to the dominant institutional paradigm on purely instrumental grounds.

[In a group discussion at the end of the fifth year]

PW — Sketch for me the future of one of 'the lads'.

Nigel — Prosperity and gloom (. . .) anybody that leaves school will be prosperous the first two years when we're at college, and if you see them, they've got plenty of money. I think the difference will start to show the year after you leave college (. . .) I think we'll have a, generally, we'll have a better selection for work (. . .) watch ourselves climb up the ladder, while 'the lads', if they don't like their jobs, they'll be swapping around (. . .) It was forty five minutes of talk [his personal interview with the careers master] and that, everything was a bit more information for me. There was no stops in it, complete, nothing but talk and all the time he was telling me everything I wanted to know. He summed up my character, he told me why I wouldn't fit into certain jobs, why I'd be better suited to others. I really found that helpful. You know I walked in (. . .) half wanting to go to work, half wanting to stay on and I came out completely satisfied that I'd stay on.

The working class 'lads' ' settlement of their own future cannot be so easily diverted.

Post-differentiated relationships

We should not underestimate the hostilities which can develop in the *post-differentiated* school situation. Just because we have looked at the 'richness' of the cultural response of 'the lads' we should not forget what that response is to. Where knowledge becomes devalued or worthless, authority, stripped of its educational justifications, can appear very harsh and naked. That is why it is opposed. The teaching paradigm is seen more and more in its coercive mode. The total experience of school is something 'the lads' most definitely want to escape from.

One of the most oppressive forces is the belittling and sarcastic attitude of some teachers. This attitude arises from the particular conjunction of class and institution as it is exposed after *differentiation*. We may call it the 'class insult': it occurs in class but its referent is social class. Understandably enough, many teachers are outraged when the received educational paradigm breaks down. They register this breakdown as an affront: a breach in those manners which they expect as a matter of course. As we have seen, one of the essential equivalents in the educational exchange is respect. For good reasons of their own, therefore, after *differentiation* 'the lads' stop being polite to staff – at least as the main mode of their relationship, and this change is expressed at the very heart of the general style of their culture. All some staff see, of course, is wholesale impertinence and rudeness – not the logic of a changed relationship. Their frustration and anger takes the form of withdrawing their own equivalent, 'knowledge' – or, more precisely, revaluing its nature to make it utterly beyond the reach of 'the lads' anyway no matter whether they offer anything in exchange or not. Now whilst this has a certain logic of its own, and may even be successful in reasserting the old relationship where *differentiation* has not gone too far, its essentially *institutional* dynamic is perceived as a *class* dynamic by 'the lads'. There is a double articulation of meanings which is absolutely characteristic of institutions in a class society. We are faced with a mystifying and exacerbating process of the conversion and reconversion of institutional into class, and class into institutional, meanings. The teacher's frustration and attempts to re-orientate himself to the changed relationship and the changed notion of 'knowledge' at stake between him and his pupils, though taking place within the institution, are taken by 'the lads' as insults, not to their institutional identity, but to that whole class identity which they have turned to and reworked. These class insults are given an extra bite by the facility with which they are delivered. The teacher still has the mastery of formal words and expression. It is an area increasingly abandoned by 'the lads'. Examples of this kind of ridicule are extremely common:

| Various teachers to class | *'The Midwich Cuckoos* is about children with frightening mental powers – that won't concern us here.' |
| | 'X has just asked me about this exam question, "Discuss, how can you do that sir there's only one of us".' |

'Y has just asked me, 'Do you have to do both sections?' The first section is instructions'.

'It's a good job you didn't have to learn to breathe, Y, you wouldn't be here now'.   *

'The lads' are very sensitive to this kind of approach. Where it fails, of course, or is incompetently executed (as in 'Shut your mouth when you're talking to me'), they make hay of it. Often, though, it really strikes home. It is the most hurtful barb of what they increasingly take to be the essentially arbitrary nature of authority in school.

Spanksy	What gets me about teachers [is] when they try and embarrass you in class, like [they did with] Fuzz, for instance.
Bill	In front of all your mates.
Spanksy	They says to him, you know, 'I'll get a sand pit for you next week', don't they? [Laughter] They started reading my essay out and it was really crap it was.
Derek	Made it sound worse than it was.

In an increasingly vicious circle 'the lads' respond to the overall pressure on their culture with attempts to hit back in any way that is open to them:

Joey	You do anything you can here to, you know, go against them. Well, I mean, you vandalise books.
Spike	Yeah, you smash chairs up, take the screws out of . . .
Joey	Really afterwards, you think, 'Well, stuff me, our old lady paid for that lot out of tax', but at the time you're doing it, you don't think and you don't really care.
PW	But do you think of it in the same way as smashing bottles or thieving?
Joey	It's opportunity, getting your own back on the teachers when you're caned or something. If you think, if you can get your own back on *him* you'll do anything you can (. . .) revenge, sort of thing, getting revenge.

As the pressure increases, so does misbehaviour, opposition to authority, vandalism, and the exploitation of any weakness or mistake on the part of the staff. They threaten to overwhelm the staff particularly towards the end of term. But the mark of commitment and of the 'good' school is the refusal to give way:

A senior teacher	You're faced with a tide, you can't stop it, we try, we try to stem it . . . at some places they let the tide go over them.*

At the highest levels of the staff hierarchy something very like the old paradigm can be maintained, though with a somewhat altered balance of coercion and consensus and perhaps a shift towards the 'right attitudes' variant of the exchange relationship. The progressive distance of the head of the upper school, deputy

78

head, and finally headmaster from day to day class life means they are held in a degree of awe. The weight of the material structure and organisation of the school and the knowledge that what formal and coercive power there is resides here, makes 'the lads' generally subdued, if not exactly tamed, in front of them. Over really fundamental issues senior staff have to hold the line. The basic paradigm is enforced if only as a lesson to others and as a general defence of the legitimacy of the institution. After the last lunch-time when 'the lads' return drunk from the pub senior staff are determined that they should not get away 'scot free':

Head of upper school	What they don't realise is that they are still at school on that last afternoon, we can still reach them. We can go to see their parents, and they're very surprised when we do that, 'You can't come here, I've left school', and we can put it on their reports, or give no report.

After the fire extinguisher incident the head of upper school uses the final 'confession' of 'the lads' to make his own points to the rest of the school. The suppression of Joey's objections, he explains afterwards, is the crucial point where the line is held. 'The lads' know it too, and they cannot break it:

[In a group discussion]

Joey	I was just dead angry that Peters had been trying to make out, Peters had got us all there, he was talking about the 'big boys', he wanted to dispel the idea that any kids could get away with something, and that any kids were the big boys, so knowing all the first years was there, knowing it would make an impression, he tried to make out we were all snivelling and crying. Nothing happened [i.e. during 'the confession'] (. . .) he [the head] says, 'What about the name of the school?' I said, 'You ain't The Plough [a local pub] here', I says, 'You ain't got to go for popularity polls (. . .) you gotta go for how you teach the children, no matter how many fire extinguishers you lose'. I was gonna tell 'im [the head of the upper school in the hall] it was a load of cobblers, I put my hand up and I told him. 'Er', he says, 'Does anyone want any points clearing up?' I put my hand up and I says 'Yeah, I want this point cleared up about us', I says, 'We weren't crying or nothing, we weren't grovelling'.
Derek	'Now shut up', he says.
Joey	Snuffed it out he did.

Where senior staff take individual classes containing members of 'the lads' something of their larger authority remains, and disruption is rare. The culture of 'the lads' is suppressed on such occasions, and a reified form of the traditional paradigm enforced.

The most horrific classroom breakdowns seem to occur where more junior teachers try to assert the old educational paradigm when it is simply not tenable:

the moral basis for the educational exchange having disappeared. Nothing brings out the viciousness of certain working class cultural traits like the plain vulnerability of the mighty fallen. Nothing annoys senior staff more than being brought in to try to sort out the wreckage.

In such classes advertising jingles are sung in unison to break the period up like a television programme. Regular 'news flashes' contain wicked mixtures of all that is known to give the teacher apoplexy. In one case the teacher has told 'the lads' never again to mention the school moped which they had been pestering him to let them ride, and never again to mention Picasso whom he had once unwisely been drawn into describing at length. A raucous advertising jingle – 'Beer at home means Davenports' – is interrupted for an 'important announcement': 'Picasso has just been seen riding through the school gate on a stolen school moped'. It takes the teacher twenty minutes to get the five offenders to the head's office because they keep circling back to their seats after he has lined them up by the door.

On another occasion 'the lads' are reading a play, and in a fine symbolic homologue of their submersion of the educational paradigm, slowly begin to take over the play and substitute their own. It begins with individual words, 'bastard' for 'blasted' and 'jam rag' for 'towel', to the insertion of whole lines, 'my mother bought a sink from a supermarket', and whole jokes, 'daddy bear says "Who's been eating my porridge", baby bear says, "who's been eating my porridge", and mummy bear says, "shut your 'ole, I ain't made it yet",' to a final chaotic climax of simulated battle scenes with bangs and clashes, loud rapping desk knuckles, and stomping feet.

In this permanent guerrilla war 'the lads' give no quarter to a weak opponent. Their own culture provides a commonsense map by which to judge what they take to be a failure in nerve and authority:

[In a group discussion]

Eddie   Anybody these days who puts up with what he does, they'll be played up for the rest of his life. If you don't show your authority straight away when somebody starts to pick on you, like, they'll keep on all the time, like, all the kids if they know somebody you can pick on like, or summat, they'll play on him for the rest of their life as long as they know him, they'll keep playing up. You gotta show him that you ain't gonna stand for it in the first place.

Spike   It happens with us, like Spratt in the first and second year, I used to be a right cunt I did. I was shit scared of everybody I was, I was a right little wanker, especially him, Spanksy, he used to push me around left, right and centre Spanksy did (. . .) Then one day, I'd had enough and 'cos Spratt was one of the hard boys then, you know, he was a little tufty, and we was in Science, and he got me fucking mad, he kicked me in the fucking back, and everything, so I chased him round and I fucked him, really,

I really done him, y'know all his face was smashed up and ever since then, y'know, if you show a bit of authority, show you ain't fucking scared of 'em.

In a mutation of the basic paradigm many teachers operate with a schizophrenic notion of the pupil. In a half-recognition of the basic shift of 'the lads' from an institutional to a class identity they are seen as simultaneously carrying sets of referents to both. This acts as a double-bind on 'the lads'. Typical comments are: 'I'll start helping you when you start helping yourself'; 'You're your own worst enemy'; 'Would you give me just some common decency, you haven't even got manners to listen to me, so why should you be treated like men?'. It is as if pupils were composed of two people one of whom is supposed to save the other. They are continually exhorted to behave in precisely those ways of which they are supposedly incapable of behaving. This nagging vestigal but insulting attempt to reassert the old authority further disqualifies the authority of the school in the eyes of 'the lads'.

The most 'successful' teachers, those who survive with 'the lads' and do not burden senior staff with their problems (the main criterion of success in the view of hard-pressed senior staff), are those who have adapted, somewhat, the basic paradigm whether or not it is their usual style just enough to contain the counter-culture without provoking incidents on the one hand or collapse on the other. This tactical withdrawal for strategic containment is often dignified with the rubric of progressivism and 'relevance'. The justification concerns 'individual learning', 'discovery', 'self-direction' and 'relevance' but their logic in use concerns control. Though such classes may appear noisy, aimless and undisciplined, they rarely degenerate into chaos or psychic, symbolic or real violence towards the teacher.

For 'the lads' such classes are a matter of 'riding' the formal to extend, use and celebrate their own values of independence, the 'laff' and opposition, without pushing the teacher to the point of a final confrontation in which they might suffer. If things have gone too far there is a momentary return to the old paradigm. Priming questions or sudden interests die, though, as soon as the threat of an explosion has been averted. The following of instructions becomes mindless and literal so that the teacher is forced to qualify or even contradict himself. 'The lads' know the nature of the informal dimension much better than the staff, and especially the techniques for playing it off against the formal and its weaknesses. 'The lads' are experimenting and playing with themes of authority and of the containment of authority. The following examples are from a general science class discussion about a possible syllabus for the coming term:

Fuzz	Please sir, Joey's talking to Bill.
Teacher	Why are you telling me?
Fuzz	Oh, I just felt like doing a bit of tell-taling sir.
Eddie	Let's measure the football pitch, and then the girls' netball pitch . . . then the girls' hall.

Teacher	Yes, right, that's a fairly small job . . . what are you going to do then, what are you going to do with the results?
Spanksy	[Sarcastically] Well it's like this sir, we'll get a big piece of paper – green paper if you like – then we'll draw out the pitch and the semicircles and everything, [Laughter] and then we'll put little footballers on and play Subbuteo. [More laughter]
Fuzz	No sir, we can find the area of the semicircles, and all that, and the different areas of the pitch.
Teacher	What's your long term aim then . . . what are you trying to do?
Spanksy	We can go all round the school measuring and that.
Teacher	Now (to Spanksy) I don't want you to approach it with silliness, or a couldn't care less attitude, it's got to be useful.
Fuzz	It would sir, we'd have to find out all the areas of everything and go into the girl's school and take measurements [Laughter]
Joey	I'd prefer to stay in sir. The way I see it we might as well waste time here in the warm as outside in the cold.
(. . .)	
Teacher	Well, you'll need some equipment if you're going to do a survey . . . perhaps I can get you some. If you're serious about doing it I can get you the equipment.
Fuzz	I'll go and get a tape now sir [marches towards the door] .
Teacher	What's this, where are you going?
Fuzz	To get a tape sir, to do the measuring.
Teacher	Where from?
Fuzz	From the youth wing sir, I know there's one there.
Teacher	But you can't get up just when you like and go out (. . .)
Fuzz	[Still standing] But you said we needed some equipment sir. And I know where a tape is.
Spanksy	We want to do something sir, take some action on the decision, not talk about it all day.
Teacher	I know you just want to get out of the class.
Fuzz	We don't sir, we just want to do the measuring, working out all the measuring and that.
Teacher	Will you sit down please, I'll organise the equipment.
Fuzz	It's useless this is, I only wanted to make a start.*

Here 'the lads' are talking about such classes:

PW	(. . .) Just how far can you push the teacher around without them coming right down on you?
Joey	Really, it's an instinctive thing, really. Actually you always know (. . .) Mr Archer, you don't play him up 'cos you can have a laugh with him, but you don't have to play up. Mr Bird, he's got a sort of effect about him, like, he'll shout when you're playing up and

	uh ... we carry on talking when we go in his lesson, just sit there talking to Bill and as long as you aren't disrupting the rest of the class, he doesn't mind (...).
PW	Can you tell when you've gone too far?
Joey	You can tell by just looking at 'em, really by what he sez to you, what you can say back.
Spanksy	Or when they start getting mad, y'know like this in the face [straining].
Joey	Mr Samuels, his neck goes all red, it's his neck.
Fuzz	His neck, not his face, just about that far [indicating a point on his neck].
(...)	
PW	I mean when you say you can 'talk' to somebody are you really talking seriously or are you just playing them along a bit?
-	Playing along.
-	Playing along, trying to get on the good side.

Techniques which attempt to get too close to 'the lads' are simply rejected because they come from 'teachers' and are embued with what 'teaching' already stands for in the institution.

Spanksy	Some teachers try to get down to your level like, and try to be like, you know ... like Chapman, he gets us all in the gym.
Spike	He calls him Eddie.
Eddie	Yeah, I can't stand that, a teacher to call me Eddie.
Spanksy	He was talking to us, he was goin' 'Bloody' you know, he was saying, 'The boss', you know Simmondsy.
PW	What did you think of that?
Spanksy	We thought it was good at the time, you know, now we realise he was only trying to bring us round to his ways, you know what I mean? Split us all up.
Fred	Reagan used to come over and sit by me and he used to talk to us. I got really fed up with it one time. I just told him to fuck off. He says, 'Go to the headmaster', I had four [canings] war'n it?

For all their much lauded differences, in the real situation both traditional and modern techniques are basically about winning a form of consent from students within as tightly controlled an axis as possible. It is quite wrong, as we have seen, to assume that the traditional paradigm is about any simple domination of the students. Indeed an overcompliance with the teacher's wishes is registered as 'girlishness' and 'lack of backbone' even in the traditional model. The crucial relationship even here is predicated on the *consent* of the pupils to reciprocate – willingly and from their own resources – in acts of educational exchange. Progressivism as it is usually practised can be seen as a continuation of traditionalism in the sense that it attempts to preserve a version of the consent which has always been at the heart of the older method. In the concrete situation progressivism is a broadening of its terms in the face of reality, not an overthrow of traditionalism.

One of the main consequences of the 'new' methods has been to partially legitimise and routinise the counter-school culture and therefore also the processes which it sponsors. Though an outright confrontation and explosion of the culture is prevented by these techniques, the clogging of its processes with concessions and tactical withdrawals actually gives it a much more massive and less illicit presence in the long run. Not only this, but prolonged skirmishes of classroom interaction give it masses of continuous material with which to work up its forms in a way which would be curtailed in a swifter resolution of conflict.

In this sense we can see that progressivism has a particular part to play in what constitutes the specialness of the school in relation to working class culture in general. The really distinctive difference between the school and the shopfloor, for instance, is precisely the protected and even indulgent nature of the former. RSLA and the often sincere liberal aims of educationalists all create more protected space in the school than is possible in the factory. I am in no simple sense arguing for 'de-schooling'. At one real level the school is there to help kids such as the ones under study. However, the nature of this 'help' is far from obvious and seems to have produced some unintended effects. Instead of bringing these kids into the safe camp of conformism and progress in the dominant mode, the altruistic and ano-dyne aspects of the school have been re-interpreted and claimed in particular forms by the class culture. It is hard to believe that working class kids are not very much more developed now and that RSLA (after the initial violent fluctuations), and more liberal school regimes have produced youngsters who are more mature and confident on leaving. The direction and meaning of this greater maturity is, how-ever, far from settled. Instead of feeding into the conventionally approved pool of qualities and feelings, it is quite possible that the direction of these changes will be towards strengthening inherited aspects of an oppositional class culture. In particu-lar, for instance, 'the lads' of this study have adopted and developed to a fine degree in their school counter-culture specific working class themes: resistance; subversion of authority; informal penetration of the weaknesses and fallibilities of the formal; and an independent ability to create diversion and enjoyment.

Any school year is, of course, a complex mixture of individuals ranging from 'lads' to 'ear'oles'. The non-conformists are in a minority – though often not as small as is made out – and there are other patterns and threads to the teacher/pupil relationship not brought out here – particularly that operating on the sports field.[8] In large working class comprehensive schools the situation is likely to be more confused and diversified as the chances increase of a phalanx of working class kids trying to achieve something academically whilst still keeping their dues paid up with 'the lads'. Furthermore, in schools where a sizeable proportion of working class kids are properly upwardly mobile and going on to university, the option of being something of an 'ear'ole' might be seen somewhat differently. All of these things may well act to blunt the starkness of the opposition we have uncovered in the Hammertown school between the conformists and non-conformists, and to make the social map more complex. Furthermore, in those schools where there is a genuine mix of social class – again, much rarer than is often claimed – there may be some interesting convergences between middle class and working class 'ear'ole' values, and between working class and middle class 'lads' ' values.

In addition, as many schools become multi-racial institutions, we may expect further patterns both of opposition and cross influences between parallel West Indian, Asian and white groups in the school. Of particular importance here is the recent rapid emergence of what we might think of as a *hyper* 'lads' culture developed by young West Indians in inner city schools. They differ from white varieties of counter-school culture principally in that *differentiation* of the institution has occurred with respect to themes borrowed from the West Indies. It is particularly clear in this case that the new culture is not a mere reproduction of the old, but a re-working of some old themes in the specific context, and with the specific problems in mind, of the particular institution (and later on, of course, of the specific employment situation faced by West Indians). Although these new counter-cultural forms are clearly West Indian, they are more strident, developed and anglicised than their parent cultures, and often a source of considerable alarm to West Indian parents. The consequences of these new cultures for the preparation of labour power and attitudes to work are even more profound than those arising from the parallel white forms. In particular, the theme of wagelessness and survival without a job borrowed from the underdeveloped context may well be in the process of being converted into the theme of refusal to work in the developed context. We are facing for the first time in this society the possibility of the rejection of contemporary forms and structures of work by at least a significant minority of our second generation immigrant population.[9]

We cannot be concerned with every variety of student culture and teaching relationship here, but this does not mean that our focus on the white male working class non-conformist element assumes rigid and exclusive divisions in actual school populations. The non-conformist culture is a vital tool with which to think through the nature of other positions. Any classroom situation is a complex combination of elements: acceptance, opposition, legitimacy, and the particular way in which the teacher inhabits the educational paradigm. The aim of this book is to separate out some of the central, strong patterns in the grey and confusing daily pattern of institutional life. I see no contradiction in saying that the reader's aim (especially where he is a practitioner) should be the opposite: to test reality with the concepts outlined; to contextualise; to see what role different fundamental processes play at different strengths in different situations at different times.

Notes

[1]   F. Taylor, *Scientific Management*, Greenwood Press, 1972.

[2]   In a speech at Ruskin College, Oxford, in October 1976, the Labour prime minister commented on problems and fears in current educational practice. He

called for a 'great debate' on educational issues which was subsequently taken up by the DES who organised a number of regional conferences and a background paper outlining four main areas of concern: the school curriculum, 5-16; the assessment of standards; the education and training of teachers; school and working life. DES, *Educating our Children*, January 1977.

[3] This/goes some way to explaining why teaching is so often likened to, and experienced as, a performance. There is, in a sense, an external script, and it is this realisation which marks the breakthrough of the young teacher, and which is most certainly not taught in colleges and departments of education. As a senior teacher in the school said of team teaching: 'If the new teacher can see that the older ones are acting, then he will perhaps realise earlier than he would have done under normal circumstances that everybody acts in their own way.'

These considerations also strengthen the sense in which we can speak of teachers as a group with distinctive characteristics, no matter what their particular collection of personalities and idiosyncrasies, and of teaching as a discrete activity. It is in this unity that we can partly understand the practice of education as a semi-autonomous social region not directly reducible to class relations.

[4] William Tyndale Junior School in London broke down during the summer and autumn of 1975 after complaints by some staff and parents about indiscipline and the ineffectiveness of the new teaching methods, a staff strike and an inspectors' report. See R. Auld, *William Tyndale Report*, July 1976; J. Gretton and M. Jackson, *William Tyndale: Collapse of a School - or a System*, Allen & Unwin, London 1976; T. Ellis, J. McWhirter, D. McColgan, B. Haddow, *William Tyndale: the Teachers' Story*, Writers and Readers Publishing Co-operative, London 1976.

[5] Joey during a purge: 'We might as well have dog collars, we might as well have leads on, running up a wire from the playground to the bogs.'

[6] This has been conducted partly in a succession of official reports. R. H. Tawney, *Secondary Education for All*, Allen and Unwin, 1922; Hadow Report, *Report of the Consultative Committee on the Education of the Adolescent*, HMSO, 1926; Spens Report, *Report of the Consultative Committee on Secondary Education with Special Reference to Grammar School and Technical High Schools*, HMSO, 1938; Norwood Report, *Curriculum and Examinations in Secondary Schools: Report of the Committee of the Secondary School Examination Council*, HMSO, 1943; Central Advisory Council for Education (England), *Early Leaving*, HMSO, 1954; G. Crowther (Chairman), *Fifteen to Eighteen*, Report of the Central Advisory Council for Education (England), HMSO, 1959-60; Newsom Report, *Half Our Future: A Report of the Central Advisory Council for Education (England)*, HMSO, 1963; Robbins Report, *Higher Education*, HMSO, 1963; Plowden Report, *Children and their Primary Schools: A Report of the Central Advisory Council for Education (England)*, HMSO, 1967.

[7] This lad is interesting. He is working class, rejects school, but has a total commitment to upward mobility through his chosen sport of golf.

[In an individual interview at work]

Boy   I'm fighting to establish myself as a higher class of person almost (. . .) you see so many people doing better, like, of my father's age group, doing so much better, they've got good jobs, and you are in fact envious of them, and of the provisions they can make for their families, so you just go out and try to achieve that.

PW   [What's] a better person?

Boy   It's having respect for people, I mean my father has got very little respect as a factory worker, and, you know, generally you find that your middle class has got more respect.

Very typically of upwardly mobile working class lads, however, his rejection of his own culture does not amount to an acceptance of the middle class one:

PW   Are they [middle class people] still 'they' or do you already feel you've . . .

Boy   No, I still treat them as 'they' (. . .) you know I sort of talk to them (. . .) thinking to myself you know, 'Piss off, my God you're a right one aren't you', things like that, you know. When some of them come in, like that bloke you saw having those new irons, the grey-haired guy, you know, the stiff upper lip, and all that, I mean, I really despise him. He signifies to me a supremacy over other people.

Sport is his way to the top. In a very real sense the 'killer instinct' is a class instinct:

> I wanted to prove that somebody without their, you might call it intellectual or financial, well you might say greatness, could be beaten by somebody years younger and intellectually weaker, and a very much poorer background (. . .) you have to have a killer instinct (. . .) when I play I couldn't care less who it's against, I'll try and beat them, I couldn't care less if they are paying me and they want a friendly game, I'll beat 'em (. . .) it's the hunger to win, probably a primitive feeling, almost like the hunger for food. You grab out for food and some people will grab out to win, they will try and practise and try and try until they win (. . .) middle class people don't have the killer instinct, they don't have the natural aggressiveness to get out there in the cold and practise.

[8]   Sport is a very important zone which distinguishes the 'ear'oles' and 'the lads' and where the staff are able to control a certain independence, with its roots in 'the lads' culture, by operating a paradigm containing elements both of conventional teaching and of the oppositional culture: principally toughness, masculinity and physical dexterity. The following extract comes from a recognised school sportsman:

> If it was true I wouldn't mind admitting I was an ear'ole, but I think I come somewhere in between . . . I suppose in the first year I was a bit of an ear'ole, you know, and, like more, I've got on with the sports teachers, because

I enjoy me sport and I've progressed, because I don't mind having a joke. I don't take it too serious but sometimes I crack a joke about the teachers, you know to their face sort of thing, and they see the funny side of it all. They don't seem to have relationships like that with the ear'oles. They teach 'em, nice good lads. They seem to treat me as somebody to talk to like.

[9]   See the article by Farrukh Dhonely in *Race Today*, 4 June 1974. This whole area urgently needs to be researched along the lines set out in this book.

4 Labour power, culture, class and institution

Having examined the general setting and experience of being working class and disaffected in the state institution of the school, we are now in a position to look more closely at that process of the subjective preparation of labour power which produces the most profound particular outcome of the culture and is its main logic and dynamic.

Official provision

There is now a statutory obligation on all local authorities in England and Wales to provide a vocational guidance service for persons in full time education, and an employment service for those leaving it.[1]

Traditionally, careers work has concentrated on smoothing out the difficulties of converting the academic into the occupational gradient. It was a question of matching the individual pupil's abilities and talents with the jobs available. Careers teachers and officers characteristically regularised this process, perhaps with the use of psychological tests[2] to 'objectively' ascertain ability and aptitude as a basis for advice to the individual to shift his aspirations up or down.

In recent years, and especially under a strong influence from American writers,[3] vocational guidance has been changing. It has been reacting to the human sterility of the conventional academic gradient and its implications for occupational choice. The basis of the new wave of vocational guidance is to add a horizontal grid to this model. Human potential both in the school and vocational setting, it is argued, is not exhausted by academic difference. There is variety, richness and interest *laterally* at the various pegs of the conventional academic gradient.[4]

The commitment is a double one. The world of work is explored and studied to demonstrate the variety of riches and interests it holds for the attention and engagement of *all* kinds of human characteristics. In this way real scope is offered to individuals to find their various satisfactions in work even if they are at the 'bottom' of the academic gradient. After all, 'One man's poison is another man's meat'.[5]

Along with this goes an admirable interest in the pupil as a whole individual with a multitude of interests and aptitudes, rather than as a receptacle – usually cracked, it seems, in the case of working class kids – for knowledge. The 'self-concept' of the individual is developed in relation not only to a 'job' but to the whole 'lifestyle' associated with the job.[6]

The academic paradigms are now mostly social-psychological in nature. Testing still serves as a privileged instrument for the discovery and definition of individual differences, special characteristics and aptitudes. At least in the written texts, however, there is an admirable openness about psychological testing, and a suggestion that it should be used by the pupils themselves as part of the development of their own 'self-concept' rather than applied in the more traditional, exclusive and mysterious manner by 'the expert'. This democratic approach is strengthened by the use of 'client centred' and 'counselling' techniques adapted from American forms of psychotherapy, and especially the work of Carl Rogers.[7]

Perhaps the most startling earnest of the good intentions of the new vocational guidance wave is the assertion – in the recognised texts at least – that careers teaching should specifically exclude service to the economy and its manpower requirements. Their explicit responsibility is held to be to their clients.[8] Most remarkably, some commentators have suggested that, far from serving the requirements of industry, vocational guidance (through its influence on future workers and their demands for satisfaction in work) may actually challenge industry and force it to change.[9] This certainly reverses the notion, held strongly in other quarters, that education and careers work should simply service the needs of industry.

It should be noted that careers education largely fails in its own terms by simply not reaching the majority of working class kids in an effective way. A recent official survey [10] found that nearly a third of all schools devoted no time expressly to careers, and that only 14 per cent of schools had a careers teacher designated as head of department. Furthermore, 75 per cent of third year, 28 per cent of fourth year, and 52 per cent of fifth year pupils received no careers education at all. The survey concluded that careers education as a 'preparation for living' was not 'generally accepted or put into practice except by a minority of schools'.[11] The progressive notion of careers education, then, is some distance away from what actually happens in most schools in a purely quantitative sense.[12]

In the Hammertown school, however, careers teaching is a serious and conscientious business. The careers teacher is full-time, experienced and recently qualified in 'counselling'. He is perhaps the most hard-working teacher in the school and despite problems of short-staffing, which mean that he often has to deal with the whole fifth year at once, he tries to pursue and speaks the language of modern methods: child centred teaching; preparation for life; work experience and the encouragement of 'self-concepts' in relation to work.

The careers service in Hammertown helps to reinforce this approach by suggesting its own revision to the meritocratic model. At the careers office there is a large picture on the notice board of two figures. One is fairly obviously a scruffy student, and the other a well-scrubbed conventional working class lad. The caption reads 'Who gets the job?' and sets of comments are ballooned around the two figures making contrasts in the following couplets: 'dirty flop-top thatch/short well-groomed hair; 24 hour growth/clean-shaven healthy expression; 'get off my back expression'/smiling open features (good chap); picking of nasal orifice/clear direct gaze; slouch/hands firmly clasped (shows firmness and resolve); short tatty T-shirt/sober suit, clean shirt (appreciates traditional British standards), creased straight trousers; dilapidated baseball boots/highly polished black shoes'. The meaning is clear. Looks can be controlled if intelligence cannot; ability is not everything.

The old meritocratic model of the fitting of ability to work profiles massively persists of course, particularly in the lectures given by outside speakers. This speaker on the construction industry is typical:

> We take all kinds of kids, those with CSEs and those without, though if you've got CSEs of course, so much the better. If you come in at the craft level, you go to college to get the City and Guilds (. . .) that's the first level. Now if you've got your craft qualification you can go on (. . .) if you get to the final stage you can become a craft technician (. . .) and if you really want to you can carry on and there's a chance of going to Aston University to get a degree (. . .) So you can go as far as you like, and you should go as far as you can (. . .). [in answer to a question from Joey] 'Painting', what do you mean by 'painting'? You could learn to paint that wall in twenty-four hours, is that what you want? Why not think of doing something a bit more, going a bit further on than that, say an interior decorator where you have to think about your colour design, plan it out, have a job left to you, not simply stand there and splash it on (. . .) We won't stop you if you're really keen to get on.*

And inside the school where the main teaching paradigm has already been *differentiated* with respect to working class values, and where there is an obvious resistance – or, as is usually recorded, 'rudeness' – from 'the lads', this careers/ counselling approach can yield to a more abrasive approach. When patience has run out after continuous barracking, or a series of 'let downs', or a patent lack of interest, there is a typical sharp and exclusive re-evaluation of what the teacher stands for, often in the form of a blunt review of the unmodified meritocratic model – bottom end upwards. Despite the 'relevant' personal analogy the following kind of remark has a much older sting.

Careers teacher Some of you think you can just walk in and get an apprenticeship
to fifth year with your standards. Your standards! Some of you can hardly
       write and read and add up and you think you've got a right to an
       apprenticeship . . . let me tell you, you have no right at all, not
       by a long shot, you don't have a right to anything and the sooner
       you appreciate that, the better you'll do. I haven't the right to
       expect a good job myself, despite all the training, I don't have
       the right to a promotion . . . I've got to work towards it, work
       to deserve it.*

A one-sided, potent and bastardised form of relevance/progressivism is often resorted to in an attempt to hold the axis of control and pedagogic security. Since relevance is about the return to working class themes, and since working class themes importantly centre on work, there is obviously a temptation to assert attitudes and requirements appropriate to working life retrospectively on the school culture. Where the non-conformists might escape the school's net, they cannot escape the exacting requirements of industry. Working values are brought back into the school to disqualify non-conformist behaviour. This often takes the form of a blackmail which says both that, 'If you are not developing the right attitudes now you will not succeed at work', and also more practically, 'If you do not co-operate now you will not get a good leaving report'. The totalising theme of prep-aration for work therefore often joins the embattled theme of 'co-operation', making the atmosphere positively reek with the gun smoke of moral indignation for the fifth year. Everything 'the lads' do seems to come back to their being selfish, rude and unco-operative, and, finally, damning to their future working lives.

| Careers teacher to fifth year | I've just heard of a case, a lad at Easter, he got sacked after three weeks. He resented authority and wouldn't obey the rules. His attitude was wrong, the manager just sacked him, he said, 'OUT', he wasn't going to put up with it, why should he? I've told you before, bad habits at school take a lot of throwing over. If you're resentful of authority here, and have a bad attitude towards discipline, it will carry on at work, it will show there and they won't have time for it. Now's the time to start making the effort, show you are up to it now (. . .) What you'll be doing is exchang-ing one lot of problems for another worse lot of problems (when you go to work), and they're all made by your own attitudes, your attitudes at school here now will make it that much harder for you when you get to work.* |

Still, whether in new wave, 'progressive', modified or traditional mode, 'the lads' reject, ignore, invert, make fun of, or transform most of what they are given in careers lessons. The denoted [13] level of straight exhortation to take getting a job seriously, to prepare carefully for interviews, and to push and achieve in the job, or even simple information about different jobs – apart perhaps from something they have already decided to do – is most heavily filtered.

[In a group discussion on careers sessions]

Spanksy	After a bit you tek no notice of him, he sez the same thing over and over again, you know what I mean?
Joey	We're always too busy fucking picking your nose, or flicking paper, we just don't listen to him.
(. . .)	
Spanksy	He makes the same points all the time.
Fuzz	He's always on about if you go for a job, you've got to do this, you've got to do that. I've done it. You don't have to do none of that. Just go to a place, ask for the man in charge, nothing like what he says.
Joey	It's ridiculous.

PW	What do you mean, in terms of what qualifications you may need?
Fuzz	Qualifications and everything, you don't, you just ask for a job and they give you the job.
(. . .)	
PW	(. . .) They were on about how good it was to work hard and try to get on (. . .)
Will	'Tis when you're older, y'know, if you can't cope with the job, but . . . like, too hard for yer, and wanna sit down and just tell other blokes . . . when you're younger . . . 'cos the pay goes down once you go up with some jobs.
PW	How about the speaker who came from the College of Education?
Fred	They try to put you off work . . . Joey, he says to him, 'Do you want to be a painter and decorator?' Painting a wall, you can get any silly cunt to paint a wall! Or, 'You want to do the decorative pieces, signwriting'.
Spanksy	Got to be someone in society who slops on a wall . . . I wanted to get up and say to him, 'There's got to be some silly cunt who slops on a wall'.

It is certainly not true that new information is fed into a rational system of self-assessment and a developing 'self-concept' in relation to 'lifestyle' and 'job profile'. If things are remembered, they are picked up by some highly selective living principle of the lads' culture and interpreted for its own – often subversive, derisive and oppositional – ends:

[In a group discussion on careers films]

Perce	I wonder why there's never kids like us in films, see what their attitude is to it? What they'm like and what we'm like.
PW	Well, what sort of kids are they in the films?
Fuzz	All goody goodies.
Will	No, you can tell they've been told what to say. They'm probably at some acting school or summat y'know, and the opportunity to do this job – film careers for other kids, and you've gotta say this, wait for your cue, wait till he's finished his lines.
PW	I mean, how can you tell that?
Will	Well, they're just standing there, seem to be just waiting for 'im to say it, then . . .

Fuzz	You see all these films on there, right! They've all got some like stupid kid on, 'Oh yes, I'd like to do this,' 'Oh it's my turn, it's my turn to go and get the eggs.'

Spike   You ain't got a kid like, whose getting pissed up (. . .), nothing like that.

Their attitudes must of course be seen in relation to the rejection of many other aspects of the school. It would be surprising indeed if the careers teacher could hold out against the tide where others could not. It is also clear that the more aggressive careers approach which further alienates 'the lads' from what they see as a monstrously totalised morality can be triggered by the larger emergence of the whole counter-school culture, and is not properly controllable within the careers sphere alone. The thread of rejection to careers advice is part of the central thread of opposition to the school.[14]

'The lads' also basically reject the idea of qualifications. 'Qualifications' for them constitute the practical arm of the power of knowledge as it is institutionally defined. Since knowledge is opposed so must qualifications be resisted and discredited. As in other things, the principal means of discrediting formal standards is to 'see behind' them, in the informal mode, to 'how things really work'. Experience, or at least projected experience, manoeuvres around formal definition. At a certain level they really feel that they know better. It is possible to get on without qualifications and school work because what really matters is 'knowing a bit about the world', 'having your head screwed on', and, 'pulling your finger out' when necessary. Of course, the adult working class world, the air of practicality which prevails on the English shopfloor, and the distrust of theory there, considerably strengthen this kind of perspective. This is the basic cultural resource which is sharpened into a harder form during *differentiation* at school.

'The lads' feel profoundly that there must be a simpler way. Qualifications, to them, seem to be a deflection or displacement of direct activity. They feel that they can always demonstrate any necessary ability 'on the job', and that the doing of a thing is always easier than the account of it, or its representation in an exam, or its formal description seem to imply.

[In an individual discussion]

Joey   I couldn't fucking survive on the wage [in the apprenticeship], it'd be about £10 a week for the first year or two, every birthday it goes up or summat, I couldn't do that. I'm more the energetic type, I always think, why fucking walk around somewhere, when you can jump over. I'm always fucking jumping over fences (. . .) I'm quite satisfied as I am now not taking any leaving qualifications, if I'm intelligent enough, it'll fucking show through (. . .) or I'll make 'em see that I'm something. I'll make 'em see that I'm worth a bit of an investment and perhaps then I'll get on a fucking course (. . .) I mean let's face it, it's fucking easy, it's really fucking easy, 'cos all you got to do is learn how to turn a fucking lathe, once you can do that, all the measuring and that just becomes fucking routine (. . .) anybody can really be an apprentice like.

Typically it is felt that this kind of insight is denied to the 'ear'oles'. The conformists will have to 'do it the hard way'. They only need qualifications because they do not have the imagination or wit to do things any other way:

[In an individual interview]

PW   What is it you think you've got that the ear'oles haven't?

Spike   Guts, determination, not guts, cheek as well (...) we know more about life than they do. They might know a bit more about maths and science which isn't important. It's important to fucking nobody. That they've got to try and find out is ... by the time they're twenty they might know as much about life as me now. 'Cos they gotta go through it. Well I mean I've been through stages of life now, I've had ups and downs, you know disappointments. I've accepted them, I've took 'em as they've cum. That's it you know, but ear'oles when they get work, they'm, how can I put it ... just going to abide by the rules and do their fucking best (...) They'm clever in some ways, they're clever with the maths and the science and the English, but they ain't clever in life. They'm underdogs to me.

Continuities

Although the teacher's notion of the continuity between school and work is rejected by 'the lads', another kind of continuity is profoundly important to them. In terms of actual job choice it is the 'lads' culture and not the official careers material which provides the most influential guides for the future. For the individual's affiliation with the non-conformist group carries with it a whole range of changes in his attitudes and perspectives, and these changes also supply over time a more or less consistent view of what sort of people he wants to end up working with, and what sort of situation is going to allow the fullest expression of his developing cultural skills. We have seen that shopfloor culture has some of the same determinants as, and marked similarities with, counter-school culture and that shopfloor culture is importantly borne back to 'the lads' in many ways – not least in the working class home via parents. There is, in fact, often a direct link between school and work both in the minds of 'the lads' and of parents. This establishes a clear experiential continuity between disparate situations. We can see this as a continuous base line of experience and response which informs the whole of working class culture in its long arc of adaption to hostile conditions and its development of particular kinds of social relations at work:

[In an individual discussion]

Joey   He [his father] makes it all sound like a big fucking school, he makes it sound like this place. He was telling me the other day, he says, 'cos we was talking about the extinguisher actually, I think that's what it stemmed from. We was talking about messing about, and the old lady says 'Well, you shouldn't mess about', and the old man says, 'We do.' (. . .) he told us about this bloke, got this other Paki, and fucking pulled his trousers down and pulled him round the shop by his cock, like, got him by the cock and fucking yanked him around the shop, all silly things like that. You could pull him and he might fall into the furnace or fall under a fucking hammer. He says you go under and you put a, not the spade end the other end of the shovel, and you put that under their legs and pick 'em up, pick 'em up fucking under there like [indicating crotch] . . . and they can't get off. He reckons they're always fucking about like this, like and I thought it must be just like an extension of school, fucking working in factories, with the same people, the same people every day, you'd fuck about every day, you'd come there and it'd be all the same people like every day.

The located 'lads' culture, as part of the general class culture, supplies a set of 'unofficial' criteria by which to judge generally *what kind* of working situation is going to be most relevant to the individual. It has to be work where he can be open about his desires, his sexual feelings, his liking for 'booze' and his aim to 'skive off' as much as is reasonably possible. It has to be a place where people can be trusted and will not 'creep off' to tell the boss about 'foreigners' or 'nicking stuff' – in effect where there are the fewest 'ear'oles'. Indeed it would have to be work where there was a boss, a 'them and us' situation, which always carried with it the danger of treacherous intermediaries. The future work situation has to have an essentially masculine ethos. It has to be a place where people are not 'cissies' and can 'handle themselves', where 'pen-pushing' is looked down on in favour of really 'doing things'. It has to be a situation where you can speak up for yourself, and where you would not be expected to be subservient. The principal visible criterion is that the particular job must pay good money quickly and offer the possibility of 'fiddles' and 'perks' to support already acquired smoking and drinking habits and to nourish the sense of being 'on the inside track', of knowing 'how things really work'. Work has to be a place, basically, where people are 'alright' and with whom a general cultural identity can be shared.

Not only does the informal culture throw up these criteria but the informal group upon which it is based also enforces them. All of the mechanisms previously considered – the 'kidding', the 'laff', the 'pisstake' – work towards settling norms about the *future* situation as well as the present one:

[In a group discussion on future jobs]

Eddie   I wanna be a jeweller.

PW   A what? [Laughter]

Eddie   A jeweller.

PW	I dunno, what's the joke. What's funny about a jeweller. [Laughter]
-	He's a cunt.
-	He's a pisstaker.
-	'Im, he, he'd nick half of the jewels, he would.
Spike	He wants to be a diamond setter in six months.
Derek	He'd put one in a ring and six in his pocket.
PW	Do you know anything about jewellery?
Eddie	No. [Laughter]

Self-assessment techniques and psychological testing registers this cultural level much more profoundly than it registers what it is supposed to: intrinsic, individual qualities. When an expected outside speaker does not arrive, the careers teacher hands round 'self-assessment' questionnaires: items such as honest/kind/generous/ studious/clean/obedient/smart to be graded most of the time/half of the time/ almost never. When they are completed he calls for volunteers to read out their answers. In a revealing physical demonstration of their habitual symbolic jostling 'the lads' are nudging each other, looking over each other's shoulders, changing answers on each other's sheets, comparing notes, making fun of answers, and generally enforcing a collective line on the test. When volunteers read out their answers 'the lads' make their own and *differentiated* standards clear. A 'nearly all the time' answer for 'obedience' is received with sneers and jeers. Bill calls out from the floor 'What's he answered for "clean and smart" sir?' for an 'ear'ole' widely regarded as scruffy and untidy amongst 'the lads'. There are guffaws and laughs for 'nearly all the time'. Bill himself volunteers. When he answers 'nearly all the time' for 'thoughtful' the teacher takes him up on it, 'because I've not seen much sign of that in your work and attitudes towards teachers'. But of course Bill still thinks, as he explains afterwards, that he is thoughtful about 'things that really matter, like my mates'.

The systematic cultural self-preparation of 'the lads' for a certain kind of work marks them out from the 'ear'oles', not only in terms of school work, but also in terms of their expectations. The division between conformism and non-conformism is experienced as a division between different kinds of future, different kinds of gratification, and different kinds of jobs that are relevant to these things. These differences are not random or unconnected. On the one hand they arise systematic- ally from *intra-school* group oppositions, and on the other hand they point to apparently quite distinct job groupings in the post-school situation. The 'ear'oles'/ 'lads' division is taken by those concerned as a likely future division between skilled/unskilled or white collar/blue collar work. 'The lads' themselves readily transpose the divisions of the internal cultural landscape of the school on to likely divisions at work, although they do not necessarily accept the conventional evalua- tion of the categories employed:

[In a group discussion]

Joey   (. . .) We wanna live for now, wanna live while we're young, want money to go out with, wanna go with women now, wanna have cars now, and uh think about five, ten, fifteen years time when it comes, but other people, say people like the ear'oles, they'm getting their exams, they'm working, having no social life, having no fun, and they're waiting for fifteen years time when they're people, when they've got married and things like that. I think that's the difference. We are thinking about now, and having a laff now, and they're thinking about the future and the time that'll be best for 'em (. . .) They're the ones that abide by the rules. They're the civil servant types, they'll have 'ouses and everything before us (. . .) They'll be the toffs, I'll say they'll be the civil servants, toffs, and we'll be the brickies and things like that.

Spanksy   I think that we . . . more or less, we're the ones that do the hard grafting, but not them, they'll be the office workers (. . .) I ain't got no ambitions, I don't wanna have . . . I just want to have a nice wage, that'd just see me through.

(. . .)

Joey   I don't say it's wise, I say it's better for us, people, the likes of us, we've tasted, we've tasted not the good life, we've tasted, you know, the special life what you'd have when you're older. I think we just like it too much, I know I do anyway. I don't think you can cut yourself off from it now and do an apprenticeship and all that . . . and not have much bread.

For the conformists there is a much greater degree of identification with the teacher's authority. There is also a genuine interest in careers films and materials in the vector, this time, of their intended purposes. There is even an appreciation of the harder, blackmailing approach sometimes adopted by teachers because it partly speaks for them:

[In a group discussion of careers films]

Tony   Well, they opened your eyes, sort of. Being a milkman, get up at five o'clock in the morning, get up, get out, getting up in the dark.

Nigel   The one on the Post Office, I thought it was good. They've helped people, the people who are interested in that particular line (. . .)

PW   (. . .) do you ever feel insulted when he's [careers teacher] going on at the fifth?

Nigel   No, not really, 'cos I know a lot of the time, you know, what he says is right most of the time really, because a lot of the people down there just don't bother and he, you know, when he's doing something and they're just not bothered you know, he gets riled and that.

The conformists, for their own reasons, basically accept the presentation of school and work as being on a continuum. It *is* worthwhile exerting yourself to attain the official aims of the school. It *is* the best preparation for work. In passing, however, it should be noted that although this is the conventional response, it is not realised or 'won' in its own terms without hard work, a degree of rationality and personal commitment:

[In a group discussion with conformists at Hammertown Boys]

Tony   It's your attitude in the first place really. Say, if you do well at school, you get a good report when you leave (. . .) it should be better for us, because we've had to face up to the fact that we've got to come to school. We've got to do the work, else you wouldn't get on. So you more or less train yourself to be like that. But I think the ones who haven't, you know, which aren't bothered, they'll go to work and they'll think, 'Ooh, I don't like this, I'll leave it', instead of sticking at it. They won't get on well in it.

Nigel   I expect it to follow on really, you know, if you enjoy things all your life, just keep on getting on, but if you don't enjoy school, you don't intend to work. I think it just follows on into work, you won't do enough (. . .) [work] is like going to school, after you've left school, say, like I'm goin' to get an apprenticeship, you've got your apprenticeship, you'm qualified, just get, just keep on learning for the rest of your life, that' what I think (. . .) like you know, some of 'em, they don't really need school, 'cos they become a milkman or something like that.

Jobs

Altogether, in relation to the basic cultural groundshift which is occurring in relation to the school and the development of a comprehensive alternative view of what is expected from life, *particular* job choice does not matter too much to 'the lads'. Indeed we may see that with respect to the criteria this located culture throws up and the form of continuity it implies, most manual and semi-skilled jobs *are* the same and it would be a waste of time to use the provided grids across them to find material differences. Considered therefore in just one quantum of time – the last months of school – individual job choice does indeed seem random and unenlightened by any rational techniques or means/ends schemes. In fact, however, it is confusing and mystifying to pose the entry of disaffected working class boys into work as a matter of *particular* job *choice* – this is, in essence, a very middle class construct. The criteria we have looked at, the opposition to other, more conformist views of work, and the solidarity of the group process all transpose the question of job choice on to another plane: 'the lads' are not choosing careers or particular jobs, they are committing themselves to a future of generalised labour. Most work – or the 'grafting' they accept they will face – is equilibrated by the overwhelming need for instant money, the assumption that all work is unpleasant and that what really matters is the potential particular work situations hold for self and particularly masculine expression, diversions and 'laffs' as learnt creatively in the counter-school culture. These things are quite separate from the intrinsic nature of any task.

The putative diversity of jobs (and range of qualities necessary for them) presented in the careers programme when it works at its 'best' is explicitly rejected – at least as far as their own future is concerned:

[In an individual interview]

Joey   It's just a . . . fucking way of earning money. There's that many ways to do it (. . .) jobs all achieve the same, they make you money, nobody does a job for the love of a job (. . .) you wouldn't do it for nothing. I don't think anyone would, you need the bread to live (. . .) there's a difference in the actual ways you do 'em, but it's there like, they all achieve the same end, they all achieve money, they're all the same like.

[In another interview]

Spike   Every job is the same. No, I've gone too far in saying that, every job ain't the same, because your job's different, er, a doctor's job's different, a solicitor's job's different. The jobs what are the same is where you've got to fucking graft, when you'm a grafter, see, all jobs are the same (. . .) There ain't a variety, it's the same job. There's outdoor jobs, indoor jobs.

This view does not contradict, for the moment, the overwhelming feeling that work is something to look forward to. One should not underestimate the degree to which 'the lads' want to escape from school – the 'transition' *to* work would be better termed the 'tumble' *out* of school – and the lure of the prospect of money and cultural membership amongst 'real men' beckons very seductively as refracted through their own culture.

Evidence for the stupidity of expecting real satisfaction in work, and dark and unexplored reminders of what work can become when the cultural celebration is over, are continuously supplied by the larger culture, especially through parents. The promise of the future generated in the specific school form of the class culture, however, for the moment cancels out the messages from the larger class culture of which it is part and paradoxically ultimately reproduces:

[In the same interview]

PW   Are you looking forward to work?

Joey   Yes, if everybody don't start putting me off it. Our old lady, the first thing her said when her fuckin' woke me up this morning, her said, 'Oh, I don't want to go to work'. So I says, 'I fucking

100

do, I don't mind, I'll start'. Then her fucking said, 'You'll hate it, you'll hate it'.

The view that all working situations are basically the same is demonstrated most dramatically in the way 'the lads' actually get jobs. The particular choice of a specific job really can be quite random. The following accounts of how jobs were chosen are typical. For 'the lads' all jobs mean *labour*: there is no particular importance in the choosing of a site for its giving:

[In a group discussion on jobs]

Perce I was with my mate, John's brother, I went with 'im to uh . . . he wanted a job. Well John's sister's boyfriend got a job at this place, and he sez to Allan, he sez, 'Go down there, and they might give you a job there', and he went down, and they sez, 'You're too old for training', 'cos he's twenty now, he sez to Allan, he sez, 'Who's that out there?', and he sez, 'One of my mates'. He sez, 'Does he wanna job' and he sez, 'I dunno'. He sez, 'Ask him'. He comes out, I went back in and he told me about it and he sez, 'Come back before you leave if you want it'.

 What you doing?

Perce Carpentry, joining. And a month ago I went back and, well, not a month ago, a few weeks ago, and I seen him.

PW Well, that was a complete accident really. I mean, had you been thinking of joinery?

Perce Well, you've only got to go and see me woodwork, I've had it, I ain't done woodwork for years.

[In an individual interview]

Spanksy I just more or less put a pin in you know, not because I wanted to do plumbing all the while. First I wanted to do painting and decorating, then it was bricklaying, electrician, plumber (. . .) it was on Friday - I just cum into school and our old lady says to me, 'Why don't you go down the council on your own and ask for a job?'. Well I, when I cum into school, I thought, 'I'll be a plumber then, right', so I goes into the office, and I said, 'Could I go down the council yard and ask for a job?' (. . .) Just phoned up, and got on a bike, rid up there, and they said, 'You got the job', told me when to come (. . .) and I got the job within two hours of getting to school.

The self

The central subjective realisation of the commonality of modern labour and relative indifference to its particular embodiment, is one of the most basic things that 'the lads' truly learn at the heart of their culture in a way that is invisible to the school. The culture allows this realisation to surface in one form or another because it provides an alternative to finding, and needing to find, satisfaction and particular meaning in work. It has an ability to generate extrinsic group-based satisfactions to support the self and give it value. This capacity rests in turn upon something else which is fundamental, related and thoroughly and completely subjectively appropriated and validated in the counter-school culture. This concerns the learning of a certain subjective sense of labour power and of the appropriate, essentially masculine, way of giving it.

Basically this concerns an experiential separation of the inner self from work. Labour power is a kind of barrier to, not an inner connection with, the demands of the world. Satisfaction is not expected in work. The exercise of those parts of the self which might be appropriate to intrinsic satisfaction in work is denied. It is as if one part of the self is detached for a felt greater hold on other parts. Whereas work and the prospect of work is contained, limited and minimised, all that is attached to it at a cultural and symbolic level is taken hold of, developed and made as meaningful as possible. The foreshortening of the inner demands of work means that abilities can be developed and celebrated in independent and profane ways which are relatively free from the long dead arm of duty and the puritan ethic. Status and identity are constructed informally and in the group, and from the resources of the working class culture and especially its themes of masculinity and toughness – the social region which has made parts of their selves truly active and achieving – as it has grown and taken shape in the school, and not from a detailed involvement in work tasks. As we have seen, the counter-school culture is expressly geared to the development and maintenance of cultural attitudes and practices quite separate from the official ones.

It is the sensuous human face of work as prepared for unofficially (though in a particular form) in the school, much more than its intrinsic or technical nature, which confronts the individual as the crucial dimension of his future. In the end it is recognised that it is specifically the cultural diversion that makes any job bearable:

[On the imminent prospect of work]

Will   I'm just dreading the first day like. Y'know, who to pal up with, an' uh who's the ear'oles, who'll tell the gaffer.

Joey   (. . .) you can always mek it enjoyable. It's only you what makes a job unpleasant . . . I mean if you're cleaning sewers out, you can have your moments like. Not every job's enjoyable, I should think. Nobody's got a job they like unless they're a comedian or something, but uh . . . no job's enjoyable 'cos of the fact that you've got to get up of a morning and go out when you could stop in bed. I think every job's got, has a degree of unpleasantness, but it's up to you to mek . . . to push that unpleasantness aside and mek it as good and as pleasant as possible.

For 'the lads' then, labouring in modern society is about subjective containment and not extension. This is achieved through a definition of labour as emphatically

102

manual rather than as mental. This sense of the appropriate form of the giving of labour, and its meaning, arises directly out of the counter-school culture as working class themes have been offered up, shared and shaped there.

It is the school which has built up a certain resistance to mental work and an inclination towards manual work. At least manual labour is outside the domain of school and carries with it – though not intrinsically – the aura of the real adult world. Mental work demands too much, and encroaches – just as the school does – too far upon those areas which are increasingly adopted as their own, as private and independent. 'The lads' have learned only too well the specific social form of mental labour as an unfair 'equivalent' in an exchange about control of those parts of themselves which they want to be free. In a strange unspecified way mental labour henceforth always carries with it the threat of a demand for obedience and conformism. Resistance to mental work becomes resistance to authority as learnt in school. The specific conjunction in contemporary capitalism of class antagonism and the educational paradigm turns education into control, (social) class resistance into educational refusal and human difference into class division. As Bill says of the difference between his future and that of the 'ear'oles', 'It's just the difference between pen-pushing and grafting really'. This is knowledge of a class division though it is learnt in school. It is the product of schooling though its effect is social.

In a contradictory way, however, which will be explored in Part II of the book, this sense of labour power as an essential separation of the vital self from the hope of intrinsic satisfaction in work, and as *manual* activity, does not lessen 'the lads' sense of superiority, insight and true personal learning. Nor does it dampen their optimistic expectations. As we have seen, these expectations are partly the result of the urge to get out of school no matter what. They are also the result, however, of the subjective feeling amongst 'the lads' that they have penetrated, learned, and understood through experience something that others, and in particular the 'ear'-oles' have not. This is, of course, the experiential hook – the precise, unintended, unexpected reversal of the conventional logic – which actually binds these kids into a future of manual work. It is only in the uncovering of this subjective assent that we will understand their behaviour in a way which properly presents their own full powers, and appreciates the contradictory, half real notion of freedom at stake for them (and others) in a liberal social democracy. Here we can only place a definite qualification on the minimisation of their own labour power which its definition as detached and manual by 'the lads' might be taken to imply.

Although labouring is not about an intrinsic connection with the satisfactions of the task, it does bear a certain kind of significance. Labour power is the material through which the importance of other things apart from its immediate object can be expressed. Though it closes off the experiential reverberation of the task it amplifies other experiences. After all, although manual work stands for the insulation of school and mental activity, it also signifies a more positive and active exclusion of the 'ear'oles'. 'The lads' feel that they are going to do work in the real adult world of which the 'ear'oles' are incapable. Labouring – itself meaningless –

must therefore reflect aspects of the culture around if it is to be valorised (a culture, paradoxically, which its own containment makes possible).

Thus physical labouring comes to stand for and express, most importantly, a kind of masculinity and also an opposition to authority – at least as it is learned in school. It expresses aggressiveness; a degree of sharpness and wit; an irreverence that cannot be found in words; an obvious kind of solidarity. It provides the wherewithal for adult tastes, and demonstrates a potential mastery over, as well as an immediate attractiveness to, women: a kind of machismo.

Thus the whole nature of 'really doing things', of being physically active in the world, of giving labour power in a certain way, is seen by 'the lads' not simply as a defensive measure, or as a negative response, but as an affirmation and expression of what it seems has been genuinely and creatively learned. It speaks of a distinct maturity, a practice of ability and perspective, that others are felt not to have. Despite its intrinsic meaninglessness manual labour, at least at this period in their lives, comes to mean for 'the lads' in Hammertown an assertion of their freedom and of a specific kind of power in the world:

[In an individual discussion]

Spike   (. . .) it gets me mad to see these kids working in a fucking office. I just dunno how they do it, honestly. I've got freedom, I've got . . . I can get money, it's hard to explain . . .

[In an individual discussion]

Will   Working outdoors, manual work and . . . writing and all this, and getting a pen out . . . it's freedom as well you know.

[In an individual interview]

Joey   I couldn't be a teacher (. . .) unless I teach the fucking football team, and I can't play football. See, I got to be energetic, I got to be fucking moving, fucking using . . . not using my strength . . . just fucking . . . I got to be moving all the time, too energetic to have a fucking desk job. Yet in about ten or fifteen years' time when I'm fat and flabby, maybe then I'll have a desk job.

There are, of course, very different ways of being related subjectively to the giving of labour power. The conformists in the Hammertown school are much more likely to believe in the possibility of satisfaction in work, to construct their futures through the categories supplied in work, and to see their own values and achievements expressed through the intrinsic properties of work activity. They are taken along by the current of official continuities, and expect them to lead to proper and rewarding outlets. Labouring for them expresses its own properties, not other indirect cultural values:

[In a group discussion with conformists at Hammertown Boys]

Tony [who had recently secured an apprenticeship in tool-making]	You've got to work, so work hard now, get a good job, do something you like, not like making a car or something, putting on wheels all day. You know you can get the money but it ain't really worthwhile. You're getting nothing out of life. If you'm ... say like me, I'm going to be a toolmaker, you see the finished product even if they are screws, you know you've made the mould for them. I'd enjoy something like that, see the finished product.
Nigel [who had recently secured an apprenticeship in British Rail]	(...) Until you've established yourself really firmly and all that, and you know what you're doing like the back of your hand (...) you'll be worrying about it, say, you'll be thinking about the next morning (...) When you become a train driver, you'm started off by driving ordinary bugs – different stages of training each time. From bugs you probably go on to brushers [a bigger locomotive]. You can work up on each train you know, you're a driver. I think I can see meself working meself higher, you know, way up. I've got something to look forward to.

At the opposite pole to 'the lads', work can become a ruling passion for some. For them even their innermost private life is directly expressed by the giving of their labour power. It shows the stark contrast between 'the lads' retrenchment to the absolute minimum of personal meanings in work and the possibility of total absorption in work as the essential pivot of private and emotional life. 'The lads' have learned very carefully in the recesses of their own culture to blunt and topple any such pivots. They supply their own.

Here again is the working class, high status grammar school boy who leaves school at sixteen to become an assistant golf professional. This boy totally identifies with golf as a medium for advancement and expression. In an odd ghosting of 'the lads' trajectory, he rejects school but turns *in* to work rather than *out* to a culture as a means of enhancement, self-expression and validation:

[In an individual interview]

Two months ago I was playing very bad (...) my game went to pieces. There was no way I could hit the ball off the tee. No way I could hit an iron shot, no way I could chip, no way I could putt. I really felt depressed, for a month I didn't go out of a night. It's as simple as that, you sit at home and you think 'Bloody hell'. You feel as if the bottom's really dropped out of your world. You think, 'What I am going to do next time. Move my grip over a bit, change my stance?'. You just sit there at home, thinking about your game (...) When you're playing well you become so elated that everything in the world becomes secondary, apart from your golf, you know (...) there was a spell of about two months when I was playing very, very well, you know, I would challenge anybody to play over the course with me, I was winning a lot of money, I really felt on top of the world. I was almost in like a cocoon, everybody seemed to be just that bit hazy, you were almost in dream world.

Arriving

> They'm all like kids down there, like, they bin there about ten years and they, one's been there thirty-nine fucking years. But most of 'em, they walk about making soft noises and shouting for no reason at all. And they swear like troopers at each other, and they call each other names and mek up nicknames for each other. It's just like an extension of school – they all mess about.
>
> (Joey talking about the shopfloor)

'The lads' move into jobs such as tyre fitting, carpet laying, trainee machinists in a furniture factory, plumber's and bricklayer's mate,[15] upholstering in a car seat firm, bar loading in a chromium plate factory, painting and decorating. At Easter and during the summer of 1975 they all find work fairly easily. Approximately one year later, in September 1976, half of them have left their first job. Two are in their third jobs, two cannot find work for the moment.[16] The experience of entering work and of changing jobs is not a major trauma for 'the lads'. Their unofficial and informal self-preparation for work not only directs them towards, but also makes the passage into a certain kind of work more uneventful and problem-free than for many other groups.

This is not to say that there are no problems of adaption, or that occupational and regional variations do not affect the pattern, or that jobs are at all easy to find now, or that their long term relation to work is that which has been promised in the cultural celebration of their late school and early work careers. There is not sufficient space here to consider the degree of real adequacy of their self-preparation in the long term and the material and cultural nature of shopfloor culture. But it may be noted that shopfloor culture is clearly more brutal than counter-school culture and is subject to more obvious external coercion. It also has a different pattern of social enforcement of knowledge, and different authority relations with different kinds of regulatory exchange relationships. There are also different balances and meanings between conformism and non-conformism, different edges to masculinity and domination. The central question to be answered in any future work is the degree to which the reproduction of labour power off the shop floor matches, changes or throws into contradiction the cultural forms which are already there, and adequately meets, over-runs or is irrelevant to the objective physical, mental and emotional requirements of the productive process.

The informal and formal processes of the school are obviously vital in preparing labour power in a certain way, but the home, family, neighbourhood, media and non-productive working class experience in general are equally vital for its continuous reproduction and daily reapplication to the labour process. In a converse way it is important to assess the degree to which the shopfloor, both in its objective dimensions and in the oppositional informal culture it throws up, reacts back upon the non-productive sites of the reproduction of labour power and influences them in a certain way so that, as we have seen with the counter-school culture, there may be an unseen and often unintended circle of meaning and direction which acts ultimately to preserve and maintain a particular configuration – perhaps again at a tangent to the intentions of official policy.

Though the Hammertown lads are, in September 1976, still flushed with the excitement and intensity of movement and having money, and a felt sense of cultural election, we may hazard a guess that disillusion is not far away. The working class culture of which their basic responses are part is not generally one of celebration and mastery. It is basically one of compromise and settlement: a creative attempt to make the best of hard and brutalising conditions. What the culture of 'the lads' shows us is that this culture is not all of a piece, that there are nodal points of strength as well as longer troughs of despair, weakness and naked domination. For a specific period in their lives 'the lads' believe that they dwell in towers where grief can never come. That this period of impregnable confidence corresponds with the period when all the major decisions of their lives are settled to their disadvantage is one of the central contradictions of working class culture and social reproduction, and one in which the state school, and its processes, is deeply implicated.

For no matter what the larger pattern of working class culture and cycle of its continuous regeneration, no matter what the severity of disillusion amongst 'the lads' as they get older, their passage is to all intents and purposes irreversible. When the cultural apprenticeship of the shopfloor is fully worked out, and its main real activity of arduous production for others in unpleasant surroundings is seen more clearly, there is a double kind of entrapment in what might then be seen, as the school was seen before, as the prison of the workshop. Ironically, as the shopfloor becomes a prison, education is seen retrospectively, and hopelessly, as the only escape.

In the first place, the young worker is likely to have acquired family, home and financial commitments of his own which make an unpaid return to college out of the question. In the broader sense, although it may have lost much of its attractiveness, there is still a particular form of experiential attachment to labour power, and a characteristic way of relating informally to the group, which seems to disqualify the individual from anything other than manual work. There is a certain attitude to the task – precisely that which was welcomed before as an insulation – which makes development through work an unlikely prospect. The working class lad is likely to feel that it is already too late when the treacherous nature of his previous confidence is discovered. The cultural celebration has lasted, it might seem, just long enough to deliver him through the closed factory doors. Indeed it could be argued that it is an appreciation of the contrary timeliness of ill and good fortune, of knowledge and ignorance, which finally clinches working class fatalism and immobility: the difference in innocence between counter-school culture and working class culture proper. By the time the answers are known it is too late to apply them. The obvious and the alluring achieve their opposite underneath. These are common themes in working class culture and become apocryphal on the shopfloor amongst adult workers who have always only just come into factory work to save a little, pay off a debt, or make plans to start their own business 'one day' as they work away a day to day thirty years. Missed or misunderstood real opportunities, and the treacherous appearance of accepted opportunities, become the collective myth of pre-factory life. The turn of the screw is, however, that the meaning of the myth is not clear to those who live it and have a chance to change it. This is a middle-aged shopfloor worker in an engineering factory:

> I was thirteen, like, an impressionable age, I s'pose, and this is something I've never forgotten. I was with my old man and we were at the zoo, and we saw a crowd up on the 'ill like, people were clapping, and all crowding around a gorilla's cage. We pushed to the front, like, Dad was more curious than me, like, he got right to the front, and there was this gorilla clapping and stamping, and lookin' around like, havin' a good time. All the people were clapping, egging him on like. Then he suddenly come to the front of the cage and spat a mouthful of water all over our old man. He'd been goin' to the back of the cage, like, gettin' a mouthful of water, comin' forward, clapping like, then spitting the water out all over 'em.
>
> My old man stood back really shocked like . . . then he went back in the crowd and waited for some other silly buggers to push forward. I didn't realise then, like, I was only a kid, what it meant like . . . but I do now. We don't all grow up at once, see, that's life, we don't grow up at the same time, and when you've learnt it's too late. It's the same with these kids comin' in the factory, every time, they think its great. 'Oh, what's this, I wanna be there', y'know what I mean. You'll never change it, it's the same with everything, comin' to work, getting married, anything – you name it. *

The main point here, however, is that in the short to middle term 'the lads' ' experience in the counter-school culture most certainly smoothes their transition into work and produces appetites which manual work satisfies quite well. There is a sudden jump in income so that it is possible to go out every night, buy new clothes and have a drink whenever they want. And there is an excitement in being able to work with older and tougher people in rough conditions – to survive and be accepted where others would fail.

This is not to say there is no 'cultural' apprenticeship or that 'the lads' are accepted in all things equally quickly. There is a continuous attempted physical intimidation in which picking on a young worker can soon become a spectacle for the diversion of other workers where one of the unwritten rules is that they must not be helped. A virulent sexism, outdoing even that of the counter-school culture, also seeks out the young lad in particular – much to his discomfort – as its victim:

[In an individual interview at work]

Spanksy   You don't want to seem like a little baby to them [the men at work], you want to seem that you know a bit about it, about life you know (. . .) It gets me at work, you see these blokes and they'm talking about sex and that, saying, 'I'll bet you've never

108

had it away', and I'll smile like this you know, and they'll say, 'Look at him here, smiling', you know, as if I don't know nothing about sex, you know what I mean.

Still, 'the lads' at least know from their own cultural experience that the essential tests are cultural not technical, and they also know the procedures for survival. They have learnt that adults do swear, play around like kids, and make crude sexual statements. They understand some of the elaborate ways of subverting authority, getting around the formal, squeezing some enjoyment out of a dry context and making extra cash on the side. They understand that everything is not as written in the book.

There is a feeling throughout at least the first six months at work that not everybody can do their type of work, and that there is a distinction in holding a tough job down - coming precisely from a carrying forward of the resources and skills of the counter-school culture:

[In an individual interview at work]

Will   Say if I hadn't been out drinking or hadn't been say one of the lads or I hadn't grown a sense of humour or nothing like that, goin' to work on a building site you wouldn't have got on (. . .) you need a sense of humour to work on a building site. Got to be able to take a joke you know (. . .) It's been in me, but it's developed like, it might sound funny like, you know, but it might have developed more like, getting around a bit.

[In an individual interview at work]

Bill   When you get to know everybody, you know it's almost the same
(trainee   as school, you know, you have a laff and a joke (. . .) you've
machinist in come on a bit, you get a bit cheeky when you're one of the lads,
a large   you get to know everybody you know (. . .) If you'm quiet and
furniture   shy and everything you wouldn't speak to anybody unless they
factory)   spoke to you.

There is a further, perhaps less obvious, way in which the working class boy who is one of 'the lads' is drawn into a certain kind of factory work and confirmed in his choice. This is in the likely response of his new employer and bosses to what they understand of the 'lads' culture already generated at school. The reverse side of the 'them and us' attitude generated informally by 'the lads' is an acceptance by them of prior authority relations: of the framework in which there is a 'them' and an 'us'. Although directly and apparently geared to make some cultural interest and capital out of an unpleasant situation, their culture also accomplishes a recognition of, and an accommodation to, the facts of power and hierarchy. In the moment of the establishment of a cultural opposition is the yielding of a hope for direct, or quasi-political, challenge. The 'them and us' philosophy is simultaneously a rescue and confirmation of the direct, the human and the social, and a giving up - at any conscious level – of claims to control the underworkings of these things: the real power relationships.[17]

Whilst conformists are preferred for 'skilled' work, when they enter more humdrum work unaided by cultural supports, diversions, and typical habituated patterns of interpretation they can be identified by those in authority as more threatening and less willing to accept the established status quo. For these boys still believe, as it were, in the rubric of equality, advance through merit and individualism which the school has more or less unproblematically passed on to them. Thus, although there is no surface opposition, no insolent manner to enrage the conventional onlooker, neither is there a secret pact, made in the reflex moment of an oppositional style, to accept a timeless authority structure: a timeless 'us and them'. Consequently, these kids are more likely to expect real satisfaction and the possibility of advance from their work. They expect authority relations, in the end, to reflect only differences in competence. All these expectations, coupled frequently with a real unhappiness in an individual unrelieved by a social diversion, make the conformist very irksome and 'hard to deal with'. In manual and semi-skilled jobs, then, those in authority often actively prefer 'the lads' type to the 'ear'ole' type. Underneath the 'roughness' of 'the lads' is a realistic assessment of their position, an ability to get on with others to make the day *and production* pass, and a lack of 'pushness' about their job and their future in it. Finally, 'the lads' are more likeable because they have 'something to say for themselves'; they 'stand up for themselves', but only in a restricted mode which falls short of one of 'us' wanting to join 'them'. For one of 'the lads', not only is the shopfloor more familiar than he might have expected, he is also welcomed and accepted by his new superiors in such a way that seems to allow for the expression of his own personality where the school had precisely been trying to block it – this is an initial confirming response which further marks the transition from school as an *escape* from school.

The culture of the work place, of course, enforces a certain level of productive activity as well as an elemental masculine respect. Both of these are absent from the school and mark some of the most important parameters of the transformation of the counter-school culture into a work culture. Both share similar structures but the difference in contexts cashes what has always been inherent in the school version for the purposes of relatively peaceful production at work:

[In an individual interview at work]

Will (a bricklayer's mate)	You can get the sack, you know what I mean, it's different from school. You couldn't really get the sack at school, apart from being expelled and you don't fucking mind that.
PW	How are bosses different?
Will	They treat you different, don't they. They know if they say anything to you, that you don't like, that it's, you'll put one on 'im like (. . .) but at school the teachers, they say things to you, which disheartens you like and everything (. . .) More or less, when you're at work you got the law with both of you

really. But at school you go and put one on a fucking teacher, that's it you know, they could bring the law in. It's as though the teachers are privileged to cheek you and slap you around the face and pull your hair.

In the first months of work conformist kids who are doing the job they have aimed at, and which still holds the prospect of advance for them, are also relatively content. They have followed and have been guided and rewarded by officially defined continuities. The opening months of work are taken as a kind of extension of school, although the hours are longer and they are more tired at night than they were at school. In many cases their gilt-edged apprenticeships involve full-time off the job training in the factory so that there really is a direct similarity to school. When he leaves Hammertown Boys Tony goes to a craft apprenticeship, with the possibility of conversion into a technician's apprenticeship, in a large and prestigious international engineering firm. Huge flow charts on the wall of the trainee workshop where he will spend a year show all the different stages and phases of the course, with empty panels below to be filled in with individual assessments for each apprentice as the year progresses. There is a more competitive spirit here – at least after four months at work – than there was even at school:

[In an individual interview at work]

Tony   (. . .) if something's dragging on and you're waiting for your instructor it's alright for the first ten minutes you know, you've got nothing to do, but when you're waiting for an hour or summat like that, you know, you realise that that hour you could have done a lot of work (. . .) They do mess about, but they always work as well, you know they don't skive (. . .) I mean everyone tries to get on somehow. When they've got something to do they always do it (. . .) Say someone's worried, like, they say, 'Well I ain't showin' this to Jim' [the instructor]. So they catch hold of somebody else to compare them, and they come and ask him to match his with theirs. So they take 'em back to the bench, file it off or do something with it.

Individuals who fall between these categories or cross over them are likely to experience the severest short and middle term problems. Conformists, marginals, or those on the outskirts of the counter-school culture who find themselves in certain kinds of manual work where the distinctive shopfloor culture has developed are particularly prone to problems not so much of 'transition' as of basic cultural clash, and to suffer from an unrelieved exposure to unpleasant work. They are the most open to ridicule, sarcasm and intimidation, but lack proper means to defend themselves. They become easy and regular victims. This is a kid on the edge of the counter-school culture led, but not protected, by its logic to unskilled stapling and trimming in a furniture factory:

[In an individual interview at work]

I'm not too keen on 'alf of 'em, they'm like kids. The one kid behind me, Tom, he's a big head, well, he doesn't know a lot about trimming, but he thinks there's something wrong with us, 'cos we don't know see, calls you idiots and things like that (. . .) the little bloke who sweeps up, they cut a knife out [of foam] and stuck it in his back . . . You know I'm always careful, when they do start cutting things out, watch out who's next to you (. . .) they tried to put a tail on me, but I felt them put it on (. . .) They tek it a bit too far, I mean they might do it once, its a laff and they carry on, and it gets on your nerves a bit, and they keep . . . they made the one woman cry who's in the sewing shop (. . .) they get whistling you know, I can't whistle, but they kept doing it, on and on and it got on her nerves, she started to cry. They had to get the union on about it (. . .) Like he's my mate [a friend from home working at the same place]. I wouldn't mind if none of them spoke to me ever, 'cos as long as I've got someone to speak to, I mean me and Alec, we think the same. We don't mind, we keep ourselves to ourselves (. . .) one or two of them I speak to, 'You alright?', but there's still the ones who play up.

Not only is there this difficulty with social relationships, but the lack of cultural involvement removes an important mediation between the self and work. Where that work is basically mindless and repetitive it more relentlessly racks and twists the unprotected human sensibility: boredom, meaninglessness and greyness make the day interminable, the weeks the same, and leisure a false promise. This is the same kid:

[In an individual interview at work]

The worst part of the day is about quarter to nine, in the morning, and it's really rotten, you think of the time you've still got to the end of the day, especially if that three-quarters of an hour has dragged (. . .) I start working, then I look at the clock, if it's before nine o'clock, I think it should be about half past nine, that's the time it really gets you, 'God blimey, it's dragging, the time, I wish I warn't here, I wish I could be at home in bed' sort of thing (. . .) You know, at work, say stapling sort of thing, you come, 'Cor blimey, what am I doing here?', sort of thing you know. I just imagine me in say ten years time, I'll still be doing the same thing I expect, and I just don't, you know . . . It'd send me mad I think, just keep doing it, a lifetime, I want something better out of life (. . .) The nice part of the week is Friday dinner time when I get me wages . . . they bring it on a tray, the wages. It's funny though, all week I'm thinking, 'Roll on Friday, and we can go down town Saturday', and you look forward to it. When you get to town Saturday, you think, 'What was I looking forward to?'. But I still look forward to it every week, just the same.

Whilst it would be quite wrong to suggest that 'the lads' never feel these pressures, or that they will not increasingly feel them as the protective cultural layers become thinner, it is certainly true that they have a much more disillusioned attitude to start with, and a sense of their own labour power which is precisely concerned with blocking and minimising such subjective feelings. Not only this, but they have a much more energetic and optimistic approach to the possibilities of achieving some extrinsic satisfactions from membership of the informal group at work and joining in, rather than becoming the butt of, its practices. There is also a sense in which, despite the ravages – fairly well contained at this point anyway – manual work stands for something and is a way of contributing to and substantiating a certain view of life which criticises, scorns and devalues others as well as putting the self, as they feel it, in some elusive way ahead of the game. These feelings arise precisely from a sense of their own labour power which has been learnt and truly appropriated as insight and self-advance within the depths of the counter-school culture as it develops specific class forms in the institutional context. It is difficult to think how attitudes of such strength and informal and personal validity could have been formed in any other way. It is they, not formal schooling, which carry 'the lads' over into a certain application to the productive process. In a sense, therefore, there is an element of self-domination in the acceptance of subordinate roles in western capitalism. However, this damnation is experienced, paradoxically, as a form of true learning, appropriation and as a kind of resistance. How are we to understand this?

Notes

[1]   See the Employment and Training Act, 1973. In what follows I am referring to careers teachers in schools as well as to careers officers. The main difference between them is that teachers are more concerned with preparation, and careers officers with placement (DES, *Careers Education in Secondary Schools*, Education Survey 18, HMSO, 1973, p.25). The two groups, however, share the same basic vocational guidance techniques.

[2]   Up until the mid 1960s the seven point plan developed by Alec Rodger of the Department of Occupational Psychology, Birbeck College, University of London, was widely used. The points included were: Physical make-up including appearance and any handicaps in speech or physique; Attainment; Intelligence; Aptitudes; Interests; Disposition; Domestic circumstances.

[3]   See especially E. Ginzberg et al., *Occupational Choice, An Approach to a General Theory*, Columbia University Press, 1951; D. Super, *The Psychology of Careers*, Harper and Row, 1957; and E. Ginzberg, *Career Guidance: Who Needs It, Who Provides It, Who Can Improve It?* McGraw-Hill, 1971.

[4]   For a characteristic, enlightening and specific characterisation of the usual gradient paradigm modified by the addition of this horizontal range of interest see DES, *Careers Guidance in Schools*, Education Pamphlet No. 48, HMSO, 1965, esp. pp.42 and 43. '. . . as every Youth Employment Officer is aware, a significant

proportion of all the boys and girls who enter employment take jobs which require no particular educational qualification and for which at present no training is necessary. What they need to know, they pick up when they begin work; there is often surprisingly little to pick up, and that little is easily managed (. . .) there seem to be a great number of jobs which are very much alike in that they require little or no academic ability and can be done by almost anyone, an impression strengthened by the knowledge that many adults switch from one job to another without difficulty. At a casual glance, moreover, many of the young people in these middle and lower ranges of ability appear very much alike in that they have few outstanding characteristics, no overwhelming interest in school affairs, and they willingly leave as soon as they can. If neither jobs nor pupils have marked characteristics, can careers advice be of any value? This is surely a superficial view, for the truth is that each child is an individual person, and that jobs are different and of different types, even though there may be a great many of each type. It is just as important that the less well endowed should be given a fair chance to build a satisfying life as well as that the well endowed should be encouraged to use their talents to the full'.

There is a clear connection here, I think, with the modification of the basic teaching paradigm from 'below' discussed in the previous chapter where 'right attitudes' displaced 'knowledge' as the teachers equivalent. The vocational guidance approach does, however, attempt to discover and itemise real differences in jobs and does not, in the literature at least, stress 'attitudes' in quite the same way.

[5]   Quoted in the introduction to the Careers and Occupational Information Centre of the Employment Service Agency, *Publications and Services*, Manpower Services Commission, 1976. This centre typifies the new progressive attitude to careers. The introduction also states; 'One of our current preoccupations is the need for more rigorous examination of the critical characteristics of jobs, and another, the desirability of a more imaginative approach to conveying the information we unearth'.

[6]   This is clearly outlined in the now standard British work by J. Hayes and B. Hopson, *Careers Guidance*, Heinemann, 1971.

[7]   See G. Rogers, *On Becoming a Person*, Constable, 1961; C. Rogers, *Freedom to Learn*, Chas. E. Merrill, 1969; C. Rogers, *Encounter Groups*, Penguin Books, 1970; C. Rogers, *Becoming Partners*, Constable, 1973; C. Rogers, B. Stevens et al., *Person to Person. The Problem of Being Human*, Souvenir Press, 1967.

[8]   See, for instance, Hayes and Hopson, op.cit., p. 234,

... the counsellor should not use such information [manpower data] to direct young people into particular lines of study or towards those occupations where serious shortages have been predicted. Ensuring that the community's future manpower requirements are satisfied is not the counsellor's job. His responsibility is to his students.

[9]   See M. P. Carter, 'Teenage workers: a second chance at 18?' in P. Brannen (ed.), *Entering the World of Work: Some Sociological Perspectives*, HMSO, 1975.

[10]   DES, *Careers Education in Secondary Schools.*

[11]   Ibid., p. 61.

[12]   See also, Training Services Agency, *Vocational Preparation for Young People*, Manpower Services Commission, September 1975; Social Evaluation Unit, 'All Their Future', Department of Social and Administrative Studies, Oxford University, September 1975, p. 25; and K. Roberts, *From School to Work: A Study of the Youth Employment Service*, David and Charles, 1972, which concluded of vocational guidance: 'too little is provided, and what is provided is offered too late'.

[13]   For a fuller explanation of this concept and its relation to the 'connoted' see, R. Barthes, *Mythologies*, Paladin, 1977: R. Barthes, *Elements of Semiology*, Cape, 1967. I consider the 'connoted' level of careers information in Part II.

[14]   Although they are not very influential (except as a service of information once a decision has been taken) Careers Officers seem to escape the hostility of 'the lads' mainly because they do not get into the same vicious circle – not least because they have no commitment to upholding the basic teaching paradigm, and may even have some sympathy with the post-differentiated 'lads' ' culture. Interestingly, this sometimes results in diametrically opposed assessments of particular individuals.

Careers Officer for Hammertown Boys	I might just smile when I sympathise with the kids, but I'll say, 'Oh, better not go into that', you know, so they can tell by my face that I'm sympathising with them. Sometimes they do sum up their teachers quite well (. . .) I found him quite a friendly lad (one of 'the lads'), got some personality, bit of charm (. . .), I've actually got down, 'has charm'. He displayed it to me (. . .), yet his report was absolutely awful, how they couldn't stand him, how objectionable (. . .) I found I liked all your study group more than the (. . .) ordinary kid (. . .) if I've got somebody comes into an interview and talks to me then I'm immediately, I'm prejudiced towards him, you know, I like to have somebody to talk back to. I quite enjoy it then, but if it's the sort of, I don't like the sort of interview when I've got to drag information out of kids.

[15]   These two jobs (gained by Spanksy and Will) carried formal apprenticeships even though they were offered without tests or conditions relating to leaving qualifications. Spanksy and Will were delighted that they could achieve so quickly and easily that for which the conformists were struggling so desperately. It further convinced them that they had 'known better all along'.

[16]   Though this study does not deal with youth unemployment a few comments can be made. In the same way that RSLA, it was argued, had a peculiar function of exposing the oppositional dimension of what had been a more submerged counter-school culture before, so we may expect substantial or long term structural unemployment, and the freedom and collectivity of the streets, to

further encourage and expose such oppositional cultural forms – especially in their aggressive mode. This is to say that substantial unemployment may bring about the further disaffection of segments of the young and exacerbate potentially explosive social divisions. Such developments would add a new dimension to the traditional 'problems' of careers guidance and placement.

[17] For an interesting and fuller discussion of this philosophy see Richard Hoggart's important book, *Uses of Literacy*, Chatto & Windus, 1957.

PART II

ANALYSIS

5 Penetrations

Although we have looked in some detail through case study at the experience and cultural processes of being male, white, working class, unqualified, disaffected and moving into manual work in contemporary capitalism, there are still some mysteries to be explained. In one sense it might seem that one set of random causalities – individual pathology and cultural deprivation – has simply been replaced by another – cultural creativity and continuity. We have seen how some working class lads differentiate themselves from the institution, but why is this so? We have seen the conviction with which they hold their views, insights and feelings of cultural election, but what is the basis for this subjective elevation? We have seen their attitude to the occupational structure, but how can we explain its reversal of the conventional evaluation? We have seen how their genuinely held insights and convictions lead finally to an objective work situation which seems to be entrapment rather than liberation. But how does this happen? What are the basic determinants of those cultural forms whose tensions, reversals, continuities and final outcomes we have already explored?

Elements of Analysis

In order to answer some of these questions and contradictions we must plunge beneath the surface of ethnography in a more interpretative mode. I suggest that we may approach a deeper understanding of the culture we have studied through the notions of penetration and limitation.

'Penetration' is meant to designate impulses within a cultural form towards the penetration of the conditions of existence of its members and their position within the social whole but in a way which is not centred, essentialist or individualist. 'Limitation' is meant to designate those blocks, diversions and ideological effects which confuse and impede the full development and expression of these impulses. The rather clumsy but strictly accurate term, 'partial penetration' is meant to designate the interaction of these two terms in a concrete culture. Ethnography describes the field of play in which the impulses and limitations combine but cannot isolate them theoretically or show them separately.

Penetrations are not only crucially skewed and deprived of their independence, but also bound back finally into the structure they are uncovering in complex ways by internal and external limitations. There is ultimately a guilty and unrecognised – precisely a 'partial' – relationship of these penetrations to that which they seem to be independent from, and see into. It is this specific combination of cultural 'insight' and partiality which gives the mediated strength of personal validation and identity to individual behaviour which leads in the end to entrapment. There really is at some level a rational and potentially developmental basis for outcomes which appear to be completely irrational and regressive. It is, I would argue, only this contradictory double articulation which allows a class society to exist in liberal and democratic forms: for an unfree condition to be entered freely. More concretely, the specific cultural and subjective self-preparation of labour power which we have examined involves a potential progression towards more rational alternatives, which is suspended and caught off balance, unprotected, by crucial limitations. It is precipitated finally – without a stake in the conventional nor yet in an alternative – as the subjective inhabitation of a certain definition of manual labour power. This is a precipitation, however, which nevertheless carries over with it some of the affirmation and election based on blocked or distorted cultural penetrations. The astonishing thing which this book attempts to present is that there is a moment – and it only needs to be this for the gates to shut on the future – in working class culture when the manual giving of labour power represents both a freedom, election and transcendence, and a precise insertion into a system of exploitation and oppression for working class people. The former promises the future, the latter shows the present. It is the future in the present which hammers freedom to inequality in the reality of contemporary capitalism.

The remainder of this chapter outlines some of the impulses towards penetration in the counter-school culture. The next two chapters deal with those internal and external limitations which prevent and distort their sweep down to the really determining conditions and full context of the cultural form. Much of what follows is relevant to working class culture in general. Before that, however, it is necessary to examine more closely the elements involved in the notion of 'penetration': the real form of its action in the world, the scope of this action and its base in human agency. In particular we must define in what sense cultural penetrations of the fundamental relations and categories of society can be either 'rational' or 'creative'.

The counter-school culture and its processes arise from definite circumstances in a specific historical relation and are in no sense accidentally produced. The recognition of determination does not, however, dismiss creativity. Two qualifications must be insisted upon immediately however. Creativity is in no individual act, no one particular head, and is not the result of conscious intention. Its logic could only occur, as I argue later, at the *group* level. Secondly creativity cannot be pictured as a unique capacity or one able to produce limitless outcomes. Nor can it be considered in any sense as mastery – over the future or the present. On the contrary, it leads, paradoxically, to profound entrapments barred over more by the flush of subjective certainty.

Having entered these caveats, however, it must also be insisted that this cultural form is not produced by simple outside determination. It is produced also from the activities and struggles of each new generation. We are dealing with collective, if not consciously directed, will and action as they overlay, and themselves take up 'creative' positions with respect to finally reproduce what we call 'outside determinations'. It is these cultural and subjective processes, and actions which flow from them, which actually produce and reproduce what we think of as aspects of structure. It is only by passing through this moment that determinations are made effective in the social world at all. Decisions are taken by individuals 'freely' and with 'consent' in this realm which no amount of formal external direction could produce. If working class kids on their way to work did not believe the logic of their actions for themselves, no-one outside, nor outside events, could convince them – especially in view of the conventional assessment of what they are doing and where they are going. The culture provides the principles of individual movement and action.

The penetrations produced, however, at the cultural level in the working class by what I still want to call a certain creativity are by no means quite open ended. They run along certain lines whose basic determinants lie outside the individual, the group or class. It is no accident that different groups in different schools, for instance, come up with similar insights, even though they are the products of separate efforts, and thus combine to make distinctive class bonds. All the groups are penetrating through to roughly the same really determining conditions which hold their present and future possibilities. The object, therefore, of creativity is something to be discovered, not imagined. The limits to, and internal relationships of, what is discovered are already set. In another society 'the lads' would have been shown the way, they would not have discovered their own.

Of course the whole specificity of the cultural level developed here is that such insights are not merely set lessons learned, nor passive information taken in. They are lived out and are the result of concrete and uncertain exploration. It is on the basis of such 'insights' developed in its depths that those other forms of behaviour, action and enjoyment are predicated which give the most flamboyant appearance and obvious creative life to a culture.

In a sense this most central point of reference is an absent or at least silent centre beneath the splendid bedizenment of a culture. It is impossible to prove its rationality. No amount of direct questioning will elicit it from cultural participants. The variety of forms and challenges at the surface of the culture bewilder a notion that they might have a concentric cause. This is why the ethnography of visible forms is limited. The external, more obviously creative, varied and sometimes random features must be read back to their heart. The logic of a living must be traced to the heart of its conceptual relationships if we are to understand the social creativity of a culture. This always concerns, at some level, a recognition of, and action upon, the particularity of its place within a determinate social structure.

One of the most profound reasons why this social creativity cannot be expressed rationally at the surface of the culture is that it is truly only half the story. It really *does not* proceed with a pure expressive purpose from the centre of the culture. We must posit the penetration as a clean and coherent insight in order to say what it is, but the concrete forms of cultures, as ethnography insistently reminds us, do not allow single pure dynamics. In their very formation these 'insights' are distorted, turned and deposited into other forms – such as subjective affirmation of manual labour – which make it hard to believe there has ever been, or could ever be, even a notion of a rational kernel, never mind that it should be easily expressed. This means, amongst other things, that we must distinguish between the level of the cultural and the level of practical consciousness in our specification of creativity and rationality.

The argument is not that insights are made consciously in any one mind or even in the same mind or groups of minds over time - although the spoken everyday word might illuminate aspects of it variably and in contradiction with itself or perhaps unconsciously. Direct and explicit consciousness may in some senses be our poorest and least rational guide. It may well reflect only the final stages of cultural processes and the mystified and contradictory forms which basic insights take as they are lived out. Furthermore, at different times it may represent the contradictory moments of the cultural conflicts and processes beneath it. In this, for instance, it is unsurprising that verbal questions produce verbal contradictions. Not only this but practical consciousness is the most open to distraction and momentary influence. Repetition of given patterns, attempts to please the other, superficial mimicry, earnest attempts to follow abstract norms of, say, politeness, sophistication or what is taken as intelligence, can be mixed in with comments and responses which have a true cultural resonance. Survey methods, and all forms of methods relying basically on verbal or written responses, no matter what their sophistication, can never distinguish these categories.[1]

This is not in any way to dismiss consciousness. It is a privileged source of information and meaning if properly contextualised, and ultimately the only stake in the struggle for meanings. It is part of the cultural level and relates most basically to it as the immediate expression of its law. It binds in with it, and has a consistency, validity and directly developmental role with respect to its complexity. Consciousness is in any conceivable sense 'false' only when it is detached from its variable cultural context and asked to answer questions.

The creativity and rational impulses of the counter-school culture are not then idealist or fantastic products of the imagination. Nor are they basically centred on the acting individual and his consciousness. Nor are they able to take any turn they wish. They are not finally able in any way to prefigure the future.[2] A romantic view of working class cultural forms asserts that they are experimenting in some way with the future. This implies that they provide concrete outlines for living for when capitalism is overthrown. There is no way in which such imaginings can promise what they offer or give what they promise. It is quite wrong to picture working class culture or consciousness optimistically as the vanguard in the grand march towards rationality and socialism. If anything - the central case in this book - it is these elements of rationality and of the future in working class culture, and particularly in that of the school, which act finally in their current social form and in complex and unintended ways to prevent precisely that. It is the apparent cultural ascension of the working class which brings the hell of its own real present.[3]

We must seal this list of negatives, however, by positing the one distinctive and often unrecognised potential that working class cultural creativity and insight really does have. It is embedded in the only class in the capitalist social formation which does not have a structurally based vested interest in mystifying itself. Though there are many barriers to a proper understanding, though there are many ideological inversions and distortions, and though the tools for analysis are often missing, the fact still remains that the working class is the only class not inherently structured from within by the ideological intricacy of capitalist organisation. It does not take nor, therefore, need to hold the cultural and social 'initiative' and is thus potentially freer from its logic.

The working class does not *have* to believe the dominant ideology. It does not need the mask of democracy to cover its face of oppression. The very existence and consciousness of the middle class is deeply integrated into that structure which gives it dominance. There are none who believe so well as those who oppress as honest men. What kind of bourgeoisie is it that does not in some way believe its own legitimations? That would be the denial of themselves. It would be the solution of a problem of which they were the main puzzle. It would invite self-destruction as the next logical move. The working class is the only group in capitalism that does not have to believe in capitalist legitimations as a condition of its own survival.

Clear boundaries must, however, again be marked. This potential for de-mystification falls short of an ability to prefigure other forms – that must wait for a basic structural shift to reflexively determine its own cultural practices and stable forms of pattern and circle in intention and unintention. All we can say is that the demystification of capitalist ideology, legitimations and self-delusions would be a precondition for a properly socialist society. We have yet, though, no examples of this. For the moment, and especially for our immediate object of study, this greater capacity for cultural penetration has, in its real social form, resulted in a deeper and more entangled entrapment within the capitalist order. It is far from settled whether this capacity, in any way in which it has actually been taken up, is a blessing or a curse.[4]

This is to argue, therefore, for a certain kind of creativity. It is still free-floating, however, unless we can specify the human base from which it springs and its particular form of work on the world, its form of praxis.

I suggest that the smallest, discrete unit which acts as the basis for cultural penetration is the informal group. The group is special and more than the sum of its individual parts. It has, in particular, a social dynamic which is relatively independent of issues and locations, preconceptions and prejudice. A social force which we might simply call loyalty tends to overdetermine previous attitudes and the specific conditions of the group's existence. It has been shown in American microsociology that leadership, leadership aims, maintenance of the group, and convergence of individual views, are permanent characteristics of groups (at least in Western capitalism).[5] It is a requirement for the group's continued existence that there should be strongly held group views and purposes. Social psychology calls this high morale. The power that is thus generated in the group, and its unspecified open nature, constitutes an important social force. It is partly from this source that wider symbolic cultural articulations are generated.

We have, therefore, in the informal group a relative suspension of individual interests and a commitment to the reality of the group and its aims, which is not closely specified in the membership history, or location of the group. In this sense the group can, therefore, be considered as a subject in its own right. It has an internal impulse to find an objective specific to its own level in a way not limited by the previous knowledge, experience or ideology of its individual members.[6] I want to suggest that working class counter-school culture, supported by the informal group and an infinite series of contacts between groups passing on what is best and most relevant, turns its generated and open-ended force at least in part upon a de-mystification in its own way of its members' real conditions and possibilities within a class society. This is not to assert that any such intention, or final content of understanding, is actually in any one person's head, the result of an individual subjective will, or even in the form of an individual rationality. We are dealing with the unit of the group, and the specific level of cultural 'insight'. It should also be remembered that the partiality of the penetrations made at this level anyway prevent their full rational development and expression.[7]

Having suggested the basis, force and scope of what I maintain must be seen as a kind of creativity, it remains to suggest the characteristic manner of its work upon the world, the praxis which yields what I have called cultural penetrations. The characteristic expression of this force upon the world is, I suggest, a kind of production. The cultural does not simply mechanically mark, or in some simple sense 'live out' wider social contradictions. It *works* upon them with its own resources to achieve partial resolutions, recombinations, limited transformations which are uncertain to be sure, but concrete, specific to its own level and the basis for actions and decisions which are vitally important to that wider social order.

The relevant materials are not necessarily provided from outside for this kind of work and production. Indeed the praxis I am pointing to *produces* partly its own materials for its own activity in a struggle with the constrictions of the available forms.[8] What delivers the group force into the concrete form of the specifically cultural as studied in part I of the book is importantly a deflection from the dominant mode of signification - language - into antagonistic behavioural, visual and stylistic forms of expression. Conventional words cannot properly harness and 'say' the material of penetrations made at the infrastructural unit of the group in the mode of the cultural. Words created under bourgeois sway in determinate conditions cannot express what did not go into their making. Part of the reaction to the school institution is anyway a rejection of words and considered language as the expression of mental life. The way in which these creative insights are expressed, therefore, is one of expressive antagonism to the dominant bourgeois mode of signification - language. In a real sense for the working class the cultural is in a battle with language. This is not to reduce the cultural to anti-abstract behaviour. It is to posit it, in part, as an antagonistic way of expressing abstract and mental life centred, not on the individual subject, but on the group: not on the provided language but on lived demonstration, direct involvement and practical mastery.

This is not to deny individual consciousness and language use in their dialectical connection with class practice but to suggest the possibility in a class society of an asymmetrical and distanced form of relationship between the two. Language is no less rich in the counter-school culture than in the conformist one – indeed it is a great deal more incisive and lively – but it cannot express, and is therefore not used in that mode, those mental insights which are anyway too much for the received language. Critical meanings arising from the force of creativity in informal groups are diverted back into the group and into the cultural to inform, enforce and shape many other kinds of physical and stylistic practices there. Relatively autonomous cultural practices such as transformations in clothes, habits, styles of behaviour, personal appearance and group interaction can all be seen in the light of this larger praxis.

Amongst other things this level of cultural activity 'expresses', mediates, or reports on, in its own materials and practices, a notion of the world as it is specially inhabited by the social groups who constitute its terrain. If only because of this social position and *lack* of disqualification and self-mystification discussed earlier, there are likely to be elements of (perhaps distorted or displaced) radical insight, as well as much else besides, buried in specifically cultural activities. These activities – by working on real materials in particular contexts and producing surprising, unexpected or transformed outcomes – also act to expose and cast into doubt the workings of the larger ideologies, institutions and structural relationships of the whole society.[9] This is achieved without any necessary direction, intention or purpose. It happens almost by the way, as if a by-product, in the immediate concerns of the day to day culture. It never-the-less strengthens the culture, may change its basis and increase the scope of its confidence and action. It increases the sense amongst its members of election and affirmation and provides a fuller and more finely judged grounding for cultural activities, style, and attitudes which it is felt hold a greater relevance and resonance than can be directly explained. Experientially it is an aspect of how the culture 'works' for its members in the way that others do not. The combination of these two kinds of cultural production and their interaction, especially in relation to major life decisions and transitions, help to make up what I have called cultural penetrations.

An interpretative analysis makes it possible to probe this level. One can interrogate the cultural for what unspoken assumptions lie behind it. What are the grounds that make this attitude sensible? What is the context which makes that action reasonable? What is being expressed through what kind of displacement or projection in such and such an object, artefact or symbolic complex? It is through such questions that it is possible to build up a construction of the rational impulse towards penetration of its context and conditions of the counter-school culture. We are dealing with an analytic category, of course, and our 'penetrations' can never be taken from the mouths of the social agents, but it has a concrete referent in the cultural and its specific level of collectivity. The cultural forms may not say what they know, nor know what they say, but they mean what they do – at least in the logic of their praxis. There is no dishonesty in interpreting that.

Penetrations

Education and qualifications

'The lads' ' rejection of school and opposition to teachers can be seen in the light of a penetration of the teaching paradigm outlined in chapter 3. Their culture denies that knowledge is in any sense a meaningful 'equivalent' for the generality of working class kids. It 'sees through' the tautologous and manipulative modifications of the basic paradigm – whether dignified with 'relevant'/'progressive'[10]theories or not. It 'knows' better than the new vocational guidance [11]what is the real state of the job market.

The counter-school culture thus provides an eye to the glint of steel beneath the usual institutional kerfuffle in school. It has its own specific practices but it also searches out and critically exposes some of the crucial social transactions and contradictions within education. These can be grouped in three sets. They are all addressed to unmasking the nature of the 'equivalent' on offer.

Firstly the counter-school culture is involved in its own way with a relatively subtle, dynamic, and, so to speak, 'opportunity-costed' assessment of the rewards of the conformism and obedience which the school seeks to exact from working class kids. In particular this involves a deep seated scepticism about the value of qualifications in relation to what might be sacrificed to get them: a sacrifice ultimately, not of simple dead time, but of a quality of action, involvement and independence. Immediate gratification is not only immediate, it is a style of life and offers the same thing too in ten years time. To be an 'ear'ole' now and to gain qualifications of dubious value might be to close off for ever the abilities which allow and generate immediate gratifications of any kind at any stage.

The sacrifice might, then, be exorbitant, but so too might the object of the sacrifice be meaningless. Cultural values and orientations suggest that the outcome which qualifications bring is not always an unmixed blessing. Qualifications are likely to be low anyway and not likely to affect job choice ('What's the use doing CSEs when the others have got 'O' levels – Spike) and are not seen to be such an important criterion for selection anyway in the jobs 'the lads' are likely to obtain ('I'll always be able to show 'em if I can do it' – Joey). But what would be the meaning, in any case, of academic 'success' and its likely result of moderate upwards movement in the hierarchy of jobs? The possibility of real upward mobility seems so remote as to be meaningless. For 'the lads' 'success' means going into an apprenticeship or clerical work. Such jobs seem to offer little but take a lot. And this assessment is clearly made in the cultural mode. Free cultural involvement, social collectivity, the risk of the street and factory floor, and independence of mind would all be lost for a mainly *formal* – not *real* – prize. The cultural choice is

126

for the uncertain adventure of civil society against the constricting safety of conformism and only relative or even illusory official progress.

These cultural penetrations are, I would argue, of something real. Their form is of direct cultural activity and immediacy but they expose more than they know. In the first place there is a common educational fallacy that opportunities can be *made* by education, that upward mobility is basically a matter of individual push, that qualifications make their own openings.[12] Part of the social democratic belief in education even seems to be that the aggregate of all these opportunities created by the upward push of education actually transforms the possibilities for all the working class, and so challenges the class structure itself.

In fact, of course, opportunities are created only by the upward pull of the economy, and then only in relatively small numbers for the working class. The whole nature of Western capitalism is also such that classes are structured and persistent so that even relatively high rates of individual mobility make no difference to the existence or position of the working class. No conceivable number of certificates amongst the working class will make for a classless society, or convince industrialists and employers – even if they were able – that they should create more jobs.

It may well be argued that (as penetrated at the cultural level in its own way and for its own different immediate purposes) the proliferation of various certificates for working class occupants is more about obscuring the meaningless nature of work and constructing false hierarchies and binding people into them ideologically, than it is about creating or reflecting, the growth of more demanding jobs.

Secondly the culture makes a kind of assessment of the quality of available work. Though it is questionable whether they secure employment anyway, it can be suggested that what qualifications seem to promise for their working class bearers concerning the quality of work they might expect is basically illusory in the first place. Most work in industry is basically meaningless. Again we can see the general accuracy of the cultural penetration concerning the commonality of all forms of modern labour and the dubiety of the conformist road and absorption in the job – maintaining a relevance at another level (which reflects back on the lived level of course) even as it is produced on its own, immediate, cultural terrain.

More than ever today the concrete forms of most jobs are converging into standard forms. They require very little skill or training from their incumbents, and cannot offer realistic opportunities for intrinsic satisfaction. Despite the rearguard action of job restructuring and job enrichment[13] the overwhelming weight of the evidence is that more and more jobs are being de-skilled, standardised and intensified.[14] It is quite illusory to picture the labour market as open to determination from the pool of skills and capacities amongst young workers. One need only mention the unprecedented scale of unemployment amongst young workers at the moment[15] and the worrying trend towards structural unemployment of unskilled youngsters[16] to question the power young people have in any meaningful sense over the occupational market.

Objective grounds therefore certainly exist for questioning whether it is sensible to invest the self and its energies in qualifications when both their efficacy and their object must be held in great doubt. The counter-school culture poses this problem – at least at a cultural level – for its members; the school does not.

Bourdieu and Paseron have argued that the importance of institutionalised knowledge and qualifications lies in social exclusion rather than in technical or humanistic advance. They legitimate and reproduce a class society. A seemingly more democratic currency has replaced real capital as the social arbiter in modern society. Bourdieu and Paseron argue that it is the exclusive 'cultural capital' – knowledge and skill in the symbolic manipulation of language and figures – of the dominant groups in society which ensures the success of their offspring and thus the reproduction of class position and privilege. This is because educational advancement is controlled through the 'fair' meritocratic testing of precisely those skills which 'cultural capital' provides.[17]

Insofar as this is an accurate assessment of the role and importance of qualifications, it supports the view that it is unwise for working class kids to place their trust in diplomas and certificates. These things act not to push people up – as in the official account – but to maintain there those who are already at the top. Insofar as knowledge is always biased and shot through with class meaning,[18] the working class student must overcome his inbuilt disadvantage of possessing the wrong class culture and the wrong educational decoders to start with. A few can make it. The class can never follow. It is through a good number trying, however, that the class structure is legitimated. The middle class enjoys its privilege not by virtue of inheritance or birth, but by virtue of an apparently proven greater competence and merit. The refusal to compete, implicit in the counter-school culture, is therefore in this sense a radical act: it refuses to collude in its own educational suppression.

Finally the counter-school culture makes a real penetration of what might be called the difference between *individual* and *group* logics and the nature of their ideological confusion in modern education. The essence of the cultural penetration concerning the school – made unselfconsciously within the cultural milieu with its own practices and objects but determining all the same an inherently collective perspective – is that the logic of class or group interests is different from the logic of individual interests. To the *individual* working class person mobility in this society may mean something. Some working class individuals do 'make it' and any particular individual may hope to be one of them. To the class or group at its own proper level, however, mobility means nothing at all. The only true mobility at this level would be the destruction of the whole class society.

Conformism may hold a certain logic for the individual then, but for the class it holds no rewards: it is to give up all possibilities of independence and creation for nothing but an illusory ideal of classlessness. The individual might be convinced by education's apparent resume of what is supposed to happen in society – advance through effort for all who try – but the counter-school culture 'knows' much better than the state and its agencies what to expect – elitist exclusion of the mass through spurious recourse to merit. The counter-school culture and other working class cultural forms contain elements towards a profound critique of the dominant ideology of individualism in our society. They expose at some level the consequences, possibilities, realities and illusions of belonging to a class for its members – even where its constituent individuals are still behaving perhaps individualistically and competitively in some things and in the private spheres of their lives. In particular, the counter-school culture identifies the false individualistic promises of dominant ideology as they operate in the school.

It is in the school with its basic teaching paradigm that those attitudes needed for *individual* success are presented as necessary *in general*. The contradiction is never admitted that not all can succeed, and that there is no point for the unsuccessful in following prescriptions for success – hard work, diligence, conformism, accepting knowledge as an equivalent of real value. There is a generalisation in the school from an individualistic logic to a group logic without a recognition of the very different nature and level of abstraction of the latter.

Of course the careers version and certain modifications and theoretical developments of the basic teaching paradigm hold that 'success' cannot be measured on a vertical scale of qualifications or of different job status alone. There is a horizontal quotient as well. It is possible to 'succeed' in a job conventionally registered as being of low status if it demands, utilises, or allows the expression of capacities other than the conventional ones. It is possible, for instance, that even a meaningless job could be made a 'success' if it were carried out with pride and honesty. The vertical class scale of occupation actually faced by working class kids is converted both morally and practically into a differentiated multi-dimensional structure which promises to hold riches for all.

The uneasy stretch between the presentation of hard work and conformism both as a specific way to success and as a generally desirable property; the uncertainty of presenting the academic gradient as something which is worth moving up but which by no means exhausts all sources of value and achievement; the contradictory attempt to squeeze potential for self-development and value into all human capacity even as it slides down off the graph of the school's own proper academic measures: these all recognise, in some way, the difficulty of extending an individualistic logic into a class logic, but attempt a reconstitution of the same move in yet more mystified forms. These produce the most basic wobbles in the institutional axis which the counter-school culture is quick to pick up in its own way. The cultural penetration of the contradictions at the heart of education is a powerful force for the inception and reinforcement of *differentiation* in individual biographies. The counter-school culture reasserts as one of the bases of its visible forms a version of the appropriate class logic and gives an identity to – 'explains' – the position of its members, not by an illusory accommodation in the dominant academic and occupational gradient, but by a transformation and an inversion. For the class as a class, the academic and occupational gradient measures not abilities but simply its own immovable repression. The working class *is* the bottom half of this gradient no matter how its atoms move. The wisdom of movement up the gradient as an individual is replaced by the stupidity of movement as a member of a class. By penetrating the contradiction at the heart of the working class school the counter-school culture helps to liberate its members from the burden of conformism and conventional achievement. It allows their capacities and potentials to take root elsewhere.

Labour power: a commodity like no other

The counter-school culture confronts directly the reality of the school institution and exposes something of the unfair exchange it attempts to make – especially in the light of the other kinds of exchange the culture has forged in its own name. At its own level it also explores the special nature of human labour power. It has materials with which to suggest the potentially limitless nature of commitment. In particular it demonstrates that labour power is not a fixed but a variable quantity, and that no matter how it is presented normally or officially the individual has at least some control over its expenditure.

A commitment to work and conformism in school is not the giving of something finite: a measured block of time and attention. It is the giving up of the *use* of a set of potential activities in a way that cannot be measured or controlled and which prevents their alternative use. Getting through a term without putting pen to paper, the continuous evasion of the teacher's authority, the guerrilla warfare of the classroom and corridor is partly about limiting such demands upon the self. These are important sites for the learning by individuals of a certain sense of labour power. When 'the lads' arrive on the shopfloor they need no telling to 'take it easy', 'take no notice', or that 'they [management] always want more, you've had it if you let them get their way'. Indeed, in several important ways, working class kids practised in the institutional deflection of the requirements of an external system from their own vital energy and interests are more adept than their future peers at knowing, settling and controlling their own activities. This is because, at least in part, it does not matter, in the end, whether their labour power is withheld in the school, whereas those involved in shopfloor culture are more strictly coerced to produce and cannot limit their effort beyond that relatively high point fixed by the need to reproduce at least their own subsistence.

The overthrow of the educational exchange, which parallels more basic forms of exchange in capitalism, gives the form of a cultural penetration (expressed, of course, not in words or direct statement, but particular cultural practices at their own proper level) of the fact that whilst labour power is bought and sold on the market place it is, in fact, like no other commodity. It is unlike all other commodities because it is not a fixed quantity. No matter how the matter is judged morally or politically it remains true that labour power is the only variable element in the capitalist system. It must therefore be the source of expanded capital and profit. In essence, the labourer can produce more in value than is represented by his wages.[19] Better management or capitalisation – *intensification* – of his variable capacities produces greater value.[20] Labour power is the only thing in nature that can be bought with this variable capacity. Classical Marxist theory tells

us that it is the individual labourer's blindness to the special nature of the commodity which he sells which is at the heart of the ideological legitimation of
capitalism. It conceals processes of exploitation and the source of profit. The
counter-school culture, however, responds in its own way to the special nature of
labour power. As if by instinct it limits it. In its own immediate logic this is to
maintain the pre-condition for the sensuous physical and mental involvement of
its members in its own activities.

This cultural instinct, I would argue, constitutes also a kind of penetration of
important general ideological and material relationships in our society. This success,
so to speak at another level, acts back, however, ultimately to develop the culture
in a particular way and to guarantee its long-term relevance and success.

The theoretical framework of the capitalist system is this: the labourer sells his
labour power fairly and freely on the market like any other commodity, but then
gives it – not in a finite quantity as with any other commodity – but as the full
expression of his own variable natural powers. It can therefore produce far in
excess of its price, i.e. wages. The *apparent* equivalence of wages and human power
in his own bargain with capital convinces the labourer of the freedom and independence of all before the law – the freedom and equality of the capitalist state and
Judiciary. This apparent equivalence enshrined in the paraphernalia and majesty of
the state and its laws hides from him the nature of his own exploitation and also
what he shares with his class and which might have formed the basis for class
solidarity: that same exploitation. In essence an infinite capacity has been bought
for a finite sum and socially legitimated in a way which allows this purchase and use
to continue unopposed. It is this special conjunction of legitimation of access to,
and exploitation of, a variable capacity which removes the limits of production in
capitalism, where envy and too close a knowledge of direct exploitation in the face
to face exploitative relation of Lord and serf in Feudalism, for instance, had limited
it. The productivity of capital is the liberated productivity of labour power given
not as a quantity but as a capacity.[21]

The still common weekly wage packet can stand as a revealing concrete example
of this classic ideological move. In middle class professions it is clear that the yearly
salary is paid in exchange for the use of continuous and flexible services. Remunera-
tion here is not based on the particular amount of time spent on the job and of
course those 'on the staff' are expected to work overtime and at home for no extra
cash. Such workers, their wage form makes clear, are being paid for what they *are*:
for the use of their capacities, for their general potential as managers, accountants,
etc. The social implications of the weekly wage packet are very different. The
general capacity of labour power which is recognised by the salary form is here
broken up into weekly lumps and riveted to a direct and regular award. Weekly
wages, not yearly salaries, mark the giving of labour. The quantity of the wage
packet is the quantitative passing of time. Its diminution is loss of measured time,
its increase 'overtime'. With such a riveting it is that much easier to overlook the
real continuous, sensuous and variable quality of labour power and to miss the

sense in which its full giving over time opens up enormous human energies which are actually unmeasurable.

What amounts to a fetishism of the wage packet – with carefully nurtured tight-gummed compact brown envelope precisely showing currency domination in finger flick top, heavy silvered bottom, paraded around on Thursday afternoon – breaks up the weeks, quantifies effort, and presents to consciousness the massive effort and potential of human labour power as a simple concrete weekly equivalent to the crisp 'fair' wage. Whereas a monthly cheque paid unseen into a bank account might break open, this weekly riveting contains, any realisation of the disjunction between the variable potential of long term vital effort and a fixed wage return.

Though it would be wrong to impute to 'the lads' individually any critique or analytic motive, it is clear that their collective culture shows both a responsiveness to the uniqueness of human labour power and in its own way constitutes an attempt to defeat a certain ideological definition of it. We saw in the ethnography that 'the lads', from the resources of their culture, saw their own labour power as a barrier against unreasonable demands from the world of work – rather than as a special and privileged connection with it. This feeds directly into oppositional shopfloor cultures whose object is at least partly to limit production and the potentially voracious demands of capitalist production on individuals.[22]

It should also be emphasised again that this kind of cultural penetration is connected with the whole nature of the culture and is more than a simple mental category. It is the basis of quality in the specifically cultural response. There is a clear counter and intentional use of those capacities actively freed from the demands of an open-ended commitment. This use is *characteristically* working class and is relatively free from the superstitions, puritanical reserves and mystifications which attend their usual absorption into the conformism of capitalist production.[23]

The freedom that capitalism falsely promises to the whole individual can be one-sidedly and ironically rescued by a collectivity of individuals realising in common all those parts of themselves saved from absorption into production. For 'the lads' there is a distorted freedom in the commercial dance, in the streets, in fighting, in spending money, in rejecting others which no other system but capitalism guarantees. It is no fault of the working class – quite the opposite – if such as these freedoms are, they are used for class cultural purposes.

The products of this independent ability of the working class – profane testing of the formal, sharp un-reified language, oppositional solidarity, and a humorous presence, style and value not based on formal job status – are no less the product of the capitalist era for their subversive, or potentially subversive, forms: Though these things must not be exaggerated or romanticised or seen out of proportion to the minimal real freedom and material base which allows them, they arise nevertheless not from a mere suffering of, but from a creative response to, the demands of capitalism.

General abstract labour

We saw in the section on ethnography that, to all intents and purposes, 'the lads' do not basically differentiate between particular concrete types of work which they regard as being open to them – at least at any intrinsic level. There is near indifference to the particular kind of work finally chosen so long as it falls within certain limits defined, not technically, but socially and culturally. Sometimes the actual choice is made literally by accident. This sense of the commonality of labour is in marked contrast to the sense of range and variety in jobs projected by careers advisory services and teaching.

I want to suggest here that this perspective (though produced in its own specific cultural mode) can be understood in the light of a real penetration of the role of labour in the modern structure of capitalist production. It is made on the basis of maintaining a space and vigour for cultural activity but its assumption of the commonality and meaninglessness of modern work is important in a much larger context. It is this larger validity which, of course, strengthens, maintains and adds a particular resonance and success to the cultural in the long term.

It is indeed the case that what is common to all wage-labour work is more important than what divides it. The common denominator of all such work is that labour power yields to capital more in production that it costs to buy. It surely cannot be disputed that capitalism is organised for profit rather than use. Most wants in our society are satisfied not directly but through the mediation of the 'incentive' of profit. For good or ill one thing is certain, for the businessman or manager it is this incentive which is the spring of action, not the material of human wants through which it works. It does not matter what product is made since it is money which is really being made. The labourer will be switched with alacrity from the production of one commodity to another no matter what his skills or current activity when 'market conditions' change. The sprawling nature of many conglomerates which indeed include unlikely combinations such as meat-packing and space age exploration is living proof that profit, not production of what might be needed, is the lynchpin of enterprise.

There is no inherent interest, therefore, in what objects may be used for, only in the profit to be made from their production and exchange. As we have seen, profit can only arise from the exertion of labour power. Though the exploitation of labour is of the essence, the particular form of labour involved does not therefore matter to capital any more than does the nature of the particular object produced – so long as there is a contribution to profit. Since its concrete and particular form does not matter, we may call what is common to all wage labour 'abstract labour'.[24]

The inner logic of capitalism is that all concrete forms of labour are standardised in that they all contain the potential for the exploitation of abstract labour – the unique property all labour power shares of producing more than it costs when purchased as a commodity. It is this which links all the different branches of production and forms of labour, and makes the concrete form of labour, and the specific use of its products, contingent upon the central fact of its status as abstract labour.[25]

This commonality may be clear from the point of view of capital and less clear from the point of view of labour. For, as counselling and vocational guidance [26] insist, there are real differences between, say, window cleaning, park work, catering and factory work. It is the expansion of the service and public sector and the contraction of the industrial sector which is very often the basis for claims that there is a wider range of opportunity open to young people now than ever before. Against this, however, it can be argued that the capitalist industrial model is dominant over all and sometimes very different branches of employment. The current government strategy to revive manufacturing industry and 'make it profitable' is ample evidence that the social democratic state recognises the primacy of industry over other categories of employment. Industrial capitalism is dominant in even more profound ways than this simple quantitative one, however. It enforces its central logic of the efficient deployment of abstract labour in enterprises and activities quite outside itself and in many apparently different concrete forms of labouring. It provides the central paradigm for the use of labour. In view of this central dominance the actual meaning of the new and wider range of *what is dominated* must be questioned closely - not presented as concrete proof of diversity.

The 'standard minute', in one form or another, is becoming the basic unit for all timesheets in all sectors of employment no matter what the actual form of labouring involved. Its central purpose is to break up and make comparable all kinds of work. It allows management to more directly control the expenditure of labour power so that 'skills' or customary time-wasting practices - actually important differentiating elements in particular kinds of concrete labour - are not allowed to hide slack time and impede management's utilisation of abstract labour. In this sense, even work undertaken in public corporations, public services or non-profit-making bodies is strictly comparable with industrial work directed towards profit.

Suggestions, and some operating schemes, for rationalisation and cost-effectiveness in education and the welfare services demonstrate the concrete spread of capitalist industrial logic to service and public occupational areas which are numerically larger now than manufacturing industry. This is to argue neither for a reduction nor an expansion in the service and public sectors, nor is it to deny that society needs to make decisions about its deployment of labour power. It is rather to point out that the expansion of these new areas is still basically under the sway of capitalist principles, and in particular the mediation of want through the category of the efficient use of abstract labour. It is not, as is often argued, under the sway of a nascent socialism. Under pressure of cuts in state expenditure we are seeing an even more rapid move to welfare defined as the greatest time social workers can spend with the greatest number of clients for the least cost, and education defined as maximised 'contact time' between staff and students - no matter what actually happens in these unit-costed hours. This management orientation suppresses the possibility of other approaches. Welfare and education could proceed from a direct recognition of collective needs, and an examination of those structural and cultural forms which inevitably generate suffering and 'inadequacy'. Such an approach would hinge around planning for human needs and purposes – not around the efficient use of 'abstract time'. As it is, we are approaching the day when filling in standard minutes on the timesheet every day will be, despite their different forms, the most basic reality of the working life of the teacher and social worker as it is now for the plumber and carpenter, and as it always has been for the industrial worker under capitalism.

The measure of abstract labour is, then, time. We have looked at the unit of a minute but more generally it has been widely noted that the rise of capitalism out of feudalism was associated with changed notions of time.[27] Natural logics of cyclic seasons, the position of the sun in the sky, hunger in the belly or a task to be done were replaced by clock logic as the basis of time. Not returning with the sun or the season, not a signal for the appropriateness again of an activity, but a standard finite quantity, time was remorselessly running out and taking opportunities with it. In capitalism time runs straight not in a circle. It is to be saved and used. It is the measure which allows complex tasks to be synchronised: value and profit to be measured and created. 'Time is money', but the real measure which connects the two is abstract labour.

The unified movement of an inevitable linear time characteristic of the capitalist age also has a kind of ideological effect. It suggests a sense of a homogeneous society engaged in the slow progress as it were, of the narrative which follows. There is an implied pervasive concept of maturation and continuity. This invites a gradualist, reformist perspective upon what is taken to be a unified society in which all share the same timescale and appreciate its careful warning pace. It tends to suppress a notion that different social groups may have different times, or some no times, or others attempt to pull time violently forwards.

Though it must not be exaggerated we can see elements of the counter-school culture not only as cultural penetrations but as a limited defeat of this dominant sense of time. The culture in its mostly successful informal direction of its members timetables, and subversion of the official one, is directly freeing space for cultural activities but is also rejecting artificial order and gradualist patterns of bourgeois time. In a sense 'the lads' ' events and adventures are hidden from bourgeois time. This is an effect, of course, which if not directly intended never-the-less further strengthens cultural practices in the cultural milieu.

So far we have considered the commonality of labour in the abstract. Abstract labour, however, as a living principle in real social relations is producing visible empirical forms of its tendency more obviously every day.[28] As we saw before, de-skilling is a very real process. Concrete labour is regressing more and more to a mean standard de-skilled labour. Even though there is an apparent move towards employers demanding more and higher qualifications the real move of the skill content in the jobs to which they apply is in the opposite direction. Even high craft jobs in toolshops, for instance, are yielding their varied and unitary nature to specialised repetitive flow technology.

Most mechanised factory work is standardised now and could be done by a child.[29] The giving of a real standardised labour is paced by the rhythm of the machine or the line and requires neither planning nor skill. Whether particular individuals feel sick or well, whether they have degrees of CSEs matters not at all. The particular concrete form of their individual labour power is irrelevant so long as it does not stop the line. Concrete labour power is important not for its intrinsic or particular contribution but for its withdrawal of the potential negative: it will not interrupt or disrupt production. We can see in modern machine manufacture and mass production an approach of abstract labour to the very surface of concrete labour.

The whole thrust of modern techniques of organisation and methods such as time and motion study is, in one important sense, to narrow the gap between concrete and abstract labour. The commonality between all labour in the abstract is embodied here in the concrete thrust to move all labour to the golden mean of the one best way of doing things. The capitalist Eldorado has been the one best way. The convergence of particular forms of labour to a concrete standard as the tendency of the principle of abstract labour is perhaps best exemplified in the work of the man who is usually credited with the addition of motion to time study. Gilbreth explicitly took labour in the abstract as his model for the improvement of concrete labour.[30] Previous approaches had taken the shortest *existing* way of completing a task, broken it down and standardised it. Gilbreth developed a classification of basic elementary movements he called 'therbligs' without regard to a concrete model. They were measured in ten-thousandths of a minute. Real concrete tasks could therefore be built up before their execution from these building bricks. The calculation of the best abstract method of doing a particular task before its existence reveals for us that the tendency of its existence is really towards the abstract mean. Capitalism, again, distils itself in its own advance. Such an approach – even where not finally successful in its own exacting terms – clearly has the most profoundly accelerating influence on the standardisation of particular jobs inherent within the capitalist system. The 'therblig' is the ultimate attempt to turn man into machine: his unique concrete capacities into optimal standard labour. It is difficult to argue for the variety of modern labour in the face of the 'therblig'! In its robotisation of a ten-thousandth of a minute capitalism shows us its desire to make robots of us all – all of the time.

'The lads' ' indifference to the particular form of work they enter, their assumption of the inherent meaninglessness of work no matter what kind of 'right attitude' they take to it, and their general sense of the similarity of all work as it faces them, is the form of a cultural penetration of their real conditions of existence as members of class. The perspective on work offered by the counter-school culture really is superior to that supplied officially by the school. The cultural 'recognition' of the commodity form of labour power, and of the principle of abstract labour which underlies and connects particular forms of labour, is the vital precondition for the limitation of subjective absorption in these things and for the cultural exploitation and celebration by 'the lads' of their own capacities for their own ends and purposes. This freed human ability and involvement supplies materials for the cultural level which go towards its own forms of production which maintain and develop cultural penetrations to start with. The cultural is the creative, varied, potentially transformative working out – not the suffering – of some of the fundamental social/structural relationships of society. As the counter-school culture lives against, exposes and reacts to the principle of general abstract labour it is worrying at the very heart of how the capitalist system runs and maintains itself. There is potential here for a, not merely partial and cultural, but for a total social transformation. What prevents this?

Notes

[1]   For me this is the fundamental failing of English contributions to the debate about class consciousness. The level of verbal response concerning political inclinations, and the assertion of commonsense categories of consciousness and orientation towards the political system often related to such evidence as codified in survey, may conceal real cultural dynamics which work in the opposite direction and have the opposite potential, or represent relatively arbitrary positions in relation to the real meaning of the cultural forms. I would regard, for instance, the 'privatised' worker, insofar as this is a coherent category, as one of the most advanced and potentially radical working class types, rather than the most incorporated. My analysis also suggests a reversal in the conventional evaluation of the 'traditional' worker: see J. H. Goldthorpe and D. Lockwood, 'Affluence and the British calss structure', *Sociological Review*, vol. 11, no. 2, 1963; J. H. Goldthorpe, et al., *The Affluent Worker in the Class Structure*, Cambridge University Press, 1969; J. H. Goldthorpe, et al., *The Affluent Worker: Industrial Attitudes and Behaviour*, Cambridge University Press, 1968; and M. Bulmer (ed.), *Working Class Images of Society*, Routledge and Kegan Paul, 1975.

Parkin's categories are sounder in the sense that they are related to national class cultures rather than to the empirical working up of responses at the level of practical consciousness. However, their ambit is very similar and they pose similar problems for my perspective. What is the real cultural and social base for 'the radical value system'? What forms of penetration and advance lie behind the incorporation of those within the 'negotiated value system'? See F. Parkin, *Class Inequality and the Political Order*, McGibbon and Kee, 1971.

[2]   This is the fundamental weakness of Lukacs' view of working class consciousness, and the grounds for charges of historicism levelled against his work. For me it also mars Gramsci's account of working class culture, the mass party, and the drive for cultural hegemony – in other respects compatible with the present work. The sharpest and most salutory warning against historicism and humanism is provided, of course, by the structuralists. See G. Lukacs, *History and Class Consciousness*, Merlin, 1971; A. Gramsci, *Prison Notebooks*, Penguin, 1974; Althusser and Balibar, *Reading Capital*, New Left Books, 1970; and Althusser, *For Marx*, Penguin, 1969.

[3]   It is unfortunate that in their justified conviction to discredit the simple ideological optimism of humanism the structuralists should also scotch the human. The point is not to write off the subjective as any believable force for penetration and objective analysis, but to reject its over-centred, undialectical, intended nature as outlined in a certain kind of Marxism.

[4]   The implications for consciousness of the respective structural positions of the bourgeoisie and the working class is most clearly brought out by Lukacs though it is thoroughly embedded in an historicist problematic. (See Lukacs, op. cit., esp. pp. 53-4).

In my view we should understand the specificity of the Marxist theory of the connection of base and superstructure as it is articulated around the central role of the commodity and exchange of commodities (as they supply the essential forms to be reified and separated into the juridico-political enshrinement of 'freedom', 'equality' and 'independence') as basically a theory about bourgeois consciousness and its relations to being. There is no overwhelmingly *inherent* reason for working class involvement in these characteristic and complex inversions of being and consciousness. At best the conviction of equality and independence as guaranteed by the exchange of the commodity 'labour power' lasts only as long as the worker is in the market place. Certainly it is only under capitalism that he owns his own labour power, has the right to sell it, and can contract, with protection from theft or moral dependency of any kind, to sell it to the highest bidder. As soon as his labour power is contracted, however, there is no reason for him to believe that he retains these qualities:

> There [in the market place] alone rule Freedom, Equality, Property and Bentham.
> (. . .) On leaving this sphere of simple circulation or of exchange of commodities, which furnishes the 'Free-trader Vulgaris' with his views and ideas, and with the standard by which he judges a society based on capital and wages, we think we can perceive a change in the physiognomy of our dramatis personae. He, who before was the money owner, now strides in front as capitalist: the possessor of labour power follows as his labourer. The one with an air of importance, smirking, intent on business, the other, timid and holding back, like one who is bringing his own hide to market and has nothing to expect but a hiding. (Marx, *Capital*, Allen and Unwin, 1957, Aveling and Moore translation, p. 55)

Note that it is the bourgeois who properly lives out the ideology and forms of consciousness derived from the commodity form. Of course this is the dominant form and certainly the labourer is freer than he was under feudalism, but not so free as to believe himself equal. The dominant ideology does enforce aspects of itself on subordinate behaviour, and the actual behaviour of the working class – despite mass movements and a distinctive culture of its own – has been within acceptable limits with respect to this ideology, but we do not have a theory for how all this comes about in the way that we have a satisfactory theory which links in all levels and ties in surplus abstraction, the commodity form and consciousness as well for the bourgeoisie. Structuralists who take the commodity, the juridico-political and state forms its sponsors, and the labour theory of value and surplus abstraction it conceals *for the bourgeoisie* as the only base for Marxism as a 'science' are left with no account at all of working class culture and consciousness. This category is filled simply with secondary reproductions of the dominant categories, or traces of older social relations. (See Poulantzas, 'Political Power and Social Classes', NLB, 1973, pp. 223-4.)

It seems to me that a theory of struggle between the classes and the projected proletarian overthrow of capitalism is a strange thing indeed – especially today – without a theory of advanced capitalist working class consciousness and culture *sui generis*. For me such a theory would have to demonstrate the same sort of complexity as the orthodox theory, in showing the same kinds of reversals and mediations between being and consciousness, and the same bindings in of the levels of the real relations, civil society and the state.

The form of this must, I would argue, be of the contradictory and unintended results of relatively independent working class attempts to 'see into', and adapt to, the real conditions of its existence which actually reproduce, albeit somewhat changed, these conditions in, as it were, a reverse dialectic. Such an account would be clearly off-centre, and without the stable central links up and down of the notion of the commodity form in the bourgeois theory. It would show, precisely, elements of the unstable, transitional, unpredictable nature of working class culture within the relatively stable bourgeois order. It would certainly not demonstrate a finished settled form of consciousness which projects its own material and juridico-political order. It would be to probe how a relatively separate system mutates, survives and finally accommodates – reproduces at the minimum and in somewhat modified forms – a system which oppresses it. This is not to pre-figure future social forms though. It is the recognition that there is no coherent centred system – as there was for instance in feudalism – waiting in the wings to take over from capitalism. Contemporary working class culture and consciousness is without a centre – we must falsely attribute to it the centre of the commodity – and not in any symmetrical form which shows a precise configuration, binding in and unification of all levels as in the pure capitalist model. On the other hand, it is in minute, complex and tense articulation with that capitalism which it continuously mutates and whose system it partly constitutes. Its dynamic is a partial penetration of capitalism simultaneously in the moment of its reproduction of capitalism's conditions of existence.

[5]   The group has been massively researched in American sociology, industrial sociology and industrial social psychology. See in particular R. Lickert, *New Patterns of Management*, McGraw-Hill, 1961; E. Mayo, *The Human Problems of an Industrial Civilization*, Macmillan, New York, 1933; K. Lewin, 'Group decision and social change', in G. E. Swanson, et al. (eds), *Readings in Social Psychology*, Holt, 1952; and D. Katz and R. L. Kahn, *The Social Psychology of Organizations*, Wiley, 1966.

[6]   Classic Freudian theory lies behind the social psychology of the group, of course. Though in *Totem and Taboo* Freud was principally concerned with the individual category of the super-ego, particular members of Freud's primal horde are internalising what are basically elements of a social system. In the killing and internalisation of the dead father all individuals give up some claim to individual sovereignty for group solidarity and power. This involves a relative move from the instrumental selfishness of Hobbesian man in his war of all against all to a notion of the group's interests and destiny. The internalisation of the dead father is precisely about control and displacement of individual views – what is received into the group – in favour of a logic relevant to the unit of the group. There is a real creativity in the development of the law of the dead father since it has no immediate previous source – the real father always, of course, being a myth.

[7]   My position here has been accused, with a certain mischievous merit, of a 'radicalised Hawthornism'. In fact I do not wish to imply that real informal groups can hope to make serious challenges to authority, or that their solidarity is always or even often evident. As we saw in the section on ethnography, members of the informal group can be picked on unmercifully by other members, and the group does not always hold ranks during a crisis. Furthermore, it is always possible for the creative force of the group to be turned on a range of objects other than its own social position, or diverted into reactionary or fascist explanations of its position. The shopfloor is much less protected and monitored than the school and realises these other possibilities much more frequently. The point here is not to idealise the informal group, or to counterpose it as a concrete force against structural or coercive official powers (against whom it must always lose as ethnography shows), but to pose the theoretical form and possibility of a cultural creativity which *avoids* precisely this unanchored assertive romanticism.

[8]   I am indebted here to the work in Marxist psychoanalysis of the Tel Quel group, Barthes and Kristeva in Paris. In my view they move too quickly from structural considerations to the subject without attention to the mediations of the state, institutions, class cultures and human groups. Kristeva's concepts of 'practice' and 'rejection' have, however, helped me to formulate my own more limited ideas. See Kristeva, *La Revolution du Language Poetique*, Seuil, 1974; and for an overview, J. Ellis, 'Ideology and subjectivity', *Working Papers in Cultural Studies 9*, CCS, 1976.

[9]   For a longer analysis of cultural practice and production as a kind of homology of a group's social position, identity and presence, and for further examples of how such practice also uncovers aspects of social relations eccentrically, so to speak, from their direct purposes see P. Willis, *Profane Culture*, Routledge and Kegan Paul, 1978.

[10]   The DES report on the first year of RSLA ends thus: 'The most successful schools seemed to be those where the subject option system, [where progressivism and particularly 'relevance' have been massively applied] supported by appropriate guidance, enabled pupils to feel that they were being offered *equal* but *realistic* opportunities' (my italics). The tension between 'equal' and 'realistic' speaks

volumes about the contradictions of 'relevance' and progressivism in education and for the accuracy of the penetrations which deny the equation.

[11]   Located cultural processes 'see' better than official and institutional accounts the real nature of the situation facing working class kids. Although it makes a pioneering attempt to recognise and to re-introduce the human into processes of preparation for work and job selection, vocational guidance among the non-academic and 'disinterested' does this in a way which is figured *from above*. There are actually pre-existing cultural processes within the counter-school culture which accomplish the preparation of individual labour powers, and the entry to work, and also penetrate the idealism of much vocational guidance.

Insofar as the real cultural processes are picked up by vocational guidance they are usually registered as 'blocks' to good communication. Cultural factors are identified only as 'misinformation' from family or friends, or as long standing 'predispositions' which set kids against more rational advice and decision-making procedures. (See particularly J. Maizels, *Adolescent Needs and the Transition from School to Work*, Althone Press, 1970; and M. P. Carter, *Into Work*, Penguin, 1969). In some cases these cultural processes are specifically denigrated as 'prejudice' and contrasted with 'better understandings'. (DES, Careers Guidance in Schools, pp. 43 & 44).

Recent work has taken more systematic cognisance of cultural factors as determinants of occupational choice, but even here dynamic cultural processes with complex, long term, rational dynamics are represented only in descriptive assertions as sets of attitudes. Working class kids are in the world of 'the immediate present' and the 'here and now' where 'little thought or concern can be given for the future'. They see themselves as of 'limited ability' so that normal career notions are rejected. Ultimately this sort of 'cultural' explanation is a huge tautology: it is a restatement of the same problem on a wider plane. We are given no explanation for the generation of these attitudes. Such cultural accounts can be derived simply from the well-known and conventionalised facts of the situation: 'if that is the sort of work they do, and they do not object, then that must be the sort of thing they expect at a *cultural* level'. In essence we are told that working class kids do not object to their fate because that is not the sort of thing they do. See D. N. Ashton, 'The transition from school to work: notes on the development of different frames of reference among young male workers', *Sociological Review*, vol. 21, no. 1, February 1973; D. N. Ashton, 'From school to work: some problems of adjustment experienced by young male workers', in Brannen, op. cit.; and D. N. Ashton and D. Field, *Young Workers*, Hutchinson, 1976.

[12]   It is clear, for instance, that it is impossible to define unskilled workers on the basis of their qualifications. A recent government report on the unqualified and untrained had great difficulty in defining these terms in relation to skill in work (DES, *Unqualified, Untrained, and Unemployed*, 1974). It found that a substantial number of those in apprenticeships in fact lacked qualifications. The report finally settled on a circular definition of the unskilled as those 'who are not only unqualified, but also would normally, but not inevitably, seek jobs offering relatively little

training' (p. 2). The same report also states that employers are most interested in motivation than in qualificatians (p. 22), and that lack of qualifications is no impediment to advance in most kinds of jobs open to working class kids: 'there was ... no reason why an unqualified boy or girl with the right personal qualities should not aspire to an apprenticeship or a clerical job in regions where these jobs are available' (p. 22). Clearly it is the pull of the local job market and not the push of education which is the crucial factor in working class employment.

[13] See, for instance, M. Weir (ed.), *Job Satisfaction*, Fontana, 1976; P. Warr and T. Wall, *Work and Well-Being*, Penguin, 1975; N. A. B. Wilson, *On the Quality of Working Life: A Report Prepared for the Department of Employment*, Manpower Papers, no. 7, HMSO, 1973; *Work in America*, (report of a Special Task Force to the Secretary of Health, Education and Welfare), MIT Press, 1973; W. I. Paul and K. B. Robertson, *Job Enrichment and Employee Motivation*, Gowan Press, 1970; and F. Herzberg, *Work and the Nature of Man*, Staple Press, 1968.

[14] See H. Braverman, *Labour and Monopoly Capital*, Monthly Review Press, 1974; C. Palloix, 'The labour process: from Fordism to neo-Fordism', in *The Labour Process and Class Strategies*, CSE, 1976; Brighton Labour Process Group, 'The capitalist labour process' in *Capital and Class*, no. 1, Spring 1977.

[15] Jobless school leavers in England and Wales numbered around 40,000 in February 1976. This is about five times as many as at the same time in 1975 (*New Society*, 5 February 1976). In October 1976, according to *The Guardian* they numbered 82,000 (27 October 1976).

[16] DES, *Unqualified, Untrained and Unemployed*, report of a working party set up by the National Employment Council, HMSO, 1974.

[17] Bourdieu and Paseron, *La Reproduction*, Minuet, 1970.

[18] A position also shared by the English, 'New Sociology' of Education. See N. Keddie, *Tinker, Tailor, Soldier, Sailor ... The Myth of Cultural Deprivation*, Penguin, 1973.

[19] This is a simplification, of course, but not one which damages the point. In classical Marxist theory the wage is determined by the socially necessary labour time required to reproduce the labourer in determinate social and cultural conditions. The difference between this and what he produces is surplus value. Surplus value is larger than, and includes, profit. Labour power is bought at its exchange value as determined by the law of value, but exploited on the basis of its use value (Marx, *Capital*, ch. 6).

[20] Strictly speaking this should read greater relative surplus value. In the Marxist system, without an increase in the working day, even with the aid of machinery, the worker cannot produce more value, but efficiency, by lessening unit costs, devalues the commodity produced and thus lessens the cost of reproducing the labourer with respect to the commodity he produces, i.e. it lessens the necessary labour time in relation to the surplus labour time of production (Marx, *Capital*, Parts IV and V).

[21] The book presents a case which modifies this view, of course, but the classic model will serve our purposes here.

[22]   This is one of the reasons why I have fought shy of using the term 'alienation' in this discussion. It is usually used as a measure of the *increasing* ravages of capitalism on subjectivity, and as a mark, therefore, of its destructive tendencies. I would argue for a more complex assessment which recognises the undoubted sensual ravages associated with modern work – particularly for those without a specifically cultural protection – but also that the basis for a progressive tendency. On the one hand it concretely socialises labour to a great degree, on the other, more apposite to the concerns of this book, it produces a subjective and cultural demystification of 'craft idiocy' and of the absorption of the self into work. It has the potential of releasing capacities and critical attitudes usually held in check in less 'alienating' work.

[23]   This is one way to understand the 'instrumentalism' of the 'privatised' worker some stages on from 'the lads' under consideration here. Far from becoming middle class, his tendency is towards the exorcism of capitalist mystifications. He is exploiting, one-sidedly and from the limited position of the subordinate class, some of the freedoms which capitalism really does offer. Though the form of 'privatisation' may be individual, its nature is collective. It may be considered as a form of advanced proletarian consciousness. Lockwood's traditional worker shows us merely the sentimentalism and superstition of the defensive capitalist worker without any deep subjective or cultural understanding of the system which oppresses him.

[24]   'Abstract labour' is one of the central categories of the whole Marxist analysis of the capitalist system. See Marx, *Capital*, Part I; and L. Colletti, 'Bernstein and the Marxism of the Second International' in *From Rousseau to Lenin*, New Left Books, 1972.

[25]   I take Colletti's case absolutely that abstract labour is much more than a mental category in the analyst's head. It is a central factor of real social organisation and the real basis of the exchange of commodities (including labour power), and is recapitulated every time in that exchange. Abstract labour as a social force is also indicated in subjective processes such as the separation of the self from labour dealt with in the previous section. However, Colletti's equation of abstract labour with alienation forecloses too early the fixed nature of man and denies the possibility of a progressive and contradictory edge to the split between concrete and abstract labour which capitalism enforces. I dissent from Colletti as he follows Lukacs in equating the self-consciousness of the working class with knowledge of the operative principle of abstract labour as a force for reification, and recognition of its own labour power as the source of value. It is this error which allows him to attribute the simple possibility of a correct political analysis to working class consciousness (ibid., p. 91). This is where both he and Lukacs can be justly accused of empiricism and historicism. Insofar as these things are only *partially* penetrated I suggest that such realisations act finally in a contradictory way to bind the working class into the capitalist order. They help towards the making of a sceptical settlement in working class culture which allows the reproduction of the minimum conditions necessary for capitalist production.

[26] The strength and partial success of vocational guidance and its differentiation of working situations rests upon, I would argue, a mediated and misrecognised sense of the cultural adaptions made to manual work. There is a variety here and also a degree of meaning. These do not relate, however, as the guidance perspective so often suggests they do, to the intrinsic quality of particular work – or insofar as they do the *trend* is for their separation. Vocational guidance personalises the cultural and maintains a viability by transferring it to the technical.

[27] See E. P. Thompson, 'Time, Work Discipline and Industrial Capitalists' in *Past and Present*, (38) December 1967.

[28] The fundamental principle here is that abstract labour underlies and connects all forms of labour with respect to capital. We can only derive a *tendency* from this for skilled labour to give way to unskilled labour, or for abstract labour to approach actual embodiment in concrete labour. No matter what the scope of this tendency, however, there is always a distinction between these two. Concrete labour does vary. Machine maintenance, for instance, is distinct from the operation of that machine. It is important, however, that the abstract principle is empirically observable in its tendencies. For a useful clarification on these matters see Geoff Kay, 'A note on abstract labour', CSE Bulletin, vol. 5, no. 1 (13), March 1976.

[29] Most manual work needs only a mental age of 12 or less. See G. C. Mathews, 'The Post-School Adaption of Educationally Sub-Normal Boys', unpublished MEd thesis, University of Manchester, 1963.

[30] See W. Spriegel and C. Myers (eds), *The Writings of F. Gilbreth*, Irwin, 1953. There are limits to this approach. It is the ultimate attempt to use human power as a force of production. Humans are, however, also part of the social relations of production. The informal group as the basis of a cultural class force against endless exploitation isolates these techniques and resists them. 'Gold-bricking' and 'systematic soldiering' persisted after the introduction of O and M techniques. 'Human relations' techniques following upon the empirical discovery of the importance of the human group by Mayo and his associates were an attempt to neutralise this opposition. The most recent 'new' human relations aims to utilise and win over the power of the informal group in one way or another. However, O and M still remains dominant as the single most influential management service and still best exposes the basic inner drive of capitalism.

6 Limitations

As we have seen, the counter-school culture makes certain cultural penetrations of the conditions of existence of its members. There are potential materials here for a thoroughly critical analysis of society and political action for the creation of alternatives.

In one sense the reason why these cultural penetrations and associated practices fall short of transformative political activity is simply the lack of political organisation. No mass party attempts to interpret and mobilise the cultural level. This is too facile, however. The lack of political organisation itself can be seen as a result of the partiality of the penetrations - not vice versa.[1] The cultural level is clearly partly disorganised from within.

The ethnographic account reminds us again and again that there is only one social outcome. Gigantic forces in conflict resolve into one reality - not serial realities allowing us to read back their pure determinants and forwards their proper outcomes. The pure logic of cultural penetration runs straight only on the page. In reality simultaneous forces of distortion, limitation and mystification resolve this pure logic into a partial logic. In the way in which it is actually effective in the world the half-rejection and cultural penetration of the present social organisation by the counter-school culture becomes an always provisional, bare, sceptical, yet finally accepting accommodation within the status quo. It never-the-less, however, contradictorily maintains a degree of conviction of movement, insight and subjective validation in individuals even as they accept this subordination. In the present tangled knot of ideological entrapments in contemporary capitalism the most remarkable demonstration of this contradiction is that of a nascent cultural understanding of abstract labour and class solidarity amongst disaffected working class kids being delivered into a particular subjective affirmation and 'free' giving of manual labour power.

Divisions

Cultural penetrations are repressed, disorganised and prevented from reaching their full potential or a political articulation by deep, basic and disorientating divisions. The two most important are those between mental and manual labour and those of gender. (Racism which is also significant here is dealt with in a later section.)

The rejection of the school, and the cultural penetration of the unfairness of the 'equivalent' it offers can be seen as the rejection of individualism. It is also, however, simultaneously the rejection of mental activity in general. In the moment of the defeat of individualism its mark of separation passes. Individualism is

145

defeated not for itself but for its part in the school masque where mental work is associated with unjustified authority, with qualifications whose promise is illusory. Individualism is penetrated therefore at the cost of a practical division of human capacity and a yielding of the power to properly exercise one half of it. As one kind of solidarity is won, a deeper structural unity is lost. Although 'the lads' stand together, they do so on this side of the line with individualism and mental activity on the other. The human world is divided into those who are 'good with their hands' or 'good with their heads'. The burden of the cultural penetration that all work is the same is thrown mainly on to a notion that all *manual* work is the same. Manual labouring comes to take on, somehow, a significance and critical expression for its owner's social position and identity which is no part of its own proper nature.

We can see here the profound, unintended and contradictory importance of the institution of the school. Aspects of the dominant ideology are informally defeated there, but that defeat passes a larger structure more unconsciously and more naturalised for its very furnacing in (pyrrhic) victory. Capitalism can afford to yield individualism amongst the working class but not division. Individualism is penetrated by the counter-school culture but it actually produces division.

The other great division which disorientates cultural penetration is that between male and female. It is, at least in part, an internally produced division. The male counter-school culture promotes its own sexism - even celebrates it as part of its overall confidence.

The characteristic style of speech and movement, even in the absence of females, always holds something of the masculine spectacle. The ability to take the initiative, to make others laugh, to do unexpected or amusing things, to naturally take the active complement to the appreciative passive, these are all profoundly masculine attributes of the culture, and permanent goals for individuals in it. Not only this but a more concrete hallmark of being a member of the culture is to have either sexual experience or at least aspirations which are exploitative and hypocritical. Girls are pursued, sometimes roughly, for their sexual favours, often dropped and labelled 'loose' when they are given. Girls are asked to be sexy and inviting as well as pure and monogamous: to be consumed and not be consumed. The counter-school culture emphasises sexual division at the same moment that it penetrates the artificiality of individualistic division.

In its sexism the counter-school culture reflects the wider working class culture. This is partly, of course, because it turns to some of the wider class models for guidance during *differentiation* of the school educational paradigm. As he becomes disillusioned with the school, for instance, one of 'the lads' finds one of the most deep-seated and abiding models of sexual division and domination in the working home. Members of the counter-school culture are also much more likely to find a job - out of necessity - than are the conformists, and to experience a particular kind of sexism, both directed at them personally and as an aspect of the working environment in general. It becomes for them part of the worldliness and superior style of that whole working class culture of the workplace which they admire and are busily reconstructing in relation to the particular oppositions and determinants of the school.

Although there may be an institutionalised sexism in our schools, it is not as strong as the reproduced sexism at the informal level of its working class male oppositional culture. Schools must be given some credit for holding out a degree of liberalism and formalistic equality. It is no product of the school's manifest intentions that sexism and profoundly naturalised divisions arise in more virulent forms at the moment when its own authority is broken. All the same it plays out a vital and systematic, if unintended, role in the reproduction of a class society.

Labour power and patriarchy

The cultural penetrations examined may even have survived the disorientation and schism caused by the divisions outlined above if they had remained divisions in the abstract or separate from each other. As it is, there is further complex fusion of these divisions absolutely characteristic, in micro form, of a knot of meanings central to the stability of the capitalist system itself and appearing in all of its manifestations. Let us now consider this knot.

The mental/manual distinction alone presents a fertile field for the construction of naturalised divisions in human capacities. What is surprising is that a portion, including such as 'the lads', of those who make up the social whole are content to voluntarily take upon themselves the definition and consequent material outcomes of being manual labourers. This is surprising since in the capitalist mobilisation of the mental/manual distinction it is conventionally, and according to the dominant ideology, the mental labourers who have the legitimised right to superior material and cultural conditions. Mental work is held to be more exacting and therefore to justify higher rewards. It is not difficult to explain why that which is ideologically seen as desirable and which is really rewarding materially should be pursued. The fact that all do not aspire to the rewards and satisfactions of mental labour is what is in need of explanation. Just because capitalism needs a split such as this does not explain why its need is satisfied. It is only in a perfectly reflective empirical world that the shape of a need determines the inevitability of its satisfaction. Moreover, the real mechanisms at play in the satisfaction of this need are covered over and mystified, and hidden from view by the way in which the dominant ideology, and the meritocratic view of what happens in schools for instance, really do seem to assume that all are trying to achieve broadly the same aims in life.

The way in which we are all expected to pursue the same aims suggests that those at the bottom of a class society are there apparently, and they believe it for themselves, because of their own smaller capacity to achieve these aims. All accept, so to speak, the same rules, meanings and goals of the game – and also what counts as winning and losing. In fact, of course, as the humanistic developments in education and careers counselling partly recognise but wrongly interpret, this model could never actually work under modern conditions. It assumes that the lower factions of the working class are really a sub-species. It is more feudalism than capitalism. Though it is usually misrecognised, one of the things which keeps the capitalist system stable, and is one of its complex wonders, is that an important section of the subordinate class do not accept the proffered reality of the steady diminution of their own capacities. Instead they reverse the valuation of the mental/manual gradient by which they are measured. 'The lads' under study here prefer (for the moment), and affirm themselves through, manual labour. This, of course, provides the missing link for a social chain of class distinctions. All other classes above this can celebrate, justify, and see a comparative base for their own superiority in the mental mode in the currency of the dominant ideology. The 'ear'oles' conformism, for instance, takes on a more rational appearance when judged against the self-disqualification of 'the lads'. Whether or not there is that much difference in the actual work they do, they can gain some advantage and social approval from defining it, their relationship to it, and their own identity in a relatively more mental mode.

A reverse polarisation of a too well-learned distinction neatly complements the dominant ideology and gives it a sounding board for the subjective creation of identities in labour for all those factions above the lowest. Without this clinching inversion of the ideological order at its lowest reach in relation to the giving of labour power the system could not be stable. No amount of conditioning in state agencies could provide a fully human identity for those at the bottom of the class structure: coercion or permanent struggle, not free consent in submission, would be the basis of the social order.

This important inversion, however, is not achieved within the proper logic of capitalist production. Nor is it produced in the division of labour spontaneously. It is produced in the concrete articulation on the site of social classes of two structures which in capitalism can only be separated in abstraction and whose forms have now become part of it. These are patriarchy and the distinction between mental and manual labour. *The form of the articulation is of the cross-valorisation and association of the two key terms in the two sets of structures.* The polarisation of the two structures become crossed. Manual labour is associated with the social superiority of masculinity, and mental labour with the social inferiority of femininity. In particular manual labour is imbued with a masculine tone and nature which renders it positively expressive of more than its intrinsic focus in work.

Gender and mental/manual difference provide the atavistic divisions to be worked up into contemporary concrete cultural forms and relationships, but it is only the learning that division is not always and automatically to its own disadvantage which prevents sectors of the working class from seeing division as oppression. For 'the lads', a division in which they take themselves to be favoured (the sexual) overlies, becomes part of, and finally partially changes the valency of a division in which they are disadvantaged (mental/manual labour power).[2]

It is often overlooked that where two sets of divisions are lived out in the same concrete space they cannot remain separate. The pressure of consciousness and culture which work upon their own materials in their own location and seek a kind of unity will not live separately in two systems of ideas which both occur in the compression of their own life space. Such systems can only be separated in abstraction. As ethnography reminds us it is not a theoretical capacity but an empirical imperative that there must be a conjunction of systems. The secret of the continuation of both sets of divisions in labour and gender lies, at least partly, in their lived profane conjunction under the class sytem of capitalism, and not in their own pure logics. In this crossover conjunction the masculine – in its own proper field a state or formalistic law of superior status – becomes movement, action, assertion. An essence, which, it can be argued, is trans-historical, is given a style and a concrete worldly form of expression under capitalism. Manual labour power – in its own proper field neutral or even dissociated physical work on nature – becomes dominance and a form of election. It is given an expressive purpose.

If a form of patriarchy buttresses the mental/manual division of labour, this division, in its turn, strengthens and helps to reproduce modern forms of sexual division and oppression. It is precisely because there are divisions at school and work which operate objectively to their disfavour but which can be understood and inverted in patriarchal terms that those gender terms must themselves be continuously reproduced and legitimated. If the currency of femininity were revalued then that of mental work would have to be too. A member of the counter-school culture can only believe in the effeminacy of white collar and office work so long as wives, girlfriends and mothers are regarded as restricted, inferior and incapable of certain things. As we have seen, there is ample evidence of this belief amongst 'the lads'. The ideology of domesticity they impose on girlfriends, the patterns of homely and subcultural capacity and incapacity, all underwrite the restricted role of women. It is from the ideological division of labour, not simply from the domesticity of the house or patriarchal ideology that some of the real determinants and rationales of these practices spring.[3] For our immediate purposes the result of this cross-valorisation is that the flow of cultural penetration, and particularly its nascent appreciation of general abstract labour, is diverted into a surprising affirmation of labour power. There are two important processes. In the first place the association of different kinds of work with different sexual genders confirms the nature of division in the world of work. Mental activity for 'the-lads' is not only barred because of their particular experience of the institution of the school, but also because it is regarded as effeminate. Many of their own mental activities and feelings are expressed and acted through the cultural, the stylish and the concrete. In the crucial, critical and classic shift, what they take as mental work becomes for 'the lads' mere 'pen-pushing', 'not really doing things' and, most importantly, 'cissy': it is not basically man's work or within the manly scope of action. We see at least why the 'ear'oles' are likely to be regarded as effeminate and passive 'cissies' by 'the lads', and why other names for conformists include 'pouf' or 'poufter', or 'wanker'. Despite their greater achievement and conventional hopes for the future, 'ear'oles' and their strategies can be ignored because the *mode* of their success can be discredited as passive, mental and lacking a robust masculinity.

In the second place the whole meaning of what masculinity stands for reinforces the sense in which the weight of the cultural penetration concerning labour power and the nature of modern work is thrown contradictorily on to an affirmation of manual labour power. There is a further infusion of meaning into manual labour power which is no part of its intrinsic nature.

Manual labour is suffused with masculine qualities and given certain sensual overtones for 'the lads'.[4] The toughness and awkwardness of physical work and effort – for itself and in the division of labour and for its strictly capitalist logic quite without intrinsic heroism or grandeur – takes on masculine lights and depths and assumes a significance beyond itself. Whatever the specific problems, so to speak, of the difficult task they are always essentially masculine problems. It takes masculine capacities to deal with them. We may say that where the principle of general abstract labour has emptied work of significance from the inside, a trans-formed patriarchy has filled it with significance from the outside. Discontent with work is hinged away from a political discontent and confused in its proper logic by a huge detour into the symbolic sexual realm.

The brutality of the working situation is partially re-interpreted into a heroic exercise of manly confrontation with *the task*. Difficult, uncomfortable or danger-ous conditions are seen, not for themselves, but for their appropriateness to a masculine readiness and hardness. They are understood more through the tough-ness required to survive them, than in the nature of the imposition which asks them to be faced in the first place.

Though it is difficult to obtain stature in work itself, both what work provides and the very sacrifice and strength required to do it provides the materials for an elemental self-esteem. This self-esteem derives from the achievement of a purpose which not all – particularly women – are held capable of achieving. The wage packet is the provider of freedom, and independence: the particular prize of masculinity in work. This is the complement of, and is what makes possible, the fetishism of the wage packet. A trade is judged not for itself, nor even for its general financial return, but for its ability to provide the central, domestic, masculine role for its incumbent. Clearly money is part of this – but as a measure, not the essence. As Spanksy's father says, 'You can raise a family off polishing'. The male wage packet is held to be central, not simply because of its size, but because it is won in a masculine mode in confrontation with the 'real' world which is too tough for the woman. Thus the man in the domestic household is held to be the breadwinner, the worker, whilst the wife works for 'the extras'. Very often of course, the material importance of her wage may be much greater than this suggests, and certainly her domestic labour is the lynchpin of the whole household economy. The wage packet as a kind of symbol of machismo dictates the domestic culture and economy and tyrannises both men and women.

In a more general sense in the machismo of manual work the will to finish a job, the will to really work, is posited as a masculine logic and not as the logic of exploitation. 'It's a man's want to be finished when he starts a job', says Joey's father about his heavy drop forging work. The very teleology of the process of work upon nature and the material power involved in that becomes through the conflation of masculinity and manual work a property of masculinity and not of production. Masculinity is power in its own right, and if its immediate expression is in the completion of work for another, then what of it? It has to be expressed somewhere because it is a quality of being. That is the destiny which a certain kind of self-esteem and dignity seem naturally to bring. Where the intransigence and hardness of a task might bring weakness, or collective opposition or questioning, an over-ride of masculinity – a transferred teleology of production – can cut in to push back fatigue and rational assessment of purpose.[5]

And if the nature of masculinity in work becomes a style of teleology, completion, femininity is associated with a fixed state. Its labour power is considered as an ontological state of being, not a teleological process of becoming. Housework is not completion, it is maintenance of status. Cooking, washing and cleaning reproduce what was there before. Certainly in a sense housework is never completed – but neither is it as difficult or productive as masculine work is held to be. Female domestic work is simply subsumed under *being* 'mum' or 'housewife'. 'Mum' will always do it, and should always be expected to do it. It is part of the definition of what she *is*, as the wage packet and the productive world of work is of what 'dad' is.

Far from patriarchy and its associated values being an unexplained relic of previous societies, it is one of the very pivots of capitalism in its complex, unintended preparation of labour power and reproduction of the social order. It helps to provide the real human and cultural conditions which in their continuously deconstructed, reconstructed, fragile, uncertain, unintended and contradictory ways actually allow subordinate roles to be taken on 'freely' within liberal democracy. We have the elemental, though finally illusory, reversal of real conditions in experience which is necessary for the 'free' functioning of consciousness and will in finally determinate conditions. What begins as, or has the potential to be, an insight about the commonality of the giving of labour, and of the identity of the working class, amongst 'the lads' and in the counter-school culture becomes broken down into an assertion about manual labour only, and then distorted into strange affirmation of it. Labour comes to express aspects of an essence or quality not intrinsically part of its nature or relation to capital. More concretely, in an important sense it is because 'the lads' know division and superiority in courtship, in the home, on the street, in the pub, and in the family that they understand and accept division at school and work and find short term celebration and long term accommodation within its least favourable term.

Masculinity must not, however, be too simply posed. It has many dimensions and edges. In one way it is a half-blind, regressive machismo which brings self-destructive violence, aggression and division to relationships within the working class. In another way, imparting something of what lies behind it, masculinity expresses impulses which can be progressive. Behind the expression of masculinity lies an affirmation of manual labour power and behind that (though mediated and distorted) a sense of the uniqueness of the commodity of labour power and of the way in which general abstract labour unites and connects all kinds of concrete labour. The masculine disdain for qualifications, for all its prejudice, carries still a kind of 'insight' into the divisive nature of certification, and into the way in which mental work and technicism are mobilised ideologically primarily to maintain class relations rather than to select the most efficient or to increase productive efficiency.

It is in the understanding of this contradictory complex of masculinity and the strange articulation of sexual and labour divisions that we have the beginnings of an answer to the problem outlined earlier: why that which is conventionally registered, artificially defined and ideologically imbued as the least desirable and satisfying work (manual work) should be taken on voluntarily, and even with some enthusiasm by an important group in society – at least for long enough in their youth to be trapped forever.

Manual work is *seen* significantly differently by this group. Its stigma becomes *positively* expressive. Such work is undertaken in part to express things other than its objectives or dominant ideologically ascribed identity within the capitalist system. These things are not themselves without an aetiological 'rationality' which though displaced and transposed is potentially more adequate than some of those accounts which directly define manual work as inferior.

It is the unlikely hard stone at the bottom of the social system of self-selection into manual work which allows, in the currents of ideology against it, 'new classes' to effervesce upwards in experiential relations of ascendence.[6] For instance both the conformists and the non-conformists of this study are, in fact, working class and objectively doing similar work in a similar position *vis-à-vis* the productive proceeds. Yet the conformists can believe themselves, especially equipped with qualifications, to be in 'better' jobs than, and to be a 'different kind of person' from, 'the lads'. And once such a division is founded in the working class, of course, it massively legitimates the position of the middle class: not capitalism but their own mental capacities keep them where they are.

Racialism and labour power

Racial division helps, as with labour and gender divisions, to found the whole epistemological category and possibility of division. It also provides an evident underclass which is more heavily exploited than the white working class, and is therefore indirectly and partially exploited by the working class itself (at least lessening their own exploitation); it also provides an ideological object for feelings about the degeneracy of others and the superiority of the self (thus reinforcing the dominant ideological terms which make the comparison possible). Racism therefore divides the working class both materially and ideologically.

There is also a sense, however, in which racism tones the sensual giving of labour power for sections of the white working class such as 'the lads' in a way which leads to further nuanced affirmation of a particular kind of labouring. It marks the bottom limit of the scope of masculinity and delivers it not as a vulgar assertion of everything physical and menial, but as a more carefully judged cultural category. Since immigrant racial groups are likely to take the worst and roughest jobs, they are also potentially likely to be harder and more masculine. It is untenable that another social group should take the mantle of masculine assertiveness, so such jobs are further reclassified to fall off the cultural scale of masculinity into the 'dirty', 'messy' and 'unsocial' category.

A complex map of occupations therefore develops which does not have a single principle of organisation. Very light or mental work is marked down as 'cissy' but the heaviest and most uncompromising work is not necessarily masculine. It can be marked down as dirty and unacceptable through association with immigrant labour. Racism must be understood with respect more to the complex social definition of labour power under capitalism than to any pure and inevitable ethnic hostility.

There are variations, of course, in relations and social definitions between the races. West Indian males seem to have preserved a degree of machismo from the real and imputed degradation of their conditions (it would be interesting to see how far this is related to their sense of their own labour power). Certainly some white working class hostility towards young West Indians seems to be based on a kind of sexual jealousy. Of course just as his work situation is downgraded from the masculine to the dirty, so the West Indian's supposed sexual prowess can be downgraded from the natural to the disgusting.

In the case of Asians there seems to be evidence of an opposite move on the basic cultural scale of work so that successful shopkeepers, businessmen and students are defined by many working class whites such as 'the lads' as 'cissy', passive and lacking aggression alongside conformist, effeminate whites (c.f. 'queer-bashing' and 'Paki-bashing'). Some of the virulence of this response may be accounted for by the perception of this move upwards (and into its set of character-istic prejudices) in relation to the feeling that the Asians should really belong with the rough and dirty workers anyway. There is a confusion about which category of prejudice to apply, and in a certain sense the Asians suffer from both.

If the basic general thesis of the contradictory cultural forms in which labour is prepared has any validity, however, it should also throw light upon such prepara-tion amongst immigrant groups.[7]

Certainly in the case of some young second generation West Indians their cultural responses and processes can be likened to those of 'the lads'. They are in some respects more advanced in a way which shows up aspects of the present situation more clearly. Such lads have, for the most part, grown up and been edu-cated in England and have had broadly the same experiences as their white fellow pupils at school and in and around the neighbourhood and district – from a struct-ural point of view anyway. It may be suggested that this will have led their informal culture to certain kinds of mediated 'insights' about the nature of the school and the labour market similar to those amongst the white lads. They also, however, inherit from the West Indies a culture of wagelessness and poverty. It appears to them as if there is a viable possibility of surviving without wages – or in some cases without any kind of official and visible means of support at all. This opens up the possibility, therefore, of certain accurate insights about the nature of their future being carried forward not as an affirmation of a certain kind of work but as a *refusal* of all work.

This is not to say that their culture, and the actions springing from its logic, are without mystification or are not finally distorted and made partial in their own ways. However, if they close the circle too early by a refusal to work not properly based on an analysis of, and politically articulated with, the real conditions and possibilities of this society, they highlight the half-completed nature of the white response with its contradictory mixture of penetration, rationality, distortion and final incorporation.

As structural unemployment becomes a permanent feature of this society and some sections of white youth are forced into long term unemployment there may well develop a white ethnic culture of wagelessness (borrowing very likely from the West Indian one, though compare the currently emerging phenomenon of punk rock culture). A necessity might be turned into an invention and, through the cultural mediation, the option of not working become a more widespread 'freely' chosen response. The question of the cultural reproduction of an under class is as full of significance as that of the reproduction of the manual working class. We cannot, however, pursue it here.

Notes

[1]   This is not to deny the possibility, importance and relative autonomy of political action at its own level. In my view, however, before any mass party could articulate itself properly as the representative of the working class it must understand and *learn* from working class consciousness and culture. Until that effort the dialectical relation of party and consciousness is a dead letter. If spontaneism must be condemned so must 'zombieism' – the attempt to direct working class activity from outside with no thought for (or an assumption that it is morbid or moribund) the cultural, quasi-political and political content which is there already.

This book may be criticised for its lack of direct conjunctural relevance. Certainly the analysis provided is basically organic. However, I would argue more generally that we need, so to speak, a law of value of the political before we can properly analyse the market place of the conjunctural.

[2]   The basic cross-valorisation discussed here is relevant to groups other than the male working class. The association, for instance, of femininity with mental work implies a contradiction for working class women. Masculinity is an aspect of their *class* cultural identity no matter what their feminine gender on other grounds. This association also implies for middle class women a further restriction, passivity,

and inherent absurdity of their social and cultural roles even than their gender definition implies. We have here elements towards an explanation of the women's movement, its class origin, and to forms of working class antagonism to it.

For middle class males there are also contradictions between a class and cultural (patriarchal) definition of their masculinity. They are by no means immune from the inversion of the occupational gradient accomplished and underpinned by patriarchal values in an important area of working class culture. For the class base and origins of the developing 'Men's Movement' see A. Tolson, *The Limits of Masculinity*, Tavistock, 1976).

The male working class case presented in the main text is not, of course, without contradictions. Racial complexities threaten it from one side, and the reduction of work experience which allows – even given the scope of ideological play – masculine experiences threatens it from the other.

[3]   Juliet Mitchell's important book attempts to demonstrate the strict redundancy of patriarchal forms in modern capitalism. Both as outlined by Engels in his materialist analysis (*The Origins of the Family, Private Property and the State*), and in Mitchell's account of the cultural analyses of Freud and Levi-Strauss, patriarchy now seems to be superfluous. For Mitchell, apparently, it lives on as an historical trace without any continuously and relevantly reproduced logic or justification. Not only this, but patriarchy and capitalism are preserved as two quite distinct entities by Mitchell (p. 379). This lends her to posit an untenable dualistic politics (pp. 406, 414 and 415). She asserts that the systems are in contradiction but there is no actual depiction of the process of struggle between, or dialectical transformation of, both. We are dealing here surely with a contradiction that lies ultimately within *one* complex and differentiated unit, an *internal* contradiction specific to the complex balance of modern capitalism. It is precisely the oblique conjunction of the capitalist mode of production and patriarchy which make them difficult to sort out at the level of consciousness. It is the inheritance of pre-capitalist forms and their profane and complex determinate relation with (and partly constituting it) a specific and determinant kind of capitalist mode of production which helps to divert the insights bred at the cultural level, and more properly focused on specifically capitalist relations, into reactionary, immobile or neutral forms. What does indeed confound the pure logic of the system also confounds working class culture.

More generally, this book highlights the potential danger of the women's movement being vitiated by a too-short-run notion of a patriarchal sexism which oppresses them directly in some way outside capitalism. The need is for a dialectical and connected notion of a determinate capitalist patriarchy which transforms and fixes the whole social totality. This clearly has important implications for men as well as women – though it is undoubtedly women who suffer the sharpest most obvious and visible oppression. (Juliet Mitchell), *Psychoanalysis and Feminism*, Penguin, 1974.)

[4]   Masculinity is so deeply embedded in the giving of manual labour that we might actually question the 'objectivity' of those methods which aim to intensify and increase the efficiency of labour. The role of transformed patriarchal influences

within the productive process as it has been intensified by capitalism has hardly been touched on. The intertwining of patriarchal forms in capitalism means, in fact, that there is no pure way in which we can picture abstract labour. The techniques of Ford, Taylor and Gilbreth might not be so pure as they suppose. Even the codifications and reductions of modern organisation and methods, especially as they are resisted in shopfloor culture in what are often essentially masculine forms, cannot remove atavistic traces of swagger, unnecessary movement and the expression of an essence which is essentially foreign to production *qua* production. Indeed we may say that in an unintended way some of this swagger is institutionalised and given a kind of legitimation which escapes the notice of the rate setter. Certainly we may regard it as an unpredictable area which gives space and microstrategies for time wasting, systematic soldiering and resistance to intensification of the labour process.

It may even be argued much more speculatively that the particular physical style given to production in this way has more than provided the detail of concrete forms and experiential relations to production, but has altered the course of industrialisation itself. The peculiarly obstinate and trenchant form of the *mechanical* industrial revolution we know and still largely have, and its inability to fully give way to a more cybernetic industrial process when the technical processes are at hand, suggest that there are profound cultural gearings as well as more important structural factors keeping us to a certain kind of physical, visible, and mechanical work upon nature.

[5]   It is possible that this masculine style of expression influences the form of struggle and conflict in work. Certainly the union official or shop steward uses particular shopfloor cultural forms to mobilise the men – the spectacle or bluff, or strong and combative language – which are suffused with masculine feelings. This establishes a real expression of anger and opposition which may be very effective in the short term, and is certainly a force to be reckoned with. But it may be that longer term objectives simply cannot be conceptualised in this way, and are to a certain extent made inoperative by default at the face to face grassroots level. The masculine style of confrontation demands an appropriate and honourable resolution: visible and immediate concessions. If this is its price, however, it can be bought off at it. But the visibility of the concessions won in this way, especially in the form of a larger, masculine wage packet, may actually conceal longer term defeats over the less visible issues of control and ownership. It is possible to satisfy violent and possibly even frightening demands by short term, visible and dramatic concessions without changing any of those basic arrangements which the violence might appear to threaten. There are many other important strands of course, long term and continuing historical factors which must be given precedence, and this is simply speculation, but the particular combination of an affirmation of manual labour in a masculine and immediate style may have an important, though as yet unexamined role, in the particular social democratic and short run economic perspective so characteristic of the British labour movement.

[6]   In this light the question of the emergence of new classes under capitalism is

less interesting than the question of the reproduction of the old in new conditions. My general argument carries more theoretical implications for the status of the division mental/manual in relation to the development of 'new' classes than is relevant to outline in the main text.

In my view it is important to separate the following categories: distillation upwards of skill and control in the productive powers, the mental/manual ideological division; ideological class division; and real class divisions. The distillation upwards of skill is a real thing in capitalism. Quite apart from its meaning in the ideological realm it is an objective and necessary hallmark of capitalism that it sets further back the limits on production. It removes the constraints of immediate wants and direct appropriation and opens up the variable capacity of labour to produce up to the limits of social resistance or technical competence. Pushing back the limits of technical competence under capitalism means the progressive distillation upwards of control and planning and the intensification of labour.

This real tendency in productive capitalism provides a framework for a cultural and social interpretation of a division between mental and manual labour. The classic transference of collective properties of a system onto individual differences and qualities can be seen. It is here that the scope is essentially created for the rolling back of social constraints on production. It establishes the possibility of division.

For the wage earning working class, objective differences produced by the distillation upwards of control and planning produce little internal division for themselves. The actual experience of work for most blue collar people is very similar. With de-skilling, centralisation and rationalisation there is really only a marginal difference between working at one machine in the tool room, and working at the same machine on the production line. The commonality of experience persists even through the proliferation of differentiated conditions of work. Even obvious differences (e.g. between white and blue overalls) pall into insignificance beside the standard minute and standardised procedures. For the working class, the objective differences they face are much less important than the ideological resonances these bear. These resonances concern, at least in part, an articulation of sexism upon the mutual/manual division. The form of the mental/manual division as it returns to production is therefore profoundly different from the material base which supports its interpretation – especially in its patriarchal and sexist associations. Just because capitalism needs and can benefit from ideological distortions and divisions of this kind does not mean that it will be supplied with them.

The mental/manual division is therefore artificial: it is a construction upon the real which is dislocated from its originating structure, transformed and re-applied. It is never-the-less made, however, to partly bear the weight of class divisions. These are of two sorts: (a) internal divisions of consciousness within what is objectively the working class, so that those doing the same basic kinds of work believe themselves to be socially diverse; and (b) real class divisions which it helps to present as differences only in competence. The middle class is legitimated in part with a currency arising ultimately from an objective tendency of the forces of product-ion. The real tendency of the distillation upwards of skill and control is made to serve as the basis of ideological class divisions quite out of its context in the forces of production. Social divisions are presented and defended as productive divisions and in a society where production and the economy constitute the main ideological discourse this transference of legitimation proves near impenetrable.

The vital move in all this is the ideological transformation of real productive tendencies into sexually imbued mental/manual divisions. This is accomplished not by the inner laws of capital, nor by some obscure working of all time-structural factors, but with the help of contradictory, half-rational cultural and subjective processes.

Class divisions erected upon the mental/manual basis are, therefore, an illusion upon an illusion. Even insofar as the mental/manual division is legitimate it occurs strictly only within the working class. The mental aspects of labour – personalised as concrete mental labour in the illusion – engaged in expanding capitalist product-ion through concentration and intensification are truly contributing to the expan-sion not the absorption of surplus [i.e. it is not middle class]. It is no logic of its own that such labour is taken over, simplified and re-interpreted – especially in the light of the frank adoption of what is taken to be manual labour elsewhere – and used for the purposes of maintaining and legitimising class division. The objective distillation upwards of control and skill in the production process goes through some long loops into the cultural and the subjective and is also supplemented with new and specific inputs of meaning (sexism and school associations of 'mental' labour) before it appears socially as the mental/manual division.

It is wrong, however, to reserve the role of the maintenance of the social rela-tions of production simply for the ideological. Similarly it is wrong to see the logic of capitalism as essentially that of the maintenance of the social relations of pro-duction. This occurs also, and in the same moment (and could not take place without), as the logic of expanded production works through the continuous re-organisation of the labour process, distillation upwards of skill and control, and intensification of labour. There is a dialectical relation between the two.

None of this is to deny that what we might loosely call 'mental labour' is not associated with the middle class. The work of managing capital, dividing surplus (even where some of it goes back to the working class), and maintaining the social relations of production certainly involves mental operations. It is difficult, however, to sort out activities which *look* similar but differ in having either a basically social or a productive function. The foregoing analysis does not relieve the problem of objective differentiation between classes and class factions.

However, since we have seen that the mental/manual division does not arise from production alone, but from external processes which overlay and make a certain sense of real productive tendencies but are different from them, we need not attempt to spirit away the real divisions of production as Poulantzas does in his concern to penetrate the ideological process. If the ideology at least partly arises elsewhere we can take the guilt out of seeing real demarcations in production. This should help in our identification of real class factions. See N. Poulantzas, *Classes in Contemporary Capitalism*, NCB, 1975.

[7]   This is also true of the preparation of labour power amongst working class girls. It may be suggested that specific ideologies about sex roles – from familial models to mass media stereotypes – are taken up in the school context in specific kinds of practices which have implications for the diversion of cultural penetrations and for the subjective and collective development of a certain sense and definition of labour power. Wheedling around male teachers or challenging both them and female teachers with a direct sexuality, for instance, may help girls to think of their own vital powers as applicable, not to 'work' and 'industry', but to complex and contradictory sexual manipulation, comforting and familial construction of the 'home'.

Though I could not include girls in the focus of this research, the approach outlined here is equally applicable, at least at a formal level, to the study of girls in school.

7 The role of ideology

So far we have traced certain cultural penetrations and shown how they pass through internal 'limitations' into a surprising affirmation of manual labour power.

This has, of course, been at the risk of underemphasising the impact of external forces, state institutions and dominant ideologies acting upon working class kids. Though it is impossible in one study to delineate the full complexity of the cultural level with respect to outside determinants and structures it is possible to suggest one important form of interface between culture and ideology. Basically this is that ideology works on and in, produces and is partly produced by, the cultural. Ideology is, itself, partly influenced by cultural production, and for that, contains a modality and effectivity within cultural processes.

We have seen in the section on ethnography that many forms of the conventional dominant ideology – particularly as mediated through the school – are minced up, inverted or simply defeated by the counter-school culture. The crucial divisions, distortions and transferences which have been examined arise very often not so much from ideas and values mediated *downward* from the dominant social group, but from internal cultural relationships. Certain aspects of the working class cultural affirmation of manual labour considered here are profoundly important both ideologically and materially, and are, if anything, exported upwards to a largely uncomprehending official ideological apparatus. Division, sexism, racism and expression through manual labour power all occur much more strongly in civil society than in any state institution. In fact liberal democracy seems to set its face against these things. Its agents regard them as evils to be eradicated, not as the conditions of their own existence. This, of course, does not prevent the upwards export of ideological factors being used by the state, nor does it prevent the state from helping to reproduce them in contradictory and unintended ways. Indeed the good faith of state agents in various institutions may be one of the most important conditions for this reproduction under the regime of 'freedom' and 'equality' of the capitalist order.

We cannot, however, reverse the classic flow of ideology completely and suggest that the dominant ideology, state agencies and institutions take no active part in cultural processes other than providing the contexts in which they work.

It is these more direct, or 'dominant', effects which I reserve to the received notion of 'ideology'. They play an important role in the further limitation of cultural penetrations. They arise partly from the 'ruling ideas' of the age embodied in concrete institutions, and also in more informal media (TV, radio, press, film). They can be integrated on common ground – in the school for instance. Both, but especially the second, are influenced by and utilise meanings (differentially with differential distortions) and categories fed up to them from located class cultural processes.

For our purposes the two most important 'downward' vertical impacts of ideology on the counter-school culture are those of confirmation and dislocation. They confirm (in a somewhat circular fashion) those aspects and resolutions of cultural processes which are most partial to the current social organisation of interests and production, and dislocate (bringing something new into the local system) those which retain a degree of critical penetration of that system. Though they do not directly intervene in the subjective and cultural preparation of labour power, they play over, work up, and accentuate the real experiential processes. There is no machiavellian will in this, and elements of the proffered ideology are taken up only in precise articulation with real movement of working class cultural processes which, as we have seen, are rarely properly understood from above. Though the sense and logic of ideology may lie outside the cultural process, especially as contrasted with their internal generation of meaning, they are only taken up at different times and in different ways with respect to the contours and logics of particular cultural forms.

Confirmation

Careers teaching and advice is the most explicit ideological force bearing down on 'the lads' during their preparation for work. We saw before that the denoted aspects of careers advice and work are heavily blocked and re-interpreted. Some what we may term connoted messages do get through however, especially in terms of reinforcing the naturalism of social divisions, sexism and the inevitability of certain kinds of work already forming in the culture. Often it is not intended to transmit this information. It concerns such things as the general ambience of working life; a fascination with processes and machines; the division between those who work with their hands, and those who work with their heads; the apparent timelessness and inevitability of industrial organisation; the atomised competitive nature of the world of work around the corner; the hardness and inevitability of industrial work. It is not meant to be part, and is not received as part, of the general model which is presented for a rational careers choice. It comes from the sheer exposure to a vast number of films where working class people are seen working; from the apparently bewildering variety of jobs available; from film of moving machinery shot with a cameraman's instinct for the compulsive; from the utter assumption of authority in white collars directing blue coats.

Perhaps the clearest example here is that of role differentiation between the sexes in careers films. There is no obvious discrimination, and sex role stereotyping is never the subject of comment in these films. If anything, the explicit emphasis is developing more towards equality between the sexes, but the visual images and implied assumptions remain sexually divisive and are picked up by the sexism of 'the lads'.

In a cake factory we see only girls working and the voice-over tells us as we watch a girl icing a cake, 'Yes, she really is doing it that quickly, the film isn't speeded up'. Women are always doing intricate and fiddly things. Their only relation to more heroic occupations is one of fear and concern for their menfolk. In a film on trawling the young seaman is shown leaving an anxious and uncertain mother waving on the doorstep of her own proper domain, the home. She disappears back into the house when he is out of sight apparently to wait and brood there until his return. In contrast to this obvious display of feeling the male captain on the trawler is portrayed as a remote and powerful figure 'who cannot afford to show emotion'. His attention is on the size of the catch – not on the pastoral care of his new crewman.

In another film on farming the hardness and toughness of the life is not concealed, but neither is a dignity and stature which can only be referenced against masculine themes. The voice-over tells us that 'driving a tractor is not as easy as it looks', though Tom in the film finds it easy because 'he drove earthmoving equipment in the war'. In a concluding summary what can only be assumed to be a masculine audience is told that 'it's a hard life, but not for someone who's set their heart on it'.

One of the most important general functions of ideology is the way in which it turns uncertain and fragile cultural resolutions and outcomes into a pervasive naturalism. Ideology supplies many more examples to fix the one. The least challenging and most mystified cultural productions from below are shaped, concretised and supported to form a real and lived common denominator which allows all classes to come together into a kind of consensus which is the basis for reproduction of the status quo and the stage-army show of democracy. It is a consensus which may actually work against aspects of the official ideological canons. Still this is a small price to pay for stability, and is the form of a messy ideological concession which matches the more tangible concessions made to labour and social democratic demands from below. For the working class it often marks the break from one absolutism, bourgeois ideology, to a profounder one: the law of nature, the rule of commonsense.

For 'the lads' this hegemony of commonsense surrounds them all the time. It is partly self-created and partly produced by confirmatory ideological messages downwards. It is the apparent basis of action for those around them. It supplies naturalised social divisions and an omnipresent sexual chauvinism. Perhaps most important, and in a confirming distortion of their already distorted sense of their own labour power, it supplies an overpowering feeling that the way of the world is the way of work. Work of a certain direct and concrete kind. Even in their defiant and deviant acts there is always the reminder of this way. As they run from a shop with a stolen cake the shopkeeper shouts after them, 'I've got to work for that four bob'; when they have broken a chair in the school they are told, 'Your father worked for that'; at home they are told and shown in a multitude of ways, 'if you won't work you won't eat'.

Whilst work on the world must be done there are many ways of organising it. Their buried cultural penetrations tell 'the lads' more about its real social organisation than does this assertion of the blank necessity of work. It is a reification of the most partial and limited of their cultural 'insights'. It prevents their development into an exploration of other more equal and rational organisations of production.[1]

The subversion of ordered and sequential time implicit in the rhythm of the counter-school culture, whilst potentially radical in its implications, and whilst avoiding the tyranny of the 'narrative which follows', is delivered into inertia and domination by being profoundly naturalised. Time may not be that of constructed industrialism, but nor is it that of revolutionary choice. Bourgeois time is contrasted (in the lived out cultural forms) not with relativism and possibility, but with changeless nature and its inert drift. The break from bourgeois time is to a more absolute time. The 'partial penetration' of bourgeois time, as with so many other 'insights', becomes the reduction back of the cultural and relatively arbitrary to the 'natural', not its projection forward into new forms. It is the denial of history not the claiming of history, despite the promise of its break.

Dislocation

One of the main dislocating tendencies of ideology as it is expressed through the school and careers work is characteristically unintended.

As we have seen, the dominant form of careers teaching and 'teaching for life' stresses the real differentiation of job opportunities and their capacity to satisfy the range of human aspirations and hopes in a horizontal as well as a vertical direction. This direct thrust is largely deflected and its false logic penetrated by the counter-school culture. So far as 'the lads' are concerned, all jobs are basically the same. The ideological thrust is a very strong one, however, and it helps to dislocate cultural penetrations.

Since the ideological force for differentiation is so strong, and since it cannot convince its proper object, the effect of its thrust is reversed and acts centripetally, not to make jobs various, but to decentre the cause of their sameness. The lack of variety in work does not seem to have a simple cause (the productive logic of capitalism). The bewildering variety of films, the succession of speakers and the continuous pressure from staff to make a 'choice' from 'choices' acts, not to show variety of work in the world, but rather the amazing sameness of work across such a varied area and from such a variety of determinants and causes.

It is thus no one's fault that work is boring and tiring and mostly meaningless. There is no one to blame, no action to be taken, no fellow sufferers from the *same* rod. It seems natural that very different areas such as farming, milk rounds and factory work all turn out to have bosses breathing down the worker's neck, and boring work to be done in order to obtain the magic brown envelope. This feeds into, and is strengthened by, the naturalism considered earlier. Instead of a centred world of oppression from a specific and determinate social organisation of thought, production and interests we have the naturalistic world of a thousand timeless causes. Multi-determination brings misery and is the human condition. A single enemy might be fought, but never a million little ones pricking out the contours of the human condition.

A more direct dislocation of the informal group which aids the decentring and suppression of cultural penetrations is achieved in careers work sometimes, by an explicit stress on individualism. In the Hammertown school it is common practice to use the threat of the future and the competitiveness of the world of work to drive a wedge into the solidarity of the group:

Careers teacher I've told you before, it's not often I advocate selfishness but in
to fifth year   this case I must. Forget your friends sitting around you now, you
                 might be together now, having a laugh, and it doesn't matter.
                 But all the friends in the world are no use when it comes to
                 finding a job. When it comes to that you're on your own, you've
                 got to do it by yourself and no one can help (. . .) So, just this
                 time, be selfish, don't worry what your friends are doing, you
                 get out and look after number one, sort out your own jobs and
                 don't wait for your mates.

Of course, given the situation this is good advice, especially on an individual level – and it is made honestly and with care. The run-up to the end of the last year with half the fifth without a job is a thoroughly frightening prospect for all concerned: pragmatic individual decisions do need to be made. The pressure for jobs is much worse now than it was. The fact still remains, however, that ideology has always claimed necessity for its own, and used shortness of time to forestall other perspectives and possibilities.

This force for the disintegration of the group and its perspective or more exactly for the prevention of its proper emergence, can be aided by the interview with the careers officer. Often without much direct influence on 'the lads', its individualistic and sometimes meritocratic logic can sow the seeds of dissent which can flower – despite the countervailing cultural forces – into muffled forms of individualism and demarcation.

Certainly towards the end of the last year when employment looms ahead the individualistic differentiation suggested by the dominant ideology shows some firm roots through its cultural antinomy:

[In a group discussion]
Fuzz   I went in [to the careers interview], what it was . . . she tried to
        push anything onto me, 'You wanna be a paver', her says (. . .)
        'Do you wanna be a typewriter mender', I ain't said nothing
        about typewriters [laughter]. She says, 'Well, I'll just try and
        find some places for you, and I'll let you know'.
Joey   She knows what you can do, she ain't gettin', how much, thirty
        quid a week, for nothing. She's gotta know what the strength is,
        she probably knows what you're capable of (. . .)
Fuzz   She does like, she tries to push you off the job.

164

Fred	You want, say your mind's set, she'll push it off. Yeah, I had mechanics on my mind and she put me off it (. . .) she says you ain't gonna get this because you need physics and all this lot.
Joey	Well, that's it, that's what she knows, she knows you wouldn't get it.
Spike	'Cos if you applied for a job like that, and you know what you've gotta have, her tells you you've got to have physics, well . . . it's just wasting time, unless you're willing to learn (. . .)
Will	She's putting yer on the right lines, save wasting say a year while yer training and then they chuck yer out. Know what I mean, if you ain't capable of it like.

These are the main dislocating effects of the careers dynamic on the penetrations formed at the cultural level. This ideological play across cultural radicalism in conjunction with internal weaknesses pervaded and confirmed with naturalism cumulatively helps to produce an immobility characteristic, generally, of the working class. Although inequalities are often seen, exploitation recognised, and injustices and contradictions experienced every day, none of these things seems to point in the same direction. They do not have a common cause. If some exploit and some are exploited, if some are equal and others unequal this does not happen with the systematisation of classes. All have the chance to exploit others as well as be exploited. Nor can any system ever hope to change this. Chance, fate and luck basically deal the cards in any game. A quite marked degree of disenchantment with the prevailing system and a degree of knowledge of exploitation, coupled with culturally mediated (though distorted) and partially lived out penetrations of the capitalist system, can co-exist with a calm acceptance of the system and belief that there is no systematic suppression of personal chances in life. Suppression is recognised, but as no more than a random part of the human condition. Human nature, not capitalism, is the trap. Ideology has helped to produce that – though not simply from its own resources: it is believed, because it is partly self-made.

[In an individual interview at work]

John (working in a small factory producing a range of car accessories)	There's always more stuff waiting [to work on] but I mean, even me, I mean I'm on twelve pound a week. In a day I could bring a thousand pound in for 'em. I mean everything you're doing is money.
PW	What do you make of that?
John	I think every place, the management are better off . . . everywhere you'll find the same (. . .)
PW	Yet you still say things, by and large, are fair.
John	It's fair on the whole, but I mean obviously there is points where it ain't fair, like management, but I think it's everybody's fault, everybody's too greedy, that's all it is. I mean, even the poorest

of people, if they won, say, a million quid, they'd start . . . they'd still want more money although they'd be in a situation where they know people can't eat and things, they won't start giving it away to poorer people. Just everybody in general, they got greedy. But I think it's as fair as it can be.

[In an individual interview at work]

PW   I mean do you ever feel that (. . .) you're earning that, (. . .) the director's salary or profit?

Bill (trainee machinist in a wood machine shop)   Well it happens to everybody, it's got to, I think so anyway. But there's nothing you can do about it, it happens to everybody who works in a factory, not just this factory (. . .) I'd hope I can get up there, without them thinking about me, you know . . .

The internal interlocutor

The main importance of 'ideology' for the position outlined in this book lies not perhaps so much in its direct intervention (here only partially explored) or in its institutional supports or its political context, though these are important, so much as in the whole mode of its interface with the cultural process. In our contemporary working class culture ideology can be considered as the complement of informality.

The fundamental weakness in cultural forms is the *mediated* nature of personal experience and validation as they overlay and are influenced by cultural penetrations. Though the latter are the ultimate basis of relevance and vitality in a culture they are never expressed explicitly. They are not direct resources for struggle, they only have a similarity *in the stage of our analysis* with direct political statement: they do not replace policies or the level of conscious analysis. The very concreteness, denseness, buried radicalism, and relevance of informal cultural processes, and the very substance of their claim on individuals is their greatest weakness in the larger social context. The nature of informality as a mode of opposition in this society is that it reserves itself as the exception to the rule. It is blind to all of the other exceptions which together could overthrow the rule. It is unaware of its own 'rules'. The analysis of the world which actually directs its distinctively cultural responses remains silent. It is into this silence that ideology confidently strides. Whether right or wrong, whether penetrated or not it is *the* rule, it is *the* voice. It becomes the internal interlocutor for the weakness of cultural forms. Powerful ideologies, no matter what their content, always have the gift of formality, publicness and explicit statement. They can work within the scope of consensus and consent because nothing in oppositional *cultural* processes can displace their level of action and effectiveness.

In the case of 'the lads' and the counter-school culture there is a surprising tension and contradiction between those non-conformist and oppositional views which reject the institution and conventional morality. This contradiction is not always apparent. Its subterranean presence, however, reinforces the brake on cultural penetrations, limited as they are, and helps to further disorganise them and project their meanings on to unlikely objects.

Certainly every 'lad' occupies the contradiction in his own way, with different pressures of feeling and different kinds of resolution. It is the cultural *itself* which exhibits the surprising and continuing ambiguity. The logic of non-conformism, rejection and instrumentalism certainly underlies many actions, choices and behaviour. But this logic is always susceptible to being seen as an exception to the larger morality: the logic that holds for everyone else. The strength of personal experience – knowing how things really are – may over-ride this general logic for the purposes of daily life, but it by no means defeats it. Though the culture says to the individual, 'This is right for me', it can also seem to add 'even though it may be wrong in general'. The informal guides and validates real behaviour but it is held ultimately in the larger frame of the formal. Even where the formal is explicitly rejected in concrete situations its power to classify lingers on. Opposition and alternative interpretation are endlessly reserved off into exceptions to the rule.

[In a group discussion at school near the end of the last year]

Spanksy	It's the lobes [i.e. 'ear'oles'] that make the world we live in, not us.
Fuzz	The majority of people are like the lobes, ain't they really. They'll keep it going. If it was left to us (. . .) things'd go really wild and we wouldn't be able to cope.
PW	(. . .) would you like things to go that way?
Fuzz	No, 'cos you'd just think, you wouldn't be able to own anything, somebody'd be nicking everything.
Spike	You're stabbing yourself in the back there.
Fuzz	I ain't.
Joey	You am, you said if it was left to you, it'd all go wild.
Fuzz	It would.
Joey	But you wouldn't let it go wild. Then obviously it'd be up to you to stop it.
PW	Does that mean you want to be a lobe?
Joey	I don' wanna be a lobe, I just wanna be like me.
(. . .)	
Joey	You're saying you don't want to listen [to the teachers], you've got to listen sometimes. If you walk across there, and there's a big fucking hole in the floor, you'll fall down and break your neck, and you're not listening and you go and do it, then you're killing yourself.
Spanksy	[Heatedly] I wouldn't do it, would I?
Joey	Why not? You're saying you wouldn't listen (. . .)
PW	Since you're saying all this (. . .) and you're intelligent enough to

	see it, why aren't you intelligent enough to do it [listen to teachers and conform]?
Joey	I ain't saying I'm clever. I'm saying that none of us are clever enough to do it.
PW	But you're clever enough to point it out (. . .) why not do it?
Joey	'Cos nobody else does. I'd be out then I wouldn't be one of these like if I stopped playing up and stopped drinking. I'm an integral part of the group now. I can't get out of it.
Will	The teachers are trying to turn us into ear'oles, that's what we come to war'n it, teach us all this stuff, and we don't like ear'oles, so we think, well, if we become like an ear'ole like, we don't like them ourselves, we want to stop as we am.

The oppositional code which upholds the least 'desirable' aspects of 'the lads'' culture is most exposed to the dominant ideology. In the face of the internal interlocutor oppositional internal life can become merely an answer. The point here is not that 'the lads'' attitude to, say, violence, is right or wrong – for all its brutality it is actually a kind of reflection of competitive individualism under capitalism – but that it is asked to justify itself from within. Though cultural forms and the mediated 'rationality' of concrete actions penetrate it, subvert it or reverse it, the dominant ideology remains to ask questions, the very form of which seals the political out of the cultural.

[In a group discussion]

Spanksy	Everybody gets it though, I've got it on me own, he's been bashed on his own, why shouldn't he do it to someone else?
Joey	What about wars? You end up shooting some little fat nip. He might have ten kids at home and no wife to support them.
Pete	Yeah, it ain't right is it?
Bill	You ain't gonna think about that, 'cos while you're standing there thinking about it, he'd kill you.
(. . .)	
Joey	If he isn't man enough to take care of himself, or if he isn't er . . .
Spanksy	Or if I outnumber him four to one . . .
Joey	Or if he ain't fast enough to run (. . .)
Derek	Well how about Roberts [an 'ear'ole'], when he grows up and he picks on him?
Joey	That's his fault, that's his fault for not growing up tough enough.
Derek	It ain't his fault, it's probably his mum and dad who . . .
Joey	It's his own fault . . .
Bill	Our mum and dad, I bet you, our mum and dad . . .
Joey	[Heatedly] Well OK, OK then . . . It's his mum and dad's fault for bringing him up like a big poof.
Derek	'It's his mum and dad's fault'! You just said it was his fault.

168

Joey	Or if their mum and dad bring them up like a pouf, then it's their fault. It's always somebody's fault, it always goes back to somebody . . . 'cos no matter what age I am, I'd like to see some young fucking fifteen year old mug me (. . .)
PW	(. . .) do you really believe that or is it to try and make it all right somehow?
Joey	It's to try and make it alright really.
PW	(. . .) It's important to have the story, why's that?
Joey	I dunno, you've always got to justify it. You seem a bit of a cunt if you're just doing it like, er . . . I can't explain, really you've got to justify, you've always got to make it seem alright, and there is a reason for doing it (. . .) This justification is only for me, not for the police. The police, I'd just say, 'I didn't mean to do it' and start crying and all that bollocks, trying to get yourself out of it . . . you know, I've got to have some reason for justifying it like. I always feel you'll be called to answer for it, in this life or the next. You'll always be called to answer for the things you do.
PW	But if you don't believe it yourself, is it going to help?
Joey	It helps to an extent. Some cases, like, you can really justify it and it puts it out of your mind, whereas with others (. . .) you have to try and think summat out, to try and justify it, on the surface it justifies it, but not deep down. Deep down you know that it ain't right. It's just for when anybody else talks about it, you say, 'Ah well, there's some reason, I wasn't thinking of anything cruel'.

One of the time-honoured principles of cultural and social organisation in this country as it is enacted and understood at the subjective level is that of 'them' and 'us'.[3] That the 'them' survives in 'us' is usually overlooked. This internal division should not be surprising. In a peaceful social democratic society with real class divisions, the 'them' and 'us' can never be starkly clear. This basic distinction must be rehearsal and mediated and echoed around from the largest social units to the individual person. Even the most 'us' group or person has a little of 'them' inside. It is this which allows the 'us' to properly betray itself. Ideology is the 'them' in 'us'. It has been invited. Informality and the strength of personal validation unconnected with a political practice invite it. The very strength of the cultural struggle invites it. Once there it confirms partially and dislocates penetration. It prevents the 'us' from becoming a collective, assertive 'we'. Ideology is allowed to become instead the spurious 'we', the illusory unity from whom all reserve themselves severally but yield a sovereignty in the name of all others. The hall of mirrors of the national will needs each small mirror. Here we have looked at the construction and the interface of just one.

Notes

[1]   To avoid confusion I do not use the term hegemony but in many ways it would be useful here to denote the precise state of the *relationship* between ideology and located cultural forms. This is the sense in which I take Gramsci's use of the word though I have refrained from using it myself given the uncertainty existing already about its precise meaning. See A. Gramsci, *Prison Notebooks*, Penguin, 1973; P. Anderson, 'Antinomies in Gramsci's Thought', *NLR*, no. 100.

[2]   Even amongst some potentially radical workers with a definite political position basic insights about the nature of the capitalist system are often under-layed with a commonsense, absolutist view of the (unpleasant) fixed parameters of human nature which is given no dialectical interconnection at all with determining factors and mediating cultural forms. Social advance can be pictured from this basis as the necessity of a greater authority than capitalism to centrally direct people – even against their will – for the greater good of the whole. This is a skilled 'self-taught' worker in an engineering factory with pronounced, though unaffiliated, left wing leanings:

> I'll leave you with a thought. Have you ever been fishing? Well, you know the maggots in the tin? Well, humans in their collectivity, in their tenacity, and in their underlying greed, if you like, filth, nastiness, are just like that. You won't change it. You might get them to run along straight lines [laughs] or put them into compartments, like, but they'll still be maggots like (...) Capitalism's got the glitter, you know, they'll [the people] push through to see the bright lights. They [the capitalists] know that, the bright lights, the holidays in Bermuda, the adverts on the TV. They [the people] all think it will be them, and anyway they like the glitter even though none of them will ever do anything. The capitalists know that, and they know that it will never change. They know people are greedy and all they've got to do is show a little bit of ... glamour. They don't ask the workers to come up, they say it's their fault, 'It wasn't us, they want it ...'. But they still show it. It will never change. *

[3]   See for instance the classic work by Richard Hoggart, *The Uses of Literacy*, Chatto & Windus, 1957.

170

8   Notes towards a theory of cultural forms and social reproduction

Though we have only looked at one of the specific forms of the reproduction of labour power and of the subjective attitudes which allow it to be applied to the production process, there are some broad guides in this study for the development of a more general theory of cultural forms and their role in social reproduction, or more exactly for their role in maintaining the conditions for continued material production in the capitalist mode.

In the first place it warns against a too reductive or crude materialist notion of the cultural level. [1] It is not true, for instance, that the manpower requirements of industry in any direct sense determine the subjective and cultural formation of particular kinds of labour power.[2] Nor is it true that designated institutions such as the school produce - or could produce if in some way better run - classless, standardised packages of labour power. In its desire for workers of a certain type the reach of the production process must pass through the semi-autonomous cultural level which is determined by production only partially and in its own specific terms. Its own terms include consciousness, creativity of collective association, rationality, limitation, unintentionality and division. Its particular contributions to the formation of manual labour, for instance, are a particular kind of affirmation of manual activity and a penetration and transference of sets of divisions (principally manual/mental and male/female).[3]

In a more general sense it cannot be assumed that cultural forms are *determined* in some way as an automatic reflex by macro determinations such as class location, region, and educational background. Certainly these variables are important and cannot be overlooked but *how* do they impinge on behaviour, speech and attitude? We need to understand how structures become sources of meaning and determinants on behaviour in the cultural milieu *at its own level*. Just because there are what we can call structural and economic determinants it does not mean that people will unproblematically obey them. In some societies people are forced at the end of a machine gun to behave in a certain way. In our own this is achieved through apparent freedoms. In order to have a satisfying explanation we need to see what the *symbolic* power of structural determination is within the mediating realm of the human and cultural. It is from the resources of this level that decisions are made which lead to uncoerced outcomes which have the function of maintaining the structure of society and the status quo. Although it is a simplification for our purposes here, and ignoring important forms and forces such as the state, ideology, and various institutions, we can say that macro determinants need to pass through the cultural milieu to reproduce themselves at all.

In the case of job choice amongst the unqualified working class, for instance, we can *predict* final employment quite well from class background, geographical location, local opportunity structure, and educational attainment.[4] Certainly these factors will give us a better guide than expressed intention from individuals say during vocational guidance counselling. But what is it to say in any sense that these variables *determinate* job choice? We are still left with the problem of the forms of decision taking and of the apparent basis of willing acceptance of restricted opportunities. To quote the larger factors is really no form of explanation at all. It does not identify a chain or set of causalities which indicate particular outcomes from many possible ones. It simply further outlines the situation which is still in need of explanation: *how* and *why* young people take the restricted and often meaningless available jobs in ways which seem sensible to them in their familiar world as it is actually lived. For a proper treatment of these questions we must go to the cultural milieu which has been studied in this book and we must accept a certain autonomy of the processes at this level which both defeats any simple notion of mechanistic causation and gives the social agents involved some meaningful scope for viewing, inhabiting and constructing their own world in a way which is recognisably human and not theoretically reductive. Settling for manual work is not an experience of absolute incoherence walled from enlightenment by perverse cultural influences, nor is it that of atavistic innocence deeply inscribed upon by pre-given ideologies. It has the profane nature of itself, neither without meaning nor with other's meaning. It can only be lived because it is internally authentic and self made. It is felt, subjectively, as a profound process of learning: it is the organisation of the self in relation to the future.

If a distinctive level of the cultural is to be argued for then, how are we to specify its scope and nature? In my view it is misleading to attempt such a specification in mechanical or structural terms. Culture is not static, or composed of a set of invariant categories which can be read off at the same level in any kind of society. The essence of the cultural and of cultural forms in our capitalist society is their contribution towards the creative, uncertain and tense social reproduction of distinctive kinds of relationships. Cultural reproduction in particular, always carries with it the *possibility* of producing – indeed in a certain sense it really lives out – alternative outcomes. The main relationships which cultural forms help to reproduce are those of its members to the basic class groupings of society and with the productive process. Though the cases vary markedly I do not mean to imply that the main class cultures are conceptually different at this formal level.

Within this larger specification of process it is possible to outline three specific characteristics of the cultural level in our society which help to accomplish this main purpose. In the first place the basic material of the cultural is constituted by varieties of symbolic systems and articulations. These stretch from language to systematic kinds of physical interaction; from particular kinds of attitude, response, action and ritualised behaviour to expressive artefacts and concrete objects. There are likely to be distinctions and contradictions between these forms, so that for instance, actions may belie words, or logics embedded within cultural practices and rituals may be quite different from particular expressed meanings at the level of immediate consciousness. It is these stresses and tensions which provide the text for the more interpretative analysis required 'beneath' ethnography if the account of a culture is to be in any sense full.

In the second place I suggest that these things are produced at least in part by real forms of cultural production quite comparable with material production. Indeed in such areas as the generation of a distinctive style in clothing or changes made in the physical environment the production *is* material production. The basis for, and impetus of, this production is the informal social group and its collective energies at its own proper level. These energies I suggest are expressed in two connected forms. One is direct. It is the attempt to develop some meaningful account and representation of the world (often in an antagonistic relationship with language) of cultural members' place within it and to experiment with possibilities for gaining some excitement and diversions from it. The other is the profane investigation, the unconsciously revellatory probing of the world and its fundamental organisational categories, made in the course of the first process. The symbolic construction of the cultural world and of possibilities within it (the first) involves work on materials which - especially where they are new, only partially used or not properly ideologically incorporated - can bring real and unexpected results. These importantly derive from the nature of the materials, and the construction of the world, as they are worked upon by human agency for its own purpose. The first process is relatively intentioned - though not on an individual basis. The second can be quite decentred from the particular culture and implies no particular teleology though it importantly influences direct cultural activity and is the basis for its long term relevance and resonance for particular individuals.

Finally I suggest that cultural forms provide the materials towards, and the immediate context of, the construction of subjectivities and the confirmation of identity. It provides as it were the most believable and rewarding accounts for the individual, his future and especially for the expression of his/her vital energies. It seems to 'mark' and 'make sense' of things. I suggest in particular that the individual identity is importantly formed by the culturally learned sense, and subjective inhabitation, of labour power, and, in the reverse moment, that cultural forms themselves are importantly articulated, supported and organised by their members' distinctive sense of labour power and collective mode of effectivity in the world.

These are some of the main forms, functions and distinctive practices to be found at the cultural level. Their basic nature and their own full reproduction can only be understood, however, with respect to the way in which they help to produce the major relationships of the social group to itself to other classes and to the productive process. We might think of this process of reproduction as having two basic 'moments'. In the first place, outside structures and basic class relationships are taken in as symbolic and conceptual relations at the specifically cultural level. The form of this, I suggest, is of cultural (i.e. not centred on the individual or conscious practice) penetrations of the conditions of existence of the social group who support the culture. Structural determinations act, not by direct mechanical effect, but by mediation through the cultural level where their own relationships become subject to forms of exposure and explanation. In the second 'moment' of the process, structures which have now become sources of meaning, definition and identity provide the framework and basis for decisions and choices in life - in our liberal democracy taken 'freely' - which taken systematically and in the aggregate over large numbers actually helps to reproduce the main structures and functions of society. That is: the factories are filled on Monday morning and on every Monday morning with workers displaying the necessary apparent gradations between mental and manual capacity and corresponding attitudes necessary to maintain, within broad limits, the present structure of class and production. The processes which interact with the penetrations of the first 'moment' to produce a cultural field such that life-decisions are made to reproduce and not refuse or overthrow existing structures I call limitations. Where the penetrations tend towards an exposure of inequality and the determining relationships of capitalism and the construction of a possible basis of collective action for change by the social group concerned, the limitations break up and distort such tendencies and apply them to different ends. The limitations are specific to the cultural level, prevent any essentialist reading of cultural forms, cannot be derived from the production process itself, and include both inherent functional weaknesses of cultural process, the effects of relatively independent meanings systems such as racism and sexism, and the actions of powerful external ideologies. In the case we have studied cultural penetrations of the special nature of labour in modern capitalism become a strangled muted celebration of masculinity in labour power. Cultural penetrations stop short of any concrete resistance or construction of political alternatives in an unillusioned acceptance of available work roles and a mystified use of them for a certain cultural advantage and resonance - especially concerning sexism and male expressivity. We should not underestimate the surviving degree of rationality and insight here. That working situation is given only the minimum of intrinsic interest and involvement. The self-abnegation of living subordination as equality, and in the terms of the official ideology, in the face of daily evidence and experience to the contrary, is at least denied.

The argument here, then, is that cultural forms cannot be reduced or regarded as the mere epiphenomenal expression of basic structural factors. They are not the accidental or open-ended determined variables in the couplet structure/culture. They are part of a necessary circle in which neither term is thinkable alone. It is in the passage through the cultural level that aspects of the real structural relationships of society are transformed into conceptual relationships and back again. The cultural is part of the necessary dialectic of reproduction.[5]

This view of cultural forms and reproduction is both pessimistic and optimistic. It is pessimistic in suggesting the irony that it is in the form of creative penetrations that cultures live their own damnation and that, for instance, a good section of working class kids condemn themselves to a future in manual work. It is optimistic, however, in showing that there is no inevitability of outcomes. Subordination and failure is not unanswerable. If there are moments when cultural forms make real penetrations of the world then no matter what distortions follow, there is always the possibility of strengthening and working from this base. If there has been a radical genesis of conservative outcomes then at least there exists a *capacity* for opposition. We have the logical possibility of radicalness. Structuralist theories of reproduction [6] present the dominant ideology (under which culture is subsumed) as impenetrable. Everything fits too neatly. Ideology always pre-exists and pre-empts any authentic criticism. There are no cracks in the billiard ball smoothness of process. All specific contradictions and conflicts are smoothed away in the universal reproductive functions of ideology. This study suggests on the contrary, and in my view more optimistically, that there are deep disjunctions and desperate tensions within social and cultural reproduction. Social agents are not passive bearers of ideology, but active appropriators who reproduce existing structures only through struggle, contestation and a partial penetration of those structures.[7] Quite apart from a particular society's structural characteristics, it is the type of this contested settlement which helps to give it its special nature. A society, for instance, is deeply marked by the specific forms in which its labour power is prepared.

This warning against too closed or pre-emptive a notion of cultural forms and reproduction is also a case for recognising a necessary uncertainty. Too often it is assumed that capitalism implies thoroughly effective domination of the subordinate class. Far from this, capitalism in its modern, liberal democratic forms *is* permanent struggle. What is accommodating in working class culture is also what is resistant so that capitalism is never secure. It can never be a dynasty. Insofar as it has a stability it is the dynamic one of risking instability by yielding relative freedoms to circles of unintention in the hope of receiving back a minimum consent for rule. There is thus a deep uncertainty and changing balance of ever-heightening contradictions at the heart of capitalism. Full contested cultural reproduction is more important to capitalism than to any other system but the conditions for its own survival are also the conditions for its replacement.

Capitalist freedoms are potentially real freedoms and capitalism takes the wager, which is the essence of reproduction, that the freedoms will be used for self-damnation. The dominant class could never batten down the hatch on these freedoms without help from below. And if these freedoms are not used at this time for their full subversive, oppositional or independent purposes capitalism will not take the blame. It makes its own wager on uncertainty, others can make theirs.

The profound – though not limitless – uncertainty at the heart of the system should also warn against too functionalist a view of class cultural processes. Certainly, for instance, the circles of contradiction and unintention described in this book 'work' for capitalism at this point in time. But so must any system 'work' which is stable enough to be studied. There must therefore always be a functional level of analysis in reproduction. But this must not be allowed to obscure the struggles which through uncertainties motor the working parts. Many aspects of 'the lads' culture, for instance, are challenging and subversive and remain threatening. There are many breaks, lags, antagonisms, deep struggles and real subversive logics within and behind cultural processes of reproduction which fight for out-comes other than those which satisfy the system for the moment.

This uncertainty also warns against any simple teleological notion of capitalist development. The huge growth of the state in welfare and education, for instance, is not necessarily in any 'best' interests of capitalism. It has to some extent been forced on it by competing groups using their own real freedoms for self-advance-ment as they have seen it. Of course state agencies have been utilised and modified to help cool out, or drive out, problems which capitalism produces but cannot solve. But whilst they help to solve problems these institutions cannot wholly be absorbed back into capitalism. They maintain spaces and potential oppositions, keep alive issues, and prod nerves which capitalism would much rather were for-gotten. Their personnel are in no simple sense servants of capitalism. They solve, confuse or postpone its problems in the short term very often because of their commitment to professional goals which are finally and awkwardly independent from the functional needs of capitalism. They may help, unconsciously, in unin-tended forms of class reproduction but all the same this may also involve the heightening of opposition and criticism which the dominant class could well do without. State agencies and institutions often take contradictions further, and faster, and in stranger, more displaced and disoriented forms, than any pure capital-ism could dream of. The bureaucratic educational welfare state machine so characteristic of Western capitalism must be seen in part as the result of a cumula-tive encrustment which capitalism manages to turn to its advantage rather than as the expression of its own will or straightforward domination. Its own uncertainty makes it prone to mutation and further gives it life in mutation.

Reproduction and state institutions

This study gives more precise suggestions, especially concerning the significance of systematic misrecognition and unintended consequence, for conceptualising the role of institutions in cultural and social reproduction.

In the first place we must not expect particular kinds of reproduction to take place tidily in discrete kinds of institution. Just as the school and its formal time-table lies tangential to the real processes of learning and of the preparation of manual labour power, other kinds of institution may lie awkwardly against real social functions. The particular meaning and scope of the role of institutions in reproduction may be less to do with their formal nature and manifest communi-cations than with the unintended and often unseen results of their relationships and habituated patterns of interaction with located and informal cultures. Further-more, the same institution may play very different roles in different kinds of reproduction, so that, for instance, the school is more central to the preparation of mental labour power than to manual labour power.

In the second place it suggests that institutions cannot be studied as simple unities. They have at least three levels which we might describe as the official, the pragmatic and the cultural. At the official level an institution is likely to have a formal account of its purpose in relation to its view of the main structural and organisational features of society and how they interrelate (or might be made to interrelate). In a liberal democratic society such as ours, it would be quite wrong to assume that state institutions like the school are run in any obvious or intentional way for the benefit of the dominant class (as are private schools for instance). Their conscious and centrally directed aim is not to promote two very different kinds of ideology suited to the needs of acknowledged inferior and superior classes. Their educated, concerned and honest liberal agents would not countenance that. Furthermore, this level of institutional practice is most directly related to the political realm proper and all the determinants and interests which operate there. Part of the dominant social democratic political pressure since the war has been to equalise provision, or at least to equalise access to provision through the reform and development of institutions. Convergence, not divergence, has been the main official tendency.

It is, of course, an absolute requirement for the existing social system that the same standards, ideologies and aspirations are not really passed on to all. The success of the official ideology, or what amounts to the same thing the demise of its oppositional cultural reproduction, in many institutions would be catastrophic for social reproduction in general. The 'transition' from school to work, for instance, of working class kids who had really absorbed the rubric of self-development, satisfaction and interest in work, would be a terrifying battle. Armies of kids equipped with their 'self-concepts' would be fighting to enter the few meaningful jobs available, and masses of employers would be struggling to press them into meaningless work. In these circumstances there would indeed be a much greater 'problem' of 'careers guidance' than we have now. Either a gigantic propaganda exercise of wartime proportions or direct physical coercion would be needed to get the kids into the factories. Since this is not yet required, and since social reproduction of the class society in general continues despite the intervention of the liberal state and its institutions, it may be suggested that some of the real functions of institutions work counter to their stated aims. This misrecognition, it can be suggested, helps to maintain many of the cultural processes taking place within particular institutions which contribute towards social reproduction. At the second, the pragmatic level, official ideologies and aims are mediated to the agents and functionaries of particular institutions. They are likely to appreciate something of the more theoretical rationale for the prevailing or coming 'official' ideology, but they are also mainly interested in their own face to face problems of control and direction and the day to day pressures of their own survival within the inherited institution. They run a practical eye over 'official' ideology. They will adopt newly sanctioned ideologies, for instance, only when they seem to offer real and practical help – though they may well justify the change, even to themselves, with the rubric of the purer received ideology. It is this practical engagement which very often prevents the agents from seeing what is happening below them.

At the third level 'below' the others are the cultural forms of adaption of the institution's clients as their outside class experience interacts with the practical exigencies and processes of the institution as they strike them. One of the important variants of this is likely to be an oppositional informal culture which may well actually help to accomplish the wider social reproduction which the official policy has been trying to defeat or change. As we have seen in this book, where they occur at a cultural level the destruction of official myths and illusions and a canny assessment of the world do not stop incorporation into that world. They can aid it. If the specificity of the institution and vulnerability of its ideology help to promote certain kinds of oppositional cultures and their characteristic penetrations it also helps to disorientate them into their accommodative mode by providing or strengthening powerful limitations. In particular it is likely to generate divisions especially in the area of its own proper concerns and also between the formal and informal. Though the school, for instance, is not effective in the way it hopes to be, it is an extremely important location, and proximate cause of renaissance of oppositional class culture experienced by a good percentage of working class boys during their 3rd, 4th and 5th years at school. This renaissance leads to changes and refinements in the subjective inhabitation of labour power which lead to very concrete outcomes. In contradictory and unintended ways the counter-school culture actually achieves for education one of its main though misrecognised objectives – the direction of a proportion of working kids 'voluntarily' to skilled, semi-skilled and unskilled manual work. Indeed far from helping to cause the present 'crisis' in education, the counter-school culture and the processes it sponsors has helped to prevent a real crisis.

I suggest that all major changes in institutional organisation might be thought through in terms of these three levels. In the case of education, for instance, progressivism has been developed and theorised as an official ideology by academics in conjunction with wider social democratic, political and institutional movements to increase educational provision and access for the working class. At the pragmatic level, however, progressivism is taken up in schools mainly as a practical solution to practical problems without any real shift in basic philosophies of education. At the cultural level it can be argued that often 'progressivism' has had the contradictory and unintended effect of helping to strengthen processes within the counter-school culture which are responsible for the particular subjective preparation of labour power and acceptance of a working class future in a way which is the very opposite of progressive intentions in education. It is this strengthened cultural reproduction in relation to the school which of course guarantees the future of educational experiment by always limiting the scope of its success.

This is no simple argument against, or criticism of, progressivism or other kinds of institutional reform. Any kind of educational, or other, change will encounter its own forms of unintention, contradiction, and unseen forms of reproduction in complex links to class cultures and the objective requirements of the outside system. This is rather the point: that no institutional objectives, no moral or pedagogic initiative, moves in the clear still air of good intention and Newtonian cultural mechanics. Every move must be considered in relation to its context and likely circles of effectiveness within the netherworld (usually to institutional and official eyes) of cultural reproduction and the main world of social class relationships.

Progressivism and RSLA, for instance, have actually addressed real problems, have protected kids a little longer from the harshness and inequality of industry, and have helped to give them – in unintended and unexpected ways of course – a definite kind of insight and cultural advance not available to their parents. We must not, simply, be naive about what is meant by advance. We must ask in what form, for whom, in which direction, and through what circles of unintention, with what reproductive consequences for the social system in general, particular advances are made.

Of course there is a danger in generalisation and extrapolation. Different agencies and institutions have different dominant/subordinate, professional/client relations, different lags, breaks and reversals of ideology, different moments and points of struggle, different intersections with the class system and modes of cultural reproduction. It is possible to suggest, however, that, if nothing else, many institutions may share, in some way and at some level, a self-deluding belief in the unity of their own official ideology. What is certain is that such ideology is not uncritically transmitted downwards until those at the bottom in some way receive and have and are nothing. At some point there is a break and reversal in this ideological chain which has extremely important connections with, and crucial reproductive functions with respect to, the rest of the social system. It might be suggested that in many institutions it is the characteristic sense of cultural penetration (impeded by limitations) which actually motivates members in concrete actions, and that it is often in the Parthian victory of informal mastery and control that social reproduction is decisively sealed.

Notes

[1]   Marx, for instance, never explains how labour power comes to be formed, subjectively inhabited, given an applied to the production process in a certain way. There is almost a sleight of hand in the conceptual use of the reserve army of the unemployed to explain the ideological obedience of workers. No matter what the immediate pressures and the added force of competition, we still need to understand the processes which produce large supplies of labour power of a certain kind in the first place – unemployed or not.

[2]   Though I have argued that production does not mechanically determine the cultural level and those processes there which help to form the labour power it requires, it is nevertheless clear that the workers who are produced in whatever way must broadly satisfy the global needs of production at any particular point. These requirements are to some extent influenced by the forms in which they are satisfied and vice-versa but we still need to confront the manner of articulation of their relatively independent logics and development. A few preliminary comments can be made in this complex area from the evidence of this study.

The emergence of monopoly capitalism marks an unprecedented move towards control and intensification of the labour process. Competitive capitalism with the greater centrality of the market place in commodity exchange had acted as a brake on this control. It supplied the possibility of concrete alternatives for the individual labourer if a particular job became too arduous. It also tended to set a limit on the pace of technological advance and innovation because investment in these things risked too long a cycle of capital return (or even an insufficient return if the investment were made not for optimal build up of capital but for competitive product advance) to be viable in the short run interests which prevail on the free market. (This is the same logic which prevents individual capitalists from introducing the shorter working day: see Marx, *Capital*, Aveling and Moor (translations, p. 256). The modern corporation is relatively insulated from these market pressures and can proceed with the control and intensification of the labour power it buys the use of more according to its own internal logic of production. There is a real tendency towards increased intensification of labour processes, and a further wresting of control from, and decomposition of craft skills (c.f. Braverman, *Labour and Monopoly Capital*, Monthly Review Press). Control has moved centrally and upwards for the specialised and rationalised control of large scale production. There is, therefore, a need in general (that is, apart from the still small highly skilled fraction which has control passed on to it) for a less skilled workforce open to greater systematisation and a higher working pace coupled with a degree of flexibility to allow interchange between increasingly standardised processes. In a word, monopoly capitalism requires an accelerated shift in its workforce from craft 'idiocy', pride in the job, and personal fusion in work activity.

The cultural and institutional processes described in this book – taken as a whole – tend to produce large numbers of workers approaching this type. The nature of the 'partial penetrations' we have looked at are precisely to devalue and discredit older attitudes to work, feelings of control and meaning at work. In certain respects these developments are progressive with respect to monopoly capital and are likely to supply the instrumental, flexible, un-illusioned, 'sharp', unskilled but well-socialised workers needed to take part in its increasingly socialised work processes.

The 'advancedness' of proletarian workers must not, of course, go too far. The desertion of old skills, mystiques, and protective attitudes must not become the rejection of modern work or a complete understanding of its meaninglessness. The freedom, independence and willingness to change of the new instrumental workers must not be allowed to degenerate into lack of loyalty and erosion of motivations of any kind. Most of all, the objectives social interdependence of these advanced proletarian workers – with fewer prejudices, blindnesses and limitations than any before – must not become an interdependence and solidarity of *consciousness* and political purpose.

The demands arising from modern monopolies are therefore mutually contradictory. Their need for a more advanced (or less skilled and job bound) kind of worker also invites a worker without loyalty and motivation, one who is potentially susceptible to mass critical political perspectives.

This contradiction is, however, I suggest also likely to be partly saved by the cultural forms in which labour power is supplied. If industry's needs for a more flexible and unillusioned worker are mainly satisfied by one kind of working class cultural processes (in a mediated relation to these very needs of course), this culture also provides (again in a mediated relation) other processes which produce forms of attachment, divisions and unexpected motivation which go some way towards meeting its needs for a kind of loyalty and political dislocation. The conformist cultural variants of the preparation of labour power, especially in relation to the non-conformist ones, are likely to produce workers who are committed to their activity and likely to believe in the intrinsic value of work and associated qualifications even despite their tenuous objective substance. Furthermore the mere existence of these opposed forms of attachment creates the basis for hierarchy and division in the workforce which can be exploited to break up solidarity and also legitimate, ideologically, real class divisions. These sets of cultural bifurcations and distortions which derive from the semi-autonomous cultural level make it, in fact, extremely difficult to 'see through' them to judge, expirically, actual changes in the production process. Still, it may be suggested that for the moment the needs of industry and the cultural forms of the reproduction of labour power seem to be moving in a rough if contradictory harmony. The long run contradiction cannot, however, be resolved. The ideological and material processes move in fundamentally opposite directions. The labour process itself is becoming more de-skilled and proletarianised, whilst jobs within it are apparently becoming more stratified and differentiated – especially as regards qualifications. It must remain an open question whether the elemental divisions between manual and mental labour and between sex genders in the working class will continuously reproduce and extend divisions when the objective technical divisions of the productive process are further lessening.

One of the most interesting management innovations in the control and direction of a changing workforce is the 'new' human relations: techniques of work re-structuring, job satisfaction and autonomous work groupings.* There has been a good deal of bafflement concerning the inner logic of these techniques in relation to forms of worker consciousness and resistance. In my view the most illuminating perspective on these developments is to see it as a response to an advance (in contradiction) of proletarian consciousness. Strict division of the labour process and high morale and company loyalty are becoming harder to enforce as working class cultural forms and associated actions may be seen to press through its self-imposed mental/manual barriers towards a lived understanding of abstract labour, through its own sexist barriers to the strict meaninglessness of work, to a greater informal control of work, and to a greater oppositional solidarity – at least in the powerful realm of the located and informal. The 'new' human relations marks a pre-emptive attempt by management to contain this developing consciousness, and utilise it for a greater flexibility and higher motivation.

The final price for such a strategic settlement might be quite high, both in the sense that the strict productive logic of the greatest efficiency (a prime tenet for capitalist stability) has been abandoned, and also that conditions are created more conducive to the development of more critical and challenging views amongst the workforce. In the short term it is possible that production might rise because of less disruption, and opposition decrease because of the relative atomisation of the workforce. If we characterise the whole move, however, as the ordered internalisation - on conditions - of the foreman into the informal culture which otherwise anarchically usurps and challenges his role, then we can see that there is a strict limit to dealing with opposition to, say, the managing director in this way. Concessions and devaluation of authority from the formal to the informal is a dangerous strategy, and all forms of participation are two-edged. The wager for capitalism must be whether it can come to a new stabilised division between control and obedience, or whether it is set in action on a permanent gentle slope of minor concessions. We may expect an ideological build up of division and legitimation, so to speak, further up the river, to choke off too much ambition in claims for control of the workplace.

Another way to conceptualise these changes in management technique is to picture the focus of conscious management enterprise moving from the forces of production to the relations of production. Where previously these relations had been seen simply as supplying the conditions for the operation of the forces of production, they are now being conceived of as forces in their own right.

Taylorism and Fordism are aimed at increasing the efficient and rational utilisation of the forces of production. This involves an objective socialisation of production which is likely, in its turn, to bring about what we might think of as a socialisation of consciousness where interdependence is massively recognised and used by workers to control production. Taylor was partly working in his own time against 'gold bricking' and 'systematic soldiering', but the very rationalisation and expansion of production produced by his techniques in this way creates the conditions for a greater informal control of the work process. Manipulation and control of the forces of production therefore bring real visible consequences for the social relations of production which themselves act back on the forces.

We can understand the first wave of human relations, originating in the work of Elton Mayo, as an attempt to stulify and freeze the counterproductive tendencies of the social relations of production thus affected. These 'Mark I' HR techniques in no sense consciously reorganise the forces of production to take account of social relations. They operate within the group itself - at the superstructural level so to speak - to manage, manipulate and accommodate group processes, particularly through the influence of the group leader.

The emergence of the second wave of human relations techniques marks the limits of these 'idealist' solutions. There is a more materialist conception of the informal group and workplace cultures at play. Instead of merely trying to limit the unfortunate consequences of informal group activity within a fixed labour process, the labour process itself is recognised as a determinant of the informal group, and its manipulation is entertained as a means of controlling cultural forms. The success or failure of this so far limited micro-experiment of a controlled test-tube socialism might be less important than capitalism's recognition, at certain pressure points, that it is the social relations of production which materially limit production and not the inadequate development of the forces of production. We see here the infinite variety of resources and flexibility in capitalism as it sets its acid to work on the conditions of its own supremacy. It may even be right to think yet again that the entanglements of working class radicalism will be worse confounded by free concession, and that a new level of stasis is possible within a further mutated capitalist system.

*See for instance, Mary Weir (ed.) *Job Satisfaction*, Fontana, 1976; P. Warr and T. Wall, *Work and Well-Being*, Penguin, 1975; N. A. B. Wilson, *On the Quality of Working Life: A Report Prepared for the Department of Employment*, Manpower Papers, No. 7, HMSO, 1973; Report of a Special Task Force to the Secretary of Health, Education and Welfare, *Work in America*, MIT Press, 1973; W. I. Paul and K. B. Robertson, *Job Enrichment and Employee Motivation*, Gower Press, 1970; F. Herzberg, *Work and the Nature of Man*, Staple Press, 1968.

[3]   Elements of the productive process do have to bear the weight of, reproduce in some form and return, such ideological constructions placed on its own processes.

[4]   A point made tellingly by Ken Roberts in criticism of the careers service and the centrality of vocational guidance in the school within it, 'Where is the careers service heading', *Careers Bulletin*, DE, 1976.

[5]   In this attempt to criticise a reductive or epiphenomenal reading I do not wish to imply that structures are either fully transformed into ideas and symbols – this would be to posit an historicist clarity of cultural forms which I have rejected – or do not have alternative modes of effectively on the cultural and other levels through ideology, the state and institutions. There are other forms of social reproduction than the cultural which is why I have separated the terms.

[6]   See for instance, L. Althusser, 'Ideology and Ideological State Apparatuses' in B. R. Cosin (ed.), *Education: Structure and Society*, Penguin, 1972.

[7]   Mainstream sociology too, with its notion of socialisation, and its implication of passive transmission, misses the tension and uncertainty of this process. It is not that the working class is for all time different from the middle class (for whatever reason) and passes on its disadvantages timelessly and unbreakably to succeeding generations (cf. the cycle of poverty and like theories) through ineluctable laws of socialisation.

Cultural patterns and activities and attitudes are developed in precise conjunction with real exigencies, and are produced and reproduced in each generation for its own good reasons. Patterns of the development of labour power for a specific kind of application to industry must in every generation be achieved, developed and worked for in struggle and contestation. If certain obvious features of this continuous reproduction and ever freshly struck settlement show a degree of visible continuity over time this should not lead us to construct iron laws and dynamics of socialisation from this mere succession of like things. The underworkings of these continuities are more complex, uncertain, related outwards, and liable to change than can be contained in the notion of socialisation.

9   Monday morning and the millennium

> For a mass of people to be led to think coherently (. . .) about the real,
> present world, is a 'philosophical' event far more important and 'original'
> than the discovery by some philosophical 'genius' of a truth which remains
> the property of small groups of intellectuals (. . .) it is not a question of intro-
> ducing from scratch a scientific form of thought into everyone's individual
> life, but of renovating and making 'critical' an already existing activity.
>
> Antonio Gramsci,
> from the *Prison Notebooks*,
> pp. 325 and 330

The introduction posed the question of how and why it is that working class lads
come to accept working class jobs through their own apparent choice. We can say
that for a good proportion, the disaffected – in relation to whom the conformist
case can be better understood – this is in the form of a partial cultural penetration
of their own real conditions and a mystified celebration of manual work which
nevertheless preserves something of a collective, rational, though incomplete, logic.
I have suggested that this can be understood as a form of cultural reproduction
which helps to contribute towards social reproduction in general. Some of the
theoretical implications of this position are tentatively explored in the previous
chapter. Finally I would like to consider some of the implications of this research
for the practical/political level and particularly for the two regions most clearly
involved with the concerns of this study: vocational guidance and education for
disaffected working class youth.

The whole level of cultural presentation, analysis and determination explored in
this book suggests the general possibility of effectivity at the cultural level. This
seems especially so if, as I argue, cultural processes of reproduction pass through a
moment of real penetration and potential radical solidarity. With the frequency
with which cultural forms reproduce the old they have challenged the old. A naive
reading of this position might suggest that a simple intervention might be made, or
a direct separation made in some way between the progressive and the regressive.
The problem with this interpretation is, of course, that it forgets the essential unity
of the cultural level (which the ethnographic account for instance insists upon) and
overlooks the complex ways in which the cultural has specifically internal weaknesses which are part of its nature and which are easily invaded by ideology.

Furthermore the cultural level is in no sense free-floating. It has a mediated
relationship to structural factors and often a precise material and organisational
institutional context which underwrite characteristic forms of relationship, patterns
of balance and complementarity. The couplet accommodation/resistance is riveted
tight. The terms do not often shake themselves loose and will not by mere wishing.

In terms of pedagogic or counselling practice it is wrong to assume that levers exist within the cultural milieu alone which can be operated to produce desired results. The essential meaning of the analysis in Part II was precisely that cultural forms cannot be understood with respect to themselves and upon their own base. In order to understand the counter-school culture we had to go to alternative starting points and construct the culture partly from outside: from the nature of labouring in modern capitalism; from general abstract labour; from sexism; from ideology. We cannot now naively return to discrete cultural forms and independent cultural initiatives to yield a full and properly effective programme for vocational guidance and the schooling of the disaffected working class. Interventions and reforms will pass through all the circles of unintention, contradiction and cultural reproduction in relation to structural factors which have been identified in this book.

On the other hand practitioners have the problem of 'Monday morning'. If we have nothing to say about what to do on Monday morning everything is yielded to a purist structuralist immobilising reductionist tautology: nothing can be done until the basic structures of society are changed but the structures prevent us making any changes. There is no contradiction in asking practitioners to work on two levels simultaneously – to face immediate problems in doing 'the best' (so far as they can see it) for their clients whilst appreciating all the time that these very actions may help to reproduce the structures within which the problems arise. Within the doom the latter seems to place on the former there are spaces and potentials for changing the balances of uncertainty which reproduce the living society. To contract out of the messy business of day to day problems is to deny the active, contested nature of social and cultural reproduction: to condemn real people to the status of passive zombies, and actually cancel the future by default. To refuse the challenge of the day to day – because of the retrospective dead hand of structural constraint – is to deny the continuance of life and society themselves. It is a theoretical as well as a political failure. It denies the dialectic of reproduction. The necessary tension between short term actions taken in good faith in relation to barely understood laws of growth and transformation and their unpredictable long term outcomes is a common feature of life for all social agents: it is what every mother and father is exercised in every day. There is no reason why we cannot ask those whose *work* is social and caring to operate under the tension and irony of the relationship between two levels in their activity.[1]

This whole study has shown both a degree of effectivity and a degree of non-correspondence (to structures) in the cultural level. This suggests, pace the foregoing, that there is *some* room for action at the cultural level, and certainly that there is scope here for exposing to their members more clearly what their own cultures 'tell' them about their structural and social location. At least the illusions of official and other ideologies can be exposed. An approach is possible which neither insults, nor ignores the working class and yet is tuned to the importance – though not inevitable closure – of structural factors. It would be wrong to suggest detailed programmes here. This book makes an analysis available, however, which might be thought through in the different areas by others. A number of general principles can be stated, however, and some of their obvious implications drawn out for the two main professional areas which have been encountered in this study.

*recognise the cultural level in its relative unity rather than be alienated by its most obvious and external, possibly personally insulting, elements.

*recognise the potential or submerged meanings behind attitudes and behaviour which must be, for themselves, strictly condemned.

*try to understand what reproductive functions might be accomplished by the cultural level, rather than argue naively either for the equivalence or superiority of cultural forms to the dominant ones.[2]

*learn from cultural forms and try to distinguish between their penetrations and limitations – especially in relation to dominant ideological influences. Explore how penetrations might be extended to systematic analyses of society.

*act to expose not mystify or strengthen cultural processes.

*recognise the structural limits of activity at the cultural level, and organise politically to act on behalf of, as well as amongst, your constituency if structural change is desired.

The whole area of vocational guidance is coming under increasing scrutiny now – particularly in relation to the un- (or low) qualified.[3] In one sense there seems to be more scope for action in vocational guidance than in education proper, at least by careers officers, because counsellors are not so constrained by established institutions: in this case the material context of the school and the teaching paradigm. On the other hand careers officers deal directly with the real world, with inequality, and the role of knowledge and qualifications in the distribution of job opportunities in those exchanges which help to structure the teaching paradigm in the first place. It is interesting that vocational guidance counsellors often have a remarkably detailed if submerged knowledge of the cultural level. In a certain sense the cultural milieu and its mediations is the material in their hands. It is from this basis ultimately that they make sense of the various patterns of the transition into work. Certainly they are frequently more sympathetic to such as 'the lads' than teachers are and operate often a systematic inversion or re-coding of evaluations made by the school of individuals in the counter-school culture. This different form of attunement to oppositional variants of working class culture is one of the sources of the usual tension between the school and careers officers. There is also a real attempt to register what are basically cultural values and interests in the notion of variety in individuals, in the range of their possible talents beyond the simply academic, and in the ways in which they are taken up in 'life styles', and 'patterns of leisure'.

The problem is that real forms of cultural understanding are broken up and distorted by an omnipresent ideology of individualism. Some values are detached from the cultural and projected on to individuals and their internal characteristics, other aspects of the cultural are decontextualised, atomised and associated with the intrinsic natures of particular jobs. It then becomes apparently possible to use the basic individualistic paradigm of matching individuals to work which actually has real currency only for middle class choice. The whole ideology and language of developmental psychology with its centrality of the individual and the meaningful choices open to him makes its entrance. 'Personal development', 'self concept', 'occupational choice' all gain a currency where they are only really a tautological and individualised distortion of the cultural level turning on the pivot of spurious difference – in individuals and in the jobs available.

Perhaps the main implication of this study for the practice of vocational guidance is that the cultural level can be recognised as a relatively discrete entity with its own logic and forms of – distorted – penetration of the real conditions of the social agents involved.

A number of, so to speak, short term though principled suggestions can be made. In order to contribute to longer term structural change, and to a basic change in the opportunities and quality of work faced by working class kids, it is necessary to organise more politically in professional and other bodies on behalf of the forces which are uncovered and examined in the short term.

*use a cultural perspective to identify likely 'problem cases' – those who are isolated from, or in the process of crossing between, cultural categories.

*encourage re-entry into education for working class kids for whom the 'cultural celebration' wanes and leaves them trapped. Work for higher grants for this category.

*recognise that these suggestions are ameliorative only for particular cases, and that opportunities in the economy at present are of the zero-sum variety. If some working class kids make use of existing opportunities, others lose them. For the excluded and disaffected, recognise the logic of their cultural forms in a mode not of mystification and illusion but of honesty and un-illusion. Specifically:

– recognise the strict meaninglessness and confusion of the present proliferation of worthless qualifications.

– recognise the likely intrinsic boredom and meaninglessness of most un-skilled and semi-skilled work.

– recognise the contradiction of a meritocratic society and educational system where the majority must lose but all are asked in some way to share in the same ideology.

– recognise the possibility of joblessness both as an enforced and as a chosen option in relation to the real opportunities available and to what working actually means – with and *without* the cultural level.

– use more collective practices, group discussions and projects,[4] to uncover and examine these cultural mappings of work. The group logic which cultural forms display may also be relevant to the practice of vocational guidance.

The possibilities for a principled pedagogic practice with disaffected working class youth are fraught with difficulties and must be carefully proposed. This study warns that disaffected working class kids respond not so much to the style of individual teachers and the content of education as to the structure of the school and the dominant teaching paradigm in the context of their overall class cultural experience and location. These structures and the basic patterns of relationship in the teaching paradigm are much more difficult to change than teaching style or particular kinds of content. And yet the problem remains that individual teachers do have to continue with their awkward and demoralising class contacts with disaffected kids in schools as they are presently constituted, and seek to place this day to day contact in a longer perspective. The cultural perspective outlined in this book, however, does have some implications for classroom pedagogy.

There is currently a 'crisis' in education.[5] This centres on basic standards and the adequacy of progressive teaching methods. The controversy which is developing (and which is most noticeable for the virtual absence of the views of classroom teachers and complete absence of the views of the kids) is really a supremely ideological battle which only partially and through many distortions represents the real processes of class conflict, the reproduction of labour power, and the cultural and general social processes of reproduction taking place on the site of the school. This is not to say that the battle is unreal or that sides must not be taken. However, the aims and form of a pedagogy for disaffected working class kids must be formulated with some independence from the terms of 'the great debate'. We must recognise, for instance, that there is a strong idealist strand in progressive techniques, and that these techniques are involved in ironic processes of reproduction. Conversely it must be agreed that it is a condition for working class development that working class kids do develop certain disciplined skills in expression and symbolic manipulation.[6]

As in the case of vocational guidance, the basic structural arrangements of society which in the first place throw up the problems with which education attempts to deal cannot be modified in the educational field alone - though its proper use, I argue, could provide an important precondition for such change. Such structural change could only proceed from a specifically political contribution - made perhaps, by teachers, through their professional and other collective bodies - on behalf of working class interests.

One middle range and more specifically pedagogic possibility is to exert a collective political weight for some structural change within education itself. Even though larger structures might remain broadly the same it may be possible to encourage what might be called independent working class educational institutions. Where the economic relations and basic structures of the main society ultimately enforce the state educational institute and its dominant educational paradigm, it may be that independent working class institutions could escape from some of the circles of unintention and reproduction by refusing or blunting the force of the logic of the dominant exchange relationship. The definition of the teacher might be altered by encouraging workers to take part in educational programmes. The importance of the informal in working class culture, and the processes of reproduction it sponsors, could be recognised by an unstructured and unreified approach to collective work. The exchange relationship of the dominant model could be replaced by a relationship of solidarity and self understanding. The illusory notion of 'equivalents' could be replaced by co-operation and the promise, not of the individual, but of the *social* power of knowledge. Within such a non-antagonistic institutional framework it might be possible to initiate a specifically working class contents for pedagogic practice which would drop particular notions of subjects and specialisms, and interrogate instead the nature and logic of different formal and informal working class forms and – not least important – their contradictory role in current cultural and social reproduction. There have been radical independent working class forms of education in the past [7] and a whole variety of institutions, most importantly the trade unions, exist now within the working class which could provide a basis for, and already have some on-going, educational activities. In view of the size of the educational budget (five billion sterling in the UK), and the current – however wrongly conceptualised – conviction that much of it is wasted or ineffective in relation to disaffected working class kids, it becomes feasible to argue for some devolution of state funds to independent bodies. It might be possible, as it were, to use the confusions of the current debate to mount a strictly pedagogic and educationally 'cost-effective' argument for institutions and practices which in other, ironically more liberal, times might have been seen as regressive or subversive.

These are complex issues and rather than stray too far and too naively into specialist areas I am simply trying here to make available, and suggest the relevance of, an analysis of the cultural level. To conclude certain principled short-term suggestions (which have a place in longer-term perspectives) for the immediate and tortuous problems of Monday morning can be made. Most basically I suggest that the cultural level can be recognised for itself, its particular logics traced out, and material outcomes understood. The teacher can play a sceptical, unglamorous real eye over industrial, economic and class cultural processes. Rather than being scared into a moral panic about 'disruption and violence in the classroom' (which has its own reproductive function with respect to conservative ideology) teachers can place the counter-school culture in its proper social context and consider its implications for its members own long-term future – never mind the problems which it poses for their own survival in front of the class. Within this it is possible to make more specific suggestions.

*be sensitive to the double coding of class and institutional meanings so that teaching responses and communications are not mistaken as insults to *social* class and identity.

*recognise the limits which structural factors and the dominant teaching paradigm place on pedagogic initiative and style. Try to limit the scope of the inevitable vicious circle which develops in post-differentiated relationships. This must be an essentially pedagogic question, but from this research the best suggestion seems to be of a tactical withdrawal from confrontation with the counter-school culture but which avoids any simplistic expression of sympathy and maintains a degree of institutional authority. Though it produces all the circles of unintention which we have looked at in this book, it is necessary to maintain a degree of authority in schools as they are presently materially structured in order to maintain any initiative at all in the particular direction of class activity and for what – admittedly limited – scope there is for an effectivity at the level of content. More radical teaching styles might be adopted and understood with politically conscious and organised students (cf. National Union of School Students) but it is absolutely clear that it is the disaffected who are *least* likely to be in this category. Complete withdrawal from conflict and the traditional paradigm is registered by 'the lads', for instance, in their own cultural terms, as simple defeat and humiliation of 'the enemy' – which carries its own marked set of reproductive outcomes. Such a withdrawal can indeed be seen as an abdication of a complex, contradictory, responsibility.

*use where possible small classes (implying, of course a fight for extra resources – this is in no sense a de-schooling argument) and techniques of group discussion and collective work. Such techniques are in tension with the individualistic conventional teaching paradigm, but they, at least, move towards some kind of organisational unit which might be homologous to the collective processes and forms which are to be explored.

*take cultural forms, basic transitions, social attitudes sometimes as the basic texts for class work. Attempt to promote real skills and discipline in the pursuit of a form of social self-analysis. This is not a simple 'relevance' in the existing sense because it does not assume an equivalence between cultural forms, or uncritically accept all aspects of cultural activity. It would differentiate penetrations from limitations and study both in relation to a dominant culture and ideology. In a sense its focus would be a failure: the working class reproduction of its own submission and contribution towards social reproduction. Specific topics (especially for white male groups, though they would no doubt be similar for female and ethnic groups) might include:

- what the counter-school culture implies about qualifications, the meaning of work, and the nature and role of labour power in modern society.
- how the division mental/manual labour power comes about at the cultural level and what costs this brings.
- why it is that manual work is associated with masculinity and mental work with femininity.
- what are the costs and diversions of sexism.
- what does fighting and theft and intimidation mean or express.
- what is the nature of friendship, and of informal association. What are the strengths and costs of informal/cultural activities and responses. What other kinds of friendship might be possible.
- how does the cultural decode formal messages, accept or reject official and ideological messages. Does it base itself on rationality or irrationality.
- what are the real results and outcomes of the accumulation of decisions based on informal cultures.

Accepting all of the structural constraints and bearing in mind the connectedness of cultural forms, the essential thrust of these conclusions and of the book in general can be seen as one form of exploration of the unity of theory and practice. The identification and understanding of the cultural level is an action to bring it closer to self-awareness and therefore to the political, to recognise in the materiality of its outcomes the possibility of the cultural becoming a material force. Such a politicisation of culture is actually one of the pre-conditions for, and an organic element of, longer-term structural change.[8] It is specifically in the cultural area and in its characteristic relations with the ideological, that there is indeed the possibility of effectivity at the cultural level in the pedagogic mode. The recognition of commonality in cultural forms and the understanding of their own processes is already to have strengthened an internal weakness, to have begun to unravel the power of the formal over the informal and to have started a kind of self-transformation. This may not be the Millenium but it could be Monday morning. Monday morning need not imply an endless succession of the *same* Monday mornings.

Notes

[1] It is the divorce, or attenuation of the connection between these levels which makes the real basis for some recent suggestions from sociology for a relevant practice in social work. See for instance, S. Cohen, 'It's All Right for You to Talk: Political and Sociological Manifestos for Social Work Action', in R. Bailey and M. Brake (eds), *Radical Social Work*, Arnold, 1975.

[2] A dominant, if implicit, strand in the 'new' sociology of education. See for instance, N. Keddie, *Tinker, Taylor: The Myth of Cultural Deprivation*, Penguin, 1973.

[3] See for instance Ken Roberts' recent critical review of the careers service ('Where is the Careers Service Heading', in *Careers Bulletin*, DE, Spring 1976) and the government statement on vocational preparation (*Unified Vocational Preparation: A Pilot Approach*, HMSO, 1976) which has led to the formation of the Further Education Curriculum Review and Development Unit by the DES to monitor and carry out specific studies and curricular experiments. The only and original document so far available from the unit identifies the total lack of educational or training provision for 40 per cent of young workers, and calls for joint planning and provision of training and further education. The document does not, however, take up the question of *the attitude of the young* to various kinds of provision, nor does it explore the internal contradictions in approaches which ask for 'commitment' and better 'communication' in work situations which may be intrinsically meaningless to start with. Ken Roberts' criticisms of the careers service are challenging and I agree with his strictures on the notion of 'occupational choice', but he can be easily hoist with his own petard. A good 'employment exchange' service, and a 'relevant service' for the educationally disadvantaged do nothing to increase the total job opportunities available in particular areas so that we still may expect problems of a similar order to arise in any new set up. And by ignoring the

cultural level and range of actual experiential responses to these restricted opportunities he is unable to provide any suggestions about what actually *to do* in vocational guidance – no matter what the stage of its application.

[4]   The Schools Council Careers Education and Guidance Project (material tested but not yet released) makes a host of interesting suggestions about collective work and materials for group projects. They are still bound, ultimately however, by an illusory notion of individual choice and even of the individual's power over opportunities in the job market.

[5]   The Tyndale affair, recent surveys (see Bennet's *Teaching Styles and Pupil Progress*), and the Prime Minister's concern as expressed in his Ruskin College speech (11 October 1976) about parental worries over 'new' teaching methods, together with the permanent pressure of the black paperites, have called progressivism, relevance and new teaching methods firmly into question.

[6]   I hold open the question of the *form* of these skills since, as I have argued, the cultures in which, and partly from which, they might develop are in a certain sense in tension with the received, dominant language. In developing skills, however, relevant as they might be to their cultural base, discipline and rigour must still hold a place, as must a notion of how they might actually be effective against dominant forms of expression.

[7]   See R. Johnson, 'Really Useful Knowledge' in *Radical Education 7 and 8*, Winter and Spring, 1976.

[8]   There is no reason to collapse this perspective into an historicism, or into the expressive progress of a 'class in itself' to a 'class for itself'. It is simply to observe that if change is to come about which is developmental and not oppressive for the working class no matter what the conjunctural factors and effectivity of the different levels it is necessary, at some stage, for a good proportion of them to have a supportive radical analysis. It is also to suggest, not an inevitably positive, but a negative role for the working class in acting as a pragmatic check against certain kinds of 'progress' – never mind embodying its spirit. If the cultural must become more political so must the political become more cultural.

Appendix

At best, daily life, like art, is revolutionary. At worst it is a prison house. At worst, reflection, like criticism, is reactionary. At best it creates plans for escape. Taking part in detailed life in order to reflect can be to combine the worst of both. It takes the innocence out of the former to congeal the latter with guilt.

I am strictly forbidden, because of shortage of space, to discuss methodology and its relation to theory and practice at any length. My general approach to problems in this area is discussed elsewhere.[1]

I would just like to mark a recognition here that, no matter how modified, participant observation and the methods under its aegis, display a tendency towards naturalism and therefore to conservatism. The ethnographic account is a supremely ex post facto product of the actual uncertainty of life. There develops, unwilled, a false unity which asks, 'What follows next?' 'How did it end?' 'What makes sense of it?'. The subjects stand too square in their self-referenced world. The method is also patronising and condescending – is it possible to imagine the ethnographic account upwards in a class society?

I do not deny the existence or the necessary relative independence of research and enquiry as an activity, but it may well be that any application of the knowledge so gained will have to invert aspects of the PO paradigm. The silences and enforced secrecies of the method are ultimately political silences and the secretion too of a *capacity*. It is a refusal as well as an enablement.

Still we cannot invent a form out of its time. It is necessary above all to approach the real *now* in one way or another – one-sidedly, elliptically or not. The ethnographic account, for all its faults, records a crucial level of experience and through its very biases insists upon a level of human agency which is persistently overlooked or denied but which increases in importance all the time for other levels of the social whole. Although the world is never directly 'knowable', and cannot empirically present itself in the way that the ethnographic account seems sometimes to suggest, it must nevertheless be specifically registered somewhere in theory if theory pretends to any relevance at all. Theories must be judged ultimately for the adequacy they display to the understanding of the phenomenon they purport to explain – not to themselves. This book has attempted, especially Part II, to take the advantages still offered by a qualitative method to respond descriptively and theoretically to a real and difficult level of social existence whilst resisting tendencies towards empiricism, naturalism and objectification of the subject.

There follows an edited transcription of a group discussion recorded in January 1977 at the university, of some of 'the lads' from the Hammertown school who had

194

read early drafts of the book. The discussion centred on how my role as a researcher had been seen and what the 'results' of the research meant to them.

(. . .)

Bill	The bits about us were simple enough.
John	It's the bits in between.
Joey	Well, I started to read it, I started at the very beginning, y'know I was gonna read as much as I could, then I just packed it in, just started readin' the parts about us and then little bits in the middle (. . .)
Spanksy	The parts what you wrote about us, I read those, but it was, y'know, the parts what actually were actually describing the book like I didn't . . .

(. . .)

Perc	I think we got to dislike you eventually.
PW	Really.
Perc	Truthfully I was a bit fed up of yer.
Bill	Speak for yourself when you say, 'we', say 'you'.
Joey	Not 'we'.
Spanksy	It was nice to be out of lessons.
Perc	Oh yeah, that was about it wor it, nice to be out of lessons.
Spanksy	Don't say 'wor it' and look at us and expect us to say 'yeah'.
Joey	(. . .) I thought, you know, I thought he's not doin' this for his own sake, he's doin' it 'cos, y'know, somebody's put'im up to it and he wants to find out why we do it, y'know, do a 1987 [sic] thing and cut parts of yer brain out and . . . (. . .) You were virtually the answer to our prayer, because do you remember, we used to make vague attempts at writing accounts of things we'd done at school, y'know what I mean, we'd had to make an essay . . . (. . .) I thought that we were the artists of the school, because of the things we did, I thought definitely we had our own sort of art form, the things we used to get up to. And we were definitely the leaders of the school . . . and placed amongst . . . if we were all separated and placed amongst groups of the ear'oles we could have been leaders in our own right (. . .) something should have been done with us, I mean there was so much talent there that it was all fuckin' wasted. I mean X, he was as thick as pigshit really, but if someone had took him and tutored him . . . he'd got so much imagination. To do the things he did, I mean he used to play up better than most of us X had, he must have been something more than the dumb stupid animal he put on.
John	I dunno though.

[Laughter]

Bill	(. . .) I thought, y'know, we'll have to kinda watch out for this, y'know. He's gonna let Peters and all them lot know what's goin' on, and then after a bit y'know, I realised that wasn't right and then I just enjoyed it 'cos it was a skive, y'know, get out the lessens. I wasn't really interested in it at first y'know. I could get out of lessons, have a smoke for an hour or so. Then, after, I just got slowly and slowly involved in it and I really enjoyed it.
Perc	I wanted to go to you.
PW	Even though you disliked me.
Perc	I enjoy talking to people, but sometimes I used to think, y'know, he's asking some bloody, y'know, right things. I used to think you was asking a bit much, personal things y'know.
PW	Do you mean in the group discussions or the individual ones?
Perc	Individual, I'd y'know, I doe mind talkin' to yer on me own, I'd, y'know . . . when yer with yer mates yer say a lot of things yer know that don't really happen, and now, I think a lot of things were said . . .
Bill	You mean you think a lot of it was med up?
Joey	Well, I can tell yer now, straight from the fuckin' knuckle, none of it was med up.
Chris	Almost 90 per cent of what I've read in there was, I can actually remember.
Perc	O yeah I can remember a lot of things what I read.
Joey	(. . .) Even if the individual acts were exaggerated the point's still there (. . .) the feelin' was in us.
John	They seem in the book a lot tougher than they actually were.
Spanksy	It's only how they seem to us.
John	When you're with your mates everybody changes, everybody changes, they do things a lot bigger, everybody seems a lot tougher (. . .) when they was talking about what they'd done.
PW	Was it true?
John	Yeah, what they said was true, but they didn't seem that tough to me.
Spanksy	It's cos we know everybody that was, I'd never been to another school, I know places over Newtown, they'd eat me alive, they'm massive places, they'm terrible . . . I was workin' at the one school and these four kids come over to me and they was only babies, they cum up to me and they said, 'Are you a new kid?' I say, 'No, no'. They says . . . they was cumin' up to me, fists all clenched up. What I was doin' I was gettin' some big housebricks to prop this big radiator up y'know for me mate, like, and I got these housebricks, like, y'know . . . I was only in the school fifteen minutes and I'd got kids cumin' up to me, after me. (. . .)

Bill	You were staff (at first), you were somebody in between, later on I took you as one of us.
Joey	(. . .) you were someone to pour our hearts out to. You were obviously as old as most of the staff, and yet none of the staff . . . they represented . . . they were so far apart from us. They used to sit with us at dinner table but you couldn't really talk to them just 'cos of the fact that they were staff.
John	(. . .) You could understand what they was sayin' and doin' like. Anything that happened you'd understand, like, if they'd done something wrong the night before, you'd just listen, understand, whereas teachers . . . you know, they'd say, 'That's wrong' anyway, and you'd think, 'Don't say anymore about it'.
Bill	The main difference is, you listen to us, you want to know what we've got to say, they don't, none of them.
John	They want to know so that they can get on good terms with yer.
Perc	All they'm doin', they'm doin' their jobs, that's it.
Spanksy	They're tryin' to pull themselves up . . . all they'm tryin' to do is win us over, and then go up to the headmaster and say to him, 'I'm alright with them, when they'm in my class they're alright'.
Joey	When you first started asking questions something illegal must have come out and we'd told you things we'd done wrong and we never got any backlash off other members of staff which obviously meant you hadn't told anybody.

(. . .)

PW	What does closeness mean? Take Jenkins [laughter] he was trying to be close and he really cared, what was different about him?
Joey	His whole manner, the way he carried himself . . . I think that closeness has to be tempered with a correct amount of discipline.
PW	But I didn't discipline you at all.
Joey	I think if you had told us to do something, if we were playing up and you told us, we'd 'a' stopped.
Perc	Oh are.
Joey	'Cos you'd been close to us and we'd have listened to you as one of us . . . you know what I mean. What we needed was someone like us who was just older, more responsibility.
Spanksy	(. . .) If any of me mates had told me, 'Oh come on Spanksy, you'm too much there mate,' I'd 'a' said, 'OK it's gone far enough'. Comin' from you at that time, it would have seemed as if it was one of them tellin' me.
PW	Did you feel as if I should have been telling you?
Spanksy	No, we never thought about it, it's the first time we talked about it, dayn't think about it.

(. . .)

PW	Do you think 'the lads'' culture was sensible now, if it say, stopped you coming here.
Spanksy	I could never come here [the university], I couldn't stand sittin' at a desk, I couldn't stand it writin', I can't sit at a desk and write all day, I can't.
Joey	It wasn't sensible [messing about in school], it was the only thing you could do . . . it was more fun than doing fucking nothing (. . .) They gave us the responsibility and we just didn't know, no matter how much anyone told me, if they'd've hypnotised me, I still wouldn't have thought I really needed them, 'cos I read it in the book, we all thought we were gonna make it without 'O' levels, we can you know but it would have been much easier with 'em.

(. . .)

PW	If you're not having a chance is it an individual matter or does it relate to the working class (. . .) doesn't that point to politics. Nobody needs to force you lot into factories, you're all rushing out to get there.
Joey	We've just been thrust into society too soon, we've been brought up to be too selfish (. . .) we're too selfish, we couldn't care less, you see on the tele so many people fuckin' affluent, you just want to try and do that, make it, get money, you don't care about others, the working class.

(. . .)

Bill	All I want for my kids is all I've ever wanted.
PW	How you gonna get it?
Bill	Foul means or fair.
PW	You individually or you in a group?
Bill	I just wanna get it for them and I will, not perhaps everything.
PW	The question remains, how you gonna do it?
Joey	(. . .) It's been this way too long (. . .) you gotta help yourself, how many revolutions have there been that really worked? And after a revolution there's got to be someone at the top . . . and eventually would become middle class (. . .).
John	All I want for my kids is try your best, it's no use tryin' to make you do something you don't want.

(. . .)

PW	Your own mental ability might have been blocked by your own conviction that you were going to be masculine.
Joey	It wasn't that, it was just that mental work was what teachers required, to do what they wanted. If the teachers had let us play

	up, say, 'OK, off you go', if they'd 'ave said that we'd'ave wanted to do whatever they said they didn't want us to do (. . .).
Perc	Everyone wants to be tough at school, everybody likes to think people look up to them. 'He's a hard kid'.
PW	But does it help you in the end, or the working class?
Spanksy	It helps you around the streets.
Bill	It helps you get through youth (. . .) we can just see for the moment that nobody's gonna take the piss out of us.
Joey	They won't take advantage, take advantage in our sense, you know, they'll never make a fool of us in these years 'cos we're so masculine, that's all I can see. If I'd've taken the track of the 'ear'oles' all the violence in me would have petered out a bit, you know what I mean, it would have jaded a bit . . . and then 'the lads' who were still performing would take advantage of you, I could never do it.
PW	The rep., the masculine ability to fight . . .
Joey	It's our previous life, our fathers were working class, physical, their physicalness has come over to us.
John	Them that's got the brains, they'll be the bosses in time to come and people like us will be the workers.
PW	If Joey hits him 'cos he's 'dancing funny' [Joey had earlier described how he'd 'picked on' someone at a dance the previous Saturday apparently for this offence] is he winning?
John	Yeah, he is in a way, if Joey had a rich boss and he met his son at a dance and he done 'im it would be self-satisfaction for Joey.
PW	That cancels it out does it?
John	Yeah, it does in a way.
Joey	(. . .) I knew I had to be violent or I couldn't get out there on the streets. No matter how much I was gonna get in the future I'll still get a good kick out on the streets, you know what I mean (. . .).
PW	But you could go back to college.
Joey	I don't know, the only thing I'm interested in is fucking as many women as I can if you really wanna know.

Notes

[1]   For a general discussion, see 'The Man in the Iron Cage', *Working Papers in Cultural Studies*, no. 9, and the theoretical appendix of *Profane Culture*, Routledge and Kegan Paul, 1978. Some of the problems encountered during this specific research are outlined in the final report to the SSRC 'The Main Reality', available as a stencilled paper from the Centre for Contemporary Cultural Studies, Birmingham University.

Index

Alienation 143
Althusser, L. 137, 183
Anderson, P. 170
Ashton, D. N. 141
Auld, R. 86
Autonomous work groups 179–183

Balibar, E. 137
Barthes, R. 115
Bennett, 193
Bourdieu, P. 128, 142
Braverman, H. 142, 180, 183
Brighton Labour Process Group 142

Carter, M. P. 114, 141
Cash 39
Cohen, S. 192
Colletti, L. 143
Commonality of labour 101
Concrete labour 135
Conformists 13, 98, 99, 148
Counter-School Culture: comparative
  cases 58, 86–7; drinking 19:
  eveningtime 38; excitement 33;
  fighting 34; fire extinguisher
  incident 79; 'hardknocks' 35;
  informal knowledge 25; informal
  mobility 27; informing 24, 50;
  mother 45; opposition to
  authority 11, 30, 60, 81;
  parental views 21, 73; police
  20; political attitudes 165–6;
  qualifications 94–5; racism 47;
  rejection of the conformist 11;
  relation to working class culture
  52; role of the commercial dance

36; romanticism 45; rules 24;
  self direction 26; sexism 36,
  43, 102; sexual relations 15–6,
  18, 44; smoking 18; social
  landscape of the school 16; style
  12, 17; talking 33; teaching
  styles in relation to 84; teachers
  39; 'the laff' 29, 96; 'the pisstake'
  32, 96; 'them and us' 109, 169;
  theft 40; time 28, 135, 163;
  truancy 27
Crowther, G. 86
Cultural the 3, 59, 101–2, 103, 132,
  136, 153–4, 171, 185–92:
  and social reproduction in
  institutions 176–79, 185;
  creativity 120; expressive
  antagonism 124; ideology,
  relation to 166–9; individual
  and group logic 128; informal
  group 123–4; interpretative
  analysis 125; limitations 119;
  material outcomes 95, 174, 178,
  192; misrecognition 176; non-
  reductive notions of 171, 174,
  179–85, 186; partial penetration
  3, 119, 185; penetrations 119;
  political expression in relation to
  168; politicisation of 192, 193;
  practical consciousness 122;
  production 124–5, 160, 172;
  radical genesis of 175;
  rationality of 120; relative
  autonomy of 172, 186; social
  structure 121, 171–2, 173,
  185–6; structural location 123;
  structuralist theories of 175;
  subjectivity 173; symbolic